"*Inseparable* is a really powerful and very timely personal account of the Holocaust. Even for those of us who have done a lot of Holocaust research, this book is essential and so moving and compelling. And it is especially important at a time of increasing anti-Semitism and Holocaust denial. I highly recommend this book."
—**Wolf Blitzer,** Principal Anchor, CNN

"*Inseparable* documents the harrowing journey of the Hess family as they run from the Nazis, leaving their homeland of Germany and escaping to the Netherlands, only to find themselves once again victims of a relentless and merciless hunt simply for being Jewish. In the backdrop, Faris Cassell artfully describes the meteoric rise of Adolph Hitler and his savage Nazi party, showing just how easily they are able to overtake Europe with seeming impunity. This suspense-filled retelling of World War II is rendered with a compilation of detail that is breathtaking, making it all the more frightening when experienced through the lens of one intrepid family who did all they could under impossible odds to stay together. They endured, they coped, and ultimately they miraculously overcame the machinations of evil designed to crush and annihilate them. This is a Holocaust story of triumph."
—**Silvia Foti,** author of *Storm in the Land of Rain: A Mother's Dying Wish Becomes Her Daughter's Nightmare*

"Faris Cassell narrates the compelling story of the Hesses, a family of four with two very young twin children, German Jews who sought refuge in the Netherlands only to face the German onslaught, and their struggle to survive in hiding before being deported to a concentration camp. In moving testimony, she takes us on their most difficult journey and how they remained inseparable time and again despite near impossible odds. Had this been a novel, one would have rejected it as implausible, perhaps even impossible, and yet it happened. In this case truth is stranger than fiction, and once again, Cassell is indefatigable in her quest for truth. Her narrative is as compelling as the story she tells."

—**Michael Berenbaum,** author, scholar, rabbi, and filmmaker, former Project Director of the United States Holocaust Memorial Museum, and Professor of Jewish studies at American Jewish University

"In *Inseparable*, Faris Cassell has made the Holocaust relatable to audiences who have little if any prior awareness of the genocide of European Jewry during World War II—without either desensitizing the reader with unfathomable statistics or turning the work into an elegy for the murdered. Beautifully written, the saga of the Hess family from happiness to persecution to daily confrontation with death in Nazi camps such as Westerbork and Bergen-Belsen to their eventual liberation on a train bound for nowhere is counterintuitively inspirational precisely because, as the book's subtitle indicates, it is ultimately a story of resistance to oppression, understated heroism, and survival. We identify with the book's protagonists, including the twins Marion and Stefan, who were robbed of their childhood; we are given a window into their suffering; and we are left with admiration for their courage, their inner strength, and, perhaps most important, their uncompromising decency, which allowed them to remain human despite decidedly inhuman conditions. This is a book that should be required reading, especially for high school and college students of all backgrounds, ethnicities, and faiths."

—**Menachem Z. Rosensaft,** Jewish and human rights activist, professor on the law of genocide, General Counsel and Associate Executive Vice President of the World Jewish Congress, and the Founding Chairman of the International Network of Children of Jewish Holocaust Survivors

"An unforgettable story of family, devotion, and strength during impossible times. *Inseparable* reminds us that behind Holocaust statistics there are parents and children who loved, resisted, and faced unfathomable circumstances. Faris Cassell conveys the horror of the Holocaust—but the Hess family's love for one another shines through every page. You will remember this story for a long time."

> —**Rebecca Erbelding,** author of the award-winning book *Rescue Board: The Untold Story of America's Efforts to Save the Jews of Europe*, and on-camera expert in the 2022 PBS television series, *The U.S. and the Holocaust*, directed by Ken Burns, Lynn Novick, and Sarah Botstein

"*Inseparable* manages the rare accomplishment of telling a tale of epic evil and suffering with genuine intimacy and personal compassion. This is a compelling and important book."

> —**Rabbi Brad Hirschfield,** President of CLAL (the National Jewish Center for Learning and Leadership) and Co-Founder and Executive Editor of TheWisdomDaily.com

"*Inseparable* is an important story compellingly, masterfully, and sensitively told. Faris Cassell is not only a talented storyteller with a keen eye for detail and a talent for bringing characters to life. She is also a meticulous—and tenacious—researcher. The result is history that lives and breathes, a book with both intelligence and heart."

> —**Lauren Kessler,** author of *Free: Two Years, Six Lives, and the Long Journey Home* and *Stubborn Twig: Three Generations in the Life of a Japanese American Family*, an Oregon Reads selection

"In her compelling and suspenseful account of the miraculous survival of one Jewish family, Faris Cassell also unfolds the larger story of the Holocaust in Holland and beyond. Based on memoirs, interviews, and extensive research, she cogently recounts the extraordinary experiences of Ilse and Karl Hess and their twins, Marion and Stefan, in Amsterdam, Westerbork, and Bergen-Belsen, on the famous 'Lost Train,' and, finally, their bleak Netherlands homecoming. Her cogent writing vividly exposes a nightmare landscape in which love and resourcefulness continually struggled against a seemingly endless onslaught of inhumanity and betrayal."

—**Judith R. Baskin,** Philip H. Knight Professor of
Humanities Emerita, University of Oregon

"As the violence of World War II rages around them, one family finds the courage, endurance, and unshakeable love to fight and survive the horrors of Hitler's extermination policies. Faris Cassell has written a haunting and unforgettable book; one I think very important for today."

—literary figure **Faye Kesey McMurtry**

"*Inseparable* is the inspiring survival story of young twins, Marion and Stefan Hess, their father, Karl, and their mother, Ilse. As if watching a movie, readers are riveted by their parents' cleverness, desperation, and luck as they evade the Nazis, suffer capture, and fight for their survival. In an account made vivid and engaging through the father's journals, the mother's memories, and the twins' interviews, award-winning journalist Faris Cassell shows her special talent for illuminating the struggles, triumphs, and special moments in one imprisoned—and liberated—Jewish family."

—**Elizabeth Lyon,** bestselling author and editor and recipient of the Stewart H. Holbrook Literary Legacy Award

"A father's heroism, a mother's protective love, the resilience of two toddlers, and, finally, blind luck are the ingredients for survival in Faris Cassell's new book, *Inseparable*. As in her earlier work, *The Unanswered Letter*, on the fate of an extended Viennese Jewish family, Cassell skillfully weaves together a detailed and personal account of the Hesses' journey through the murderous morass of the Holocaust with the history of a specific time and place, in this case, the lesser-known Dutch experience. At times heart-breaking, at others thrilling and dumbfounding, *Inseparable* is both an exciting and an important read."

—**Barbara Corrado Pope,** historian and author of
The Blood of Lorraine, a novel of the Dreyfus era
and Europe in turmoil

"*Inseparable: The Hess Twins' Holocaust Journey through Bergen-Belsen to America* connects with my family story directly, as my relatives were also interned at Westerbork. When I was given an advance copy of the book, I eagerly read it over a single weekend. It's terrific—thoughtful, empathetic, engaging. This is a really superb account."

—**Daniel Rosenberg,** Professor of History, University of
Oregon, and co-author of *Cartographies of Time: A
History of the Timeline* with Anthony Grafton and
Histories of the Future with Susan Harding

"*Inseparable* affected me greatly. I find myself thinking about it—unexpectedly—at different times of the day and night. We cannot imagine survival under these circumstances, just as we dare not imagine the intimate details of daily life that such survival entailed. Yet Faris Cassell lays it out so directly that we must imagine it—all of it. Without sentimentality, the survival, intact, of a family of four unfolds: the testimonies and memories of parents and children against the deafening drumbeats of those who would wipe out their families, their people, and their history. These are voices that must be heard and an extraordinary story that must be told."

— **Rabbi Shira Milgrom,** Congregation Kol Ami, Westchester County, New York, board member of the Parents Circle of Bereaved Families and supporter of Combatants for Peace, the two organizations that sponsor the annual Joint Palestinian-Israeli Memorial Day ceremony

"With indefatigable research and a detective's eagerness for one family's truth, Faris Cassell has written an extraordinary book of survival, perseverance, and sheer willpower amid the horrors of the Hitler-triggered Holocaust. If her debut book, *The Unanswered Letter*, packed award-winning power, this, I believe, is even better. In the context of World War II, *Inseparable* is destined to be to Holocaust stories what *Unbroken* was to POW stories."

— **Bob Welch,** author of *Saving My Enemy: How Two WWII Soldiers Fought Against Each Other and Later Forged a Friendship That Saved Their Lives*

"I thought I knew every story of twins surviving the Holocaust— then I read Faris Cassell's extraordinary telling of the Hess family, Karl and Ilse, and their young twins, Stefan (Steven) and Marion. *Inseparable* is an extraordinary tale of love and hate, fear and uncertainty, horror and heartache that spans the family's carefree days in Germany, harrowing escape to Holland, terrifying transports to German concentration camps, and ultimate refuge in America. It is an unforgettable story that will stay with me for years to come."

— **Nancy L. Segal,** Professor of Psychology, California State University at Fullerton, and author of *The Twin Children of the Holocaust: Stolen Childhood and the Will to Survive,*

Deliberately Divided: Inside the Controversial Study of Twins and Triplets Adopted Apart, and *Gay Fathers, Twin Sons: The Citizenship Case That Captured the World*

"*Inseparable: The Hess Twins' Holocaust Journey through Bergen-Belsen to America*, by Faris Cassell, is a riveting testament to a family's sheer resilience and the strength of the human spirit in the face of unrelenting evil. Cassell takes the reader on a harrowing journey, following the trials of Ilse and Karl Hess as they fiercely protect their young twins through Nazi occupation in the Netherlands, imprisonment in concentration camps, and cruel displacement following the Second World War. It's an incredible, impossible story of survival."

 —Isabel Vincent, investigative reporter, *New York Post*, and author of *Overture of Hope*

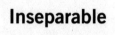

Inseparable

INSEPARABLE

The Hess Twins' Holocaust Journey through Bergen-Belsen to America

Faris Cassell

National Jewish Book Award–Winning Author of *The Unanswered Letter*

REGNERY
HISTORY
Washington, D.C.

Regnery History™ is a trademark of Salem Communications Holding Corporation
Regnery® is a registered trademark and its colophon is a trademark of Salem Communications Holding Corporation

Cataloging-in-Publication data on file with the Library of Congress

Hardcover ISBN: 978-1-68451-274-4
Paperback ISBN: 978-1-68451-468-7
eISBN: 978-1-68451-427-4

Published in the United States by
Regnery History, an imprint of
Regnery Publishing
A Division of Salem Media Group
Washington, D.C.
www.RegneryHistory.com

Manufactured in the United States of America

10 9 8 7 6 5 4 3 2 1

Books are available in quantity for promotional or premium use. For information on discounts and terms, please visit our website: www.RegneryHistory.com

To Sidney:
Wing to wing,
Oar to oar.

And to Sarah, Daniel, Jonathan, Mark, and Sam,
who were always curious and encouraging.

They asked probing questions and offered bright smiles.

The truth is all we have that stands
between us and tyranny.

—Jonathan Freedland

The whole world bled its blood....
Those kinds of things don't happen
No more, nowadays.

—Bob Dylan, "Long Ago, Far Away"

CONTENTS

IN THESE PAGES, YOU WILL MEET...

KARL HESS—a dashing, successful, self-made German-Jewish businessman in his thirties. Karl was a manager and wholesale sales representative at Europe's largest silk weaver, United Silk Corporation.

ILSE HESS—Karl's wife, a happy, outgoing young mother in her twenties. Ilse was strong-willed and resourceful, surrounded by friends and relatives, and known for her beauty.

MARION AND STEFAN HESS—the Hesses' bright and active toddler twins, born in Amsterdam in 1938. The trajectory of their young lives would be forever altered when they were caught up by crimes against humanity that they could not begin to fathom.

MARRETJE PASTERKAMP—Stefan and Marion's loving Dutch nanny, "Marry," who would do what she could for the children and their family as the Nazi persecution closed in on them.

ABRAHAM ASSCHER—copresident of the Jewish Council in Amsterdam, he was the pre-war owner of one of the largest diamond-cutting businesses in Europe, an immediate target of the invading Germans. Germany's weak economy depended on seizing properties of occupied countries.

ARTHUR SEYSS-INQUART—an Austrian Nazi and a virulent antisemite who served as *Reichskommissar* of the German-occupied Netherlands. He would order more than eight hundred executions in the last months of the war as the Allied victory seemed increasingly inevitable.

ABRAHAM PULS—loyal member of the Dutch Nazi Party (NSB), entrepreneur, and collaborator. Puls owned the notorious Abraham Puls & Sons "moving" company. He profited handsomely from the Holocaust, contracting with the Germans to clear out apartments of deported Jews, then turning over the spoils to the Germans' appointed liquidator, Einsatzstab Reichsleiter Rosenberg.

LEO FISCHER—a well-regarded German-Jewish photographer and a member of the Dutch Resistance who took pictures of the twins— and of other Jews in need of false identity documents. He would be arrested by the dreaded German "Green Police," transported to a windswept North Sea beach with seventeen other prisoners, and shot dead.

J. L. LENTZ—a Dutch civil servant and head of the Population Registration Office in The Hague, Lentz's infamous "List of Family Names of Persons of Jewish Blood" would prove critically important in rounding up Jews to be murdered.

LOLKE WILDERS—the seven-year-old was playing with other children in a Jewish neighborhood in Amsterdam when they were rounded up to be sent to Auschwitz; most were immediately gassed, but the blond and blue-eyed Lolke would survive Nazi medical experiments.

ERICH AUGUST PUTTKAMMER—a banking lawyer for the Eichmann-supervised Rotterdam Banking Association, he set up an office in Amsterdam where he sold his desperate Jewish "customers" passes purporting to exempt them from deportation to "the East."

WALTER SÜSKIND—Karl's close friend and fellow Jewish Council worker, Walter and Karl helped smuggle some eleven hundred imprisoned Jewish children and many adults out of the Jewish *Schouwburg*, a former Amsterdam theater the Germans converted to a stark collection and imprisonment site for Jews prior to their deportation.

ETTY HILLESUM—a Jewish diarist from Amsterdam and keen observer of her times, she was confined in the Westerbork transit camp during the same time as the Hess family.

LOUIS BANNET—a Dutch Jew widely considered Europe's foremost jazz trumpeter and bandleader, he would perform at the bizarre Tuesday night concerts encouraged by Westerbork's commandant to tamp down Jewish prisoners' panic and terror after the weekly deportations to Sobibor, Auschwitz, and other camps.

ANNE FRANK AND HER SISTER, MARGOT—the beloved young diarist and her older sister would both die of typhus in Bergen-Belsen, the concentration camp that the Hesses survived.

KAZIMIERZ CEGIELSKI—he was one of the most feared *Kapos* at Bergen-Belsen.

JOSEF WEISS—to save fifty fellow Bergen-Belsen prisoners from group punishment for his "bad job performance," Weiss—the camp's Elder— accepted a penalty of four breadless days.

JAN KARSKI—a member of the Polish Underground and witness to the horrors of the Warsaw ghetto and deportation to Belzec extermination camp, he carried the first eyewitness report of Holocaust atrocities to President Roosevelt. A courageous, unsung hero of the Holocaust.

RAPHAEL LEMKIN—a Jewish lawyer who escaped from Poland to the United States, Lemkin would coin the term "genocide."

KONSTANTY ROKICKI—this Polish diplomat, under constant threat of being betrayed, forged hundreds of Paraguayan passports that would be instrumental in the survival of Jews rounded up and deported by the Germans—including the Hesses.

...AND MORE...

AUTHOR'S NOTE

People have asked whether writing my first book about the Holocaust, *The Unanswered Letter: One Holocaust Family's Desperate Plea for Help*, made work on this second book about that time easier. It did not. Delving into the Holocaust is always an emotional experience, a journey into the landscape of good and evil that reverberates with urgency today. It is difficult to be immersed in that world.

Yet when I learned about the courageous Hess family—Karl and Ilse and their twin children, Marion and Stefan—I found their story powerfully compelling. Karl and Ilse's lives began in Germany, where their families had thrived for generations before being shattered by the growing Nazi menace. They fought with all their resources to elude, endure, and escape Nazi horror. Theirs is a story of the human spirit. And so I did not hesitate to say, "Yes!"

Inseparable is the story of a young family's struggle, against all odds, to stay together and survive. It could not have been written without the testimony of each member of the Hess family. Karl and Ilse have passed away, but shortly after they returned to the freedom of the Netherlands, Karl wrote a moving, detailed memoir of their life under the Nazis that has been key to this story. Quoted statements attributed to Karl Hess throughout the book were taken from his memoir. Later, Ilse gave testimony to the United States Holocaust Memorial Museum and interviews with the media, which offer her memories and perspective. Quoted statements attributed to Ilse Hess throughout the book were taken from that testimony and those interviews. (Please see the Works Consulted at the end of this book for details about these sources.)

In America, Karl would legally change his name to Charles, and Stefan would go by Steven. Central to this book has been the tireless, courageous support of the twins, Marion and Steven, who lived the story and rejected any instinct to put that history behind them and not look back. In spring 2021, over the span of two years, Marion and Steven began to tell me their story, a process that would continue over the course of two years. In narrating their story, I have used "Steven" when quoting his descriptions of the family's past, and "Stefan" when he is in their story. With generosity, depth of feeling, and careful thought, they answered hundreds of my questions, shared family documents, and enlightened me about the Holocaust as they lived it. My extensive interviews with the twins have been key to making this a compelling, often first-person, story. Quoted statements attributed to Steven (Stefan) and Marion Hess throughout the book were derived from interviews I conducted with them. This book has been written in the time of COVID-19, making travel and in-person interviews that I would normally conduct impossible. Steven and Marion bridged that divide of distance with patience and determination, imparting this story of an ordinary, yet extraordinary, family faced with overwhelming cruelty.

The issue of memory is crucial when history depends on it. Recent research suggests that our memories are not fixed, but elastic and communal—that trauma, time, and other factors may distort them. During my year of interviews with the Hess twins, their thoughts about their experience, naturally, have some differences, but their memories, supported by their extensive collection of photos and documents, are remarkably consistent.

Because Bergen-Belsen SS staff destroyed all camp records before surrendering to the British, other survivor accounts, some written in the camp, take on great importance. Testimonies, diaries, and memoirs by a number of Holocaust survivors deepen and broaden this story. In order to allow an uninterrupted flow for the reader, the voluminous reference materials, research conducted, educational endeavors, informational activities, additional interviews, and other sources used to clarify, substantiate, and supply historical context for the Hesses' story are listed in the Works Consulted at the end of this book.

As part of my research journey, I visited the Bergen-Belsen Memorial, on Germany's southern Lüneburg. I drove the narrow road past the still-working military training base and *Panzer* camp. Long stretches of chain-link fence topped with barbed wire may not have changed over the decades. I parked in the expansive parking lot and spent an entire day touring the modern cement-and-glass memorial building and extensive grounds. Supported by the German and Lower Saxony governments, the memorial receives about 250,000 visitors per year. No reconstructed barracks, no old fences or guard stations mar the landscape that has lain as hallowed ground since the camp's liberation. A forest has grown up where once there was only mud and dust. A large grass-covered field holds the remains of mass burial pits.

The quiet of the grounds was haunting, as if even our voices should remain low for fear of disturbing the resting places. Our tour was educational and moving. There was a lot to learn and try to comprehend. I found a moment to separate from our guide. I walked quietly at the edge of the path. Heavy rain was forecast and storm clouds billowed above. In the dirt beside me, a white object caught the dim light of the threatening sky. I bent down and scooped it up. In the palm of my hand lay a human tooth.

I wish I had pushed the tooth beneath the soil and said a few words, but instead I handed it to the guide, who met my eyes, took it, and put it in his pocket—to take back to the memorial building, I assumed. It was mine to ponder, not control. To whom had it belonged? What could this dirt, this young forest, or the remains of a barracks with trees growing through fallen, rotting boards tell me? I tried to listen, but heard only the wind.

■   ■   ■

In this book, I use the spelling "antisemitism," which is now becoming standard. The previously common term, "anti-Semitism," relied on the ignorant Nazi appropriation of the older word "Semite," which, in correct use, describes people—including Jews and Arabs—who speak Semitic languages. "Aryan" is a relatively more recent term, also inaccurately employed by Nazis and neo-Nazis and now burdened with eugenic racism; in fact, "Aryan" accurately refers to people who lived some four millennia ago in northern India, spoke an Indo-European language, and brought Hindu religious thought to India. In *Inseparable*, I use "Aryan" only to reflect Nazi terminology.

Nazis weaponized language—and brutally enforced their ideological distortions of it—to mold popular perceptions, because they understood that words matter and can change the world. My intent is to use words accurately to tell this inspiring story of a family who fought through one of the most evil times of human history, and never lost hope.

CHAPTER 1

In a Day
MAY 10, 1940

A s stars faded from a clear night sky over Amsterdam in the early hours of Friday, May 10, 1940, a sound like rolling thunder jolted twenty-six-year-old Ilse Hess from her troubled sleep. She had feared this moment, known it was coming. For weeks, hour after frightening hour, she and her husband, Karl, listened to the news on their wireless: *Wehrmacht troops are massing at the border. German tanks and trucks are gathering. Dutch defenses throughout the Netherlands are prepared.* The thin hope she held for her family's safety from the Germans collapsed as the roar grew louder, shook the floor in their small apartment, rattled the dishes.

"Karl!" she whispered, awakening her husband. They hurried to check on their two-year-old twin toddlers, Marion and Stefan, amazingly, still sleeping peacefully. Karl and Ilse raced to the window, cautiously opened the blackout curtains mandated by the Dutch government, then stepped onto their balcony. They peered up in horror as formation after formation of German bombers flew toward them—the German military's black cross on their wings and Nazi swastika on the tail fins seeming to glare down at the city. Some bombers turned inland from the sea, flying low and ominous, passed overhead, streaking toward towards Schiphol Airport, just six miles from the city. A phalanx of bombers swerved south toward Rotterdam. Sirens wailed. Searchlights crisscrossed the sky.

Four years before, the Jewish couple fled Germany, their homeland, for the presumed safety of the Netherlands, escaping Nazi cruelty and repression. They had said goodbye to their families. Karl had been able to transfer his well-paying position at the international German textile giant *Vereinigte Seidenwebereien*, the United Silk Corporation, to Amsterdam. The Hesses loved this beautiful, freedom-loving country. The twins were born here in 1938. Karl and Ilse took the children for long walks in the twin-size baby carriage, enjoyed admiring remarks from strangers, and drove with the children to the seaside. They visited with friends who, like themselves, had escaped the Nazis, and made new friends, Jewish and non-Jewish.

They thought they had found breathing room, a refuge from Nazi terror. But the terror had followed them, and now it was here, right outside their window.

Hurriedly they snapped on the wireless, their indispensable source of news, and waited as its radio tubes warmed up. Their favorite classical music station was off the air. Static buzzed. The children began to cry. News crackled across the airwaves. *The Netherlands is under siege! This is not a test. This is war!*

Military reserves, report to your units! The frenzied announcer continued with a spate of government orders, some aimed at the thousands of German refugees in Amsterdam, many of them, like the Hesses, Jews fleeing Nazi terror. *Stay inside your homes or face arrest*, the broadcast commanded Karl and Ilse as they huddled together. The Hesses debated what to do. They had fled the Nazis once already. Should they go further? Should they follow orders—or run for their lives?

As dawn broke on May 10 and the Hesses listened with alarm, German Heinkel bombers dropped an estimated thirty bombs on Schiphol Airport. At 6:20 a.m., Amsterdam's official radio announced, "New and large formations of planes are arriving constantly." Smoke and red-tracer trails of Dutch antiaircraft fire streaked over the Hesses' apartment as Dutch and German aircraft battled in dogfights over the city.

On May 11, a single German Junkers JU 88 bomber released four bombs on one of the most prominent canals in central Amsterdam, killing forty-four people and wounding seventy-nine. The Bethlehem Hospital, not far from the Hesses' home, was badly damaged. Karl and Ilse tended and soothed the toddler twins as best they could during the fury of the attack. It was a horrible time. They had believed that their family was safe.

The massive invasion continued relentlessly, German para-troopers dropped to the ground like swooping birds of prey, landing at airfields and key sites across the country. Some wore camouflage, the grey-green uniforms of Dutch soldiers, or the darker uniforms of local police. Some had donned monks' robes or normal street clothes, creating chaos as they swarmed through the countryside, firing on the Dutch military and civilians in their path. German troops, trucks, and artillery units sped across the border from the east, overwhelming Dutch defenses.

In an unpublished memoir written after the war for family and a few friends, Karl would describe, "After we had spent a few happy years in Holland, the first days of May 1940 turned more and more grave and full of suspense.... We learned about military developments only from the radio. It was immediately announced that no Germans, which included us, were allowed to leave their houses. For three days we sat…in great suspense. A Jewish neighbor who lived opposite us left with his family…in the direction of the coast. Other vehicles followed…."

Hitler's aggression and his fanatical following and Germany's military power had already created turmoil throughout Europe; this attack had taken neither the Hesses nor the Dutch nation completely by surprise. The previous year, Germany had invaded Poland, igniting a furor that set off World War II in Europe. Other nations, including the Netherlands, bolstered their defenses, fearing they could become Germany's next target as it built its "Thousand Year *Reich*." Listening to the news, talking with friends, Karl and Ilse packed essential belongings into a rucksack, small enough to easily carry, which they set by their door for any emergency.

A few days earlier, on May 7, the United States diplomatic corps had warned President Franklin Roosevelt about a likely German invasion of the Low Countries—the Netherlands, Belgium, and Luxembourg—and of France. The next day, breaking news from the Associated Press "from an authoritative source" alerted the Dutch that two columns of the *Wehrmacht*, units of the Sixth Army and the Eighteenth Army, were advancing toward its borders.

Even so, a German attack had felt avoidable to the Dutch, and there had been some denial, including by Karl and Ilse. After all, the Netherlands had maintained neutrality throughout World War I. The Dutch government and Queen Wilhelmina had gone to great lengths to assure Hitler that the Netherlands would remain neutral again. Furthermore, Germany was still securing its occupation of Denmark. Meanwhile, German bombs were reducing Norwegian towns to heaps of debris, and British forces in southern Norway were in full retreat in the first British-German confrontation of World War II, but Norwegians were still defending northern ports through heavy snowstorms. Germany's invasion of those northern European nations had stunned the world as the Wehrmacht unleashed the first organized airborne warfare and the first wartime deployment of paratroopers—dramatic innovations in modern war. Surrender negotiations with Norway were underway. The Hesses, like others in the Netherlands, had reason to hold to the comforting belief that Germany's resources were stretched thin, its gun sights aimed at more important targets than tiny neutral Netherlands.

German leaders had made efforts to conceal the timing of their invasion. On May 9, Hitler, Field Marshal Hermann Göring (the head of the *Luftwaffe*, the German air force), and numerous high-ranking German army officers were observed attending the theater in Berlin. Ordinary citizens flocked to the newly opened Kurfürstendamm Street Café to hear the latest hit, "The Woodpecker's Song." Foreign correspondents in Berlin, detecting no cause for alarm, left their teletypes and headed to bed. When the 1:00 a.m. curfew hour struck, Berlin was dark and still. The next morning, Hitler and his staff directed the invasion from Siegfried Line fortifications on the German-French border.

Germany's mastery of subterfuge blinded virtually everyone. American war correspondents offered conflicting analyses of Germany's three-pronged invasion: "One new probability, and many new possibilities." The most likely outcome, posited one reporter, reflecting on World War I's three and a half years of grinding trench warfare, was that "the war raging in Europe was not likely to turn into a three-or-four-year endurance contest.... The war [is] more likely than not to end within a year." After all, Germany's factories could not turn out aircraft as fast as they were being destroyed.

Journalist Walter Lippmann offered another, less buoyant perspective: "If the offensive which Hitler has now launched succeeds, we shall know no peace in our lifetime...the Allies may lose the war this summer...before the snow flies, [the United States] may stand alone...the last great Democracy on earth."

With this invasion months of preparation, debate, and worry about Germany's next move ended in disaster for the Dutch—and for the Hesses. Listening to the stream of cars on the cobblestones beneath their balcony, to people yelling to each other outside, to footsteps pounding down the stairs outside their apartment, Karl and Ilse debated: Urgently: *We have to leave now!* But if they left the apartment: *We'll be arrested.* They felt abandoned by the Dutch, but decided to follow the government orders telling all German refugees to stay home. After three days of enforced inaction, Karl and Ilse decided they could wait no longer and attempted to escape the Nazis a second time. As Karl remembered, "I had left my automobile standing in front of the door. After short deliberation, we put our twins, two years old at the time, in the car and tried like the others to reach Ymuiden [IJmuiden, the nearest port city, thirteen miles from Amsterdam] in order to escape to England.... There were eight air raids, so that all of us had to get out of the car and find shelter with the children. Either the children were lying in a ditch or we were standing with them, squeezed together in a huge crowd in some bakery or factory."

■   ■   ■

The power of the German assault shocked the Dutch. The region had long prepared, and yet not adequately prepared, for this incursion. The possibility of a German invasion had threatened for so long that the Netherlands' sharp edge of readiness had grown dull. Belgium's massive Fort Eben-Emael on the Belgian-Dutch border with Germany, completed in 1935 and considered the world's strongest fortress, stood in apparent readiness. Dutch and Belgian ground troops and air defenses on high alert along their borders extended the strategic value of that citadel.

Yet only about 750 soldiers defended the fort that May, and it was unprepared when the Germans struck. In addition to the frontal attack unleashed on the ground, German aircraft dropped new top-secret "hollow charge" bombs that pulverized the fort's supposedly impenetrable defenses. Gliders and parachutists sailed over the walls and landed inside, trapping and killing its defenders or taking them prisoner. In the countryside, the Dutch opened dikes to flood large strategic areas. The flooding slowed but did not halt the German onslaught: German ground units paddled rubber rafts across those areas. Artillery loaded on light trucks rumbled across temporary bridges, also supported by rafts. Motorcycle troops with machine guns mounted on their sidecars rolled through narrow village streets.

In one fortunate official Dutch effort, before the Germans could occupy IJmuiden and other ports, the Royal Netherlands Navy set sail for Britain; most of the fleet arrived intact. At dawn on May 13, the British warship HMS *Hereward* sailed to the Netherlands with orders to return with the Dutch royal family, the Dutch gold reserves, and diamond-filled crates that were part of the royal treasury—and to destroy the docks as they departed.

Dutch forces blew up and sank a docked passenger ship at IJmuiden, perhaps one that the Hesses could otherwise have boarded, to prevent German warships from mooring. Thirty-five miles to the south in Rotterdam, Europe's busiest seaport, bombs rocked the central city. Citizens raced to air-raid shelters. Flames shot into the sky as the city burned. Bombs continued to fall, demolishing the city's historic center. One Rotterdam resident recalled the deafening noise: "*Boom! Boom! Boom!*" There seemed no place to run—the city lay in shambles. Nearly nine hundred civilians died; thirty thousand were left homeless.

After the assault, Germans hung posters proclaiming that Germany had taken the country. The harsh message ordered the Dutch to stop fighting and laid out strict regulations for the occupied population and punishments for disobedience. On the same day that Rotterdam was bombed, German planes dropped fluttering leaflets over the nearby city of Utrecht, threatening total destruction.

By May 13, German tanks had linked up with the paratroopers. The Dutch government entreated Winston Churchill to send three British divisions. The new prime minister sent only three torpedo boats, explaining that he had no other reserves. Later that day, Dutch general Henri Winkelman advised the government that he considered the situation critical. The cabinet instructed him to avoid unnecessary sacrifices and to surrender when he saw fit.

The Dutch air force had lost 65 of its 140 aircraft, some of which were outdated biplanes. Outnumbered, outgunned, outflanked, and out-planned, the Dutch military fought fiercely, but capitulated on Tuesday, May 14. Karl and Ilse listened to their wireless in horror as General Winkelman issued a sad proclamation of defeat. "In order to [save lives]...I feel myself justified in ordering all troops concerned to suspend operations. By great superiority of the most modern means, [the enemy] has succeeded in breaking our resistance." The next day, the Netherlands signed its surrender agreement. About twenty-three hundred Dutch soldiers had been killed, seven thousand wounded. More than three thousand civilians died in the four-day siege.

The Hesses, like most people in the Netherlands, would not learn for days about the huge scale of the German invasion that simultaneously smashed into Luxembourg, Belgium, and France. Even Churchill lacked information. In May and June, he flew five times to France through heavy battle zones to assess the rapidly evolving situation, trying without success to bolster French resolve for continuing to fight. He returned from those trips shaken.

Citizens, angry and terrified, wondered aloud, *Where are our dikes, our trenches, pillboxes, mined bridges, and canals?* During and after the attacks, people fled the cities in automobiles, motorcycles, and bikes, children and the elderly sometimes pushed in wheelbarrows by younger and stronger family members, many of the vehicles heaped with household goods. Jews throughout the Netherlands joined the thousands of terrified citizens attempting to flee south, unaware that all the Low Countries and northern France had become battlefields.

Conquest of the Netherlands was only one step in Germany's *Fall Gelb*, "Case Yellow," battle plan, the *Blitzkrieg* attack—a sudden attack by an overwhelming force—whose main objective was France. France had spent years building the elaborate, costly Maginot Line of forts and outposts along its border with Germany, never envisioning that Germany would—or could—attack through the neutral Low Countries. Luxembourg's mountainous Ardennes region had long been considered impassible for modern armies—a fatal miscalculation that looked to history, not the future.

Germany had accomplished what once had seemed impossible. On June 22, after a shockingly short battle, France signed an armistice ceding its northern provinces to direct German control and leaving two southern regions nominally unconquered. That supposedly free zone, Vichy France, would be administered by a puppet French government headed by aging antisemitic World War I hero Marshal Philippe Pétain. The Italian military ruled the southeastern sector.

Time magazine abandoned its traditional reporting style to conclude its report on the invasion with something like a sigh: "Things which seemed fantastic a fortnight before, now were not only possible, but probable."

■   ■   ■

Dutch authorities stopped each car on the road to check identification papers—the Hesses' undoubtedly were German-issued documents declaring them "stateless," a term that everyone understood to describe German Jews. Adults were also often asked a trick question. Adults were requested to say, "Scheveningen," the name of a Dutch town, since native German speakers could not pronounce the Dutch *ch* and *ng*. It is not known whether Karl and Ilse were given that test on their fraught journey, but by it or by some other means, they were identified as Germans. Karl explained, "Only seven miles before our destination [the port of IJmuiden], we were stopped by Dutch guards. Since we were not Dutch, we were sent back to Amsterdam. The following day the Germans marched into Amsterdam and that night we felt more miserable than ever before in our lives. We were trapped."

■   ■   ■

Steven has a cluttered snapshot memory of that journey, typical for the memories of a young child. He explained, "Once the Germans were there, all unknown until much later to Marion and me, our father made a desperate run for the port of IJmuiden to find passage over to England. Our car was stopped by Dutch police several times as we drove through Haarlem, not far from IJmuiden. The highlight of that desperate trip was a bomb attack that sent our parents running for shelter in the famous Droste chocolate factory. As twins, we always got a lot of attention and this time it came in the form of chocolate."

Ilse recalled the events of that night more starkly: "We tried to escape by boat to England, but we were caught on the way to the coast by the police and sent back to Amsterdam. That's where the nightmare began."

Karl's thoughts were the darkest of all. As I launched into his memoir at the beginning of my research, something he had written

CHAPTER 2

"It Was a Good Life"
1902–1935

Karl and Ilse's last chance for escape to England had vanished. They may well have regretted the choices that led them to this catastrophe; they were under no illusions about Jewish life under the Nazis. Their married life in Germany had begun under the dark cloud of Nazi hatred for Jews and Hitler's increasingly harsh campaign to create a *Judenfrei* Germany, a so-called Aryan nation free of Jews.

Karl and Ilse had already seen the articles, editorials, and posters and witnessed wild rallies and book burnings inciting Germans young and old to hate Jews. They had shuddered with disbelief as Nazis blamed an international cabal of Jewish bankers for Germany's deep financial troubles. Stereotypes of Jews as rich and greedy, disloyal and dishonest had existed for centuries in Europe, and Germany's Jews would have been painfully aware of

German antisemitism reaching back to the Crusades and Martin Luther. That ugly history had, it seemed, given way to acceptance. But now those hateful ideas infected all of German life.

The Hesses had grown up in a different Germany, one that they loved. Karl was the oldest of the four children of Josef Hess, a tough German horse and cattle trader, and his wife, Rosalie, known to her descendants as intellectual, fair-minded, a lover of opera. Neither Josef nor Rosalie fit Nazi stereotypes of Jews. As a youth, Josef had wanted to become a teacher, but by age eighteen he realized that working with livestock would provide a better living. Even so, throughout his life his nickname was *Schulmeister*, "Schoolmaster." The Hess family considered themselves loyal Germans, and they certainly did not have stashes of *Reichsmarks* or own a bank. Far from wealthy, Josef focused on supporting his family.

Josef was forty-one when World War I erupted. His descendants have no record of his serving in that war, and it's likely that his livestock business was considered essential for the war effort and he continued working. The family lived in the town of Fulda in central Germany, where Rosalie and Josef were assimilated into German culture but maintained Orthodox Jewish observances, including keeping kosher and ensuring that their sons had bar mitzvahs.

Born on January 3, 1902, Karl was an adolescent when World War I devastated what had been the German Empire. Perhaps like his schoolmates he imagined himself defending the fatherland. One hundred thousand Jews had donned the steel-grey uniform of the Kaiser's army during that war. About eighteen thousand were honored with the Iron Cross for bravery, the same medal that Hitler proudly affixed to his coat.

Karl may have been deeply affected by the war's carnage. He would have seen veterans on crutches hobbling along streets in town and witnessed the humiliation, fear, starvation, and anger that followed in the wake of the war.

Karl also heard the raucous shouts of people accusing Jews of stabbing Germany in the back, promoting defeatism, and undermining the war effort. Yet twelve thousand Jews had died fighting for Germany in the Great War, as World War I was then called. The real reasons for that surrender—Germany's economic ruin, hunger throughout the country, poor military strategy, unsustainable loss of life, and the disparity of military resources between Allied nations and those of Germany and its Central Powers allies—had not kept German generals from attempting to lay blame elsewhere. They were also vociferous in criticizing the new democratic government for the military constraints on Germany, laying the groundwork for a return to authoritarianism.

Karl's family was not political. His father was practical and physical. Josef was hard on his strong-willed, blond, blue-eyed son, perhaps in the same way that he disciplined uncooperative horses, and in keeping with how other fathers of that time meted out punishment. In 1918, as the war was ending, after one such incident, sixteen-year-old Karl had enough. He left home to make his way in a world in turmoil.

■   ■   ■

The war did not end completely or decisively for the Germans when they surrendered in 1918. In the Ruhr Valley, north of Fulda, Allied troops skirmished with Germans over unresolved treaty issues until 1930. Many Germans felt shocked and betrayed by the loss of the war and the terms of the peace. As the victorious Allied nations worked to establish a new, theoretically permanent government, revolution spread from German sailors to rival political factions across the country; several thousand people died in the upheaval. Socialist groups founded a Communist party loyal to the Soviet Union.

In 1921, Germany had the highest suicide rate of any country in the world. That year more than twelve thousand Germans committed suicide. The nation was bankrupt. The Treaty of Versailles had imposed a new, unfamiliar form of government—the Weimar Republic—on their shrunken nation. Germans had never elected their head of state. Under the Weimar Republic, women gained voting rights for the first time, a jolt for some conservatives. Reeling from onerous reparations demanded by the victorious Allies, the German nation struggled to make Versailles Treaty–mandated payments it could ill afford.

In mid-1923, when Karl was twenty-one, he also would have heard angry citizens railing about the burden of inflation, as Germany's economy reeled and prices doubled as often as every three days. Workers were paid twice a day to keep pace with the changing value of the currency; restaurant prices rose while patrons were still dining. By the end of that year, 4.2 trillion marks would purchase one American dollar, the equivalent of about seventeen U.S. dollars in 2022. Some currency bills were like works of art with beautiful designs printed on fabric and leather, but they quickly became almost worthless.

Currency reforms negotiated with the Allies helped to stabilize the economy, but those hard-earned gains evaporated with the 1929 Wall Street crash, which sent waves of economic crisis across Europe. By 1932, one in three Germans had no work. Wages plunged. Food shortages contributed to widespread hunger. As the country slipped into poverty, Germans openly criticized their new government. A spectrum of political factions battled for dominance, the tumult providing fertile ground for a demagogue.

Having thought long and hard about what happened in German society in the years before Hitler came to power, as the Nazis were gaining popularity and strength, I realized that this disorder was exactly what the World War I Allied nations had struggled to prevent. In this nexus of circumstances—deep political divisions, demise of a middle class, and economic upheavals—it was, and is, predictable that people will look to a "strong man" to fill the leadership void and lead them out of the mire.

While recurring economic shock waves buffeted the country, the 1920s and early 1930s were also exciting times in Germany. A people widely divided between the affluent and desperately poor, Germans experienced a golden age of science and culture, with Berlin the world's third largest city and an important business center. Science was changing the world. The term "modern" attached to anything— from art and architecture to psychiatry and synthetic rubber for sleek automobiles and military vehicles—meant glamour, vitality, progress, and power. Medicine was changing as well; scientists studied possible uses for antibiotic drugs, sulfa, and penicillin.

Around the Western world, radios, electricity, indoor bathrooms, and automobiles were coming within reach of ordinary people. Hitler, quick to understand the value of technology for a nation, was the first modern leader to make extensive use of air travel in political campaigns.

Albert Einstein received his Nobel Prize for Physics in Germany in 1921. In 1931, German scientists created the first working electron microscope. Magnetic tape recording was developed by a section of Germany's chemical giant IG Farben in the 1930s. The Bauhaus School's strong artistic lines, bright colors, and abstract art and architecture replaced intricate classical realism harking back to the Greeks; its influence resonated around the world. Young people flocked to cabarets and Germany's experimental cinema. No longer burdened by a crushing military budget, German culture in the mid-1920s and early 1930s flourished.

■   ■   ■

Karl's family has no account of his first years on his own or how he navigated the treacherous social and political currents of that time. It is a large gap in their family history. In the early 1920s, Germans resented Allied troops still in their midst monitoring the peace and enforcing ruinous reparations. Throughout the Weimar Republic, angry Communists, Socialists, labor leaders, ultra-conservatives, and the National Socialist German Workers' Party—the Nazis—battled in the streets and at the ballot box in contentious elections for control of the *Reichstag* Parliament. All were determined to exact revenge for Germany's post-war humiliation and set the country on a new track; yet for over a decade, no consensus emerged on how to move forward.

In 1923, Hitler and six hundred armed members of the Nazi *Sturmabteilung*—the dreaded *SA*, Hitler's armed brown-shirted paramilitary "Stormtroopers"—attacked a political meeting in a Munich beer hall. The *Putsch*, an intended revolution, failed, but it created havoc. The following day, a larger band of three thousand armed Nazi supporters marching to Munich's city center were met by a fusillade of police gunfire. This raid, too, failed. Hitler fled but was captured and arrested. He dominated his internationally publicized trial, spreading his notoriety. Jews were wary of the Nazi extremists in their midst, but they had little recourse for stopping them. Probably, Jews in small, quiet towns like Recklinghausen and Fulda initially had few, if any, encounters with Nazi supporters.

In prison for less than a year, Hitler spent his time writing the first volume of *Mein Kampf*, "My Struggle," his harangue on eugenics and the Aryan master race, on strategies for propaganda and violence—a call for pride in race, or "blood." It justified German demands for *Lebensraum*, "living space" for the master race in Eastern Europe, Poland, and parts of the Soviet Union. Hitler urged Aryans to join together in a *Volksgemeinschaft*, a community bound by blood, and to back a strong one-party government. *Mein Kampf* also declared war on Jews and Bolsheviks, branded as "enemies" of the German people and ranked at the bottom of Hitler's genetic hierarchy. His tome was not written in isolation. Supporters visited Hitler in Landsberg Prison, among them Bernhard Stempfle, a virulently antisemitic Catholic priest who advocated violence against Jews and helped edit *Mein Kampf*, published in 1925.

By 1932, a rising tide of antisemitism had engulfed Germany. The Brownshirts (SA) had attracted four hundred thousand recruits, approximately twenty times the size of the regular army. They patrolled the streets harassing, beating, sometimes killing Jews, Communists, homosexuals, and political rivals in the Reichstag, the Weimar Parliament.

Karl understood that the growing popularity, power, and thuggery of German politics posed a threat, and he stayed scrupulously distant from the political arena. As he found success in his career, a third of German workers were still unemployed. Food shortages, low wages, and the stubbornly depressed economy continued to drive Germans into Hitler's ranks. Hitler's extravagant promises of prosperity and world dominance, along with his messages of blame and hatred, resonated with people seeking a way out of their difficulties and a leader they could believe in. His dramatic, carefully orchestrated speeches inspired frenzied loyalty and hope among the dispirited Germans. As the nation's Jews read about the wild speeches and felt the growing danger in the streets, they were powerless to stop the frenzy. In 1932, Nazis won enough seats in the Reichstag that with Communists, the next largest party, they comprised over half the country's lawmaking body.

Alert to the Nazis' growing strength, German president Paul von Hindenburg, known fondly as "The Old Gentleman," had resisted popular pressure to name violence-prone Hitler as Germany's next leader. Yet Hindenburg himself was deeply anti-democratic, and he sympathized with many Nazi political ideas. Eventually, on January 30, 1933, the eighty-four-year-old World War I military hero bent to the Nazis' growing popularity and named Hitler Reich Chancellor of Germany, naively believing that he could control Hitler. Hitler then convinced the Reichstag to allow him to rule by decree. One month later, shortly before a significant national election, a fire destroyed the Reichstag, Parliament's capitol building.

Communist agitators were accused of arson, and many Communists, including lawmakers, were arrested. As Communist numbers dwindled in the Reichstag, Nazis gained control, consolidating Hitler's authority. In that moment of a supposed Communist insurrection, Hitler convinced Hindenburg to grant him the authority to rule by decree. The Nazis were later accused of starting the fire, but by that time the issue was moot; Hitler had already become Germany's dictator. The Weimar Republic—cash-strapped creation of World War I's Versailles Treaty and the Allies' hope for a constrained, democratic Germany—was dead.

It is during this time that Karl emerged from the shadows of family history in his early thirties as a dashing, successful, self-made businessman. He had become a manager and wholesale sales representative at Europe's largest silk weaver, United Silk Corporation, based in Krefeld, not far from Karl's hometown, with mills operating across Germany.

The family-owned company had been founded in the eighteenth century by Mennonites, who, like the Jews, had at times been discriminated against for their religion. Originally selling linen, the family had turned to silk during a market downturn, at first producing velvet ribbons, then fine silk fabric. In the nineteenth and twentieth centuries, as silk markets burgeoned, United Silk grew substantially. By the 1920s and 1930s, the company was known across Europe for a range of high-quality textiles, including the newly popular nylon and fine silks, some with artwork printed on the fabric.

With Karl's business success came rewards, including beautifully tailored clothes and tickets to cultural events. He owned a horse and was a skilled equestrian. At a time when many Germans did not yet own automobiles and some street carts delivering produce were still horse-drawn, he drove a black Mercedes convertible. He was known as a fine dancer, perhaps mastering popular ballroom dances and the energetic swing dances that, like jazz, originated in black American ghettos. He was a man about town, an eligible bachelor in post-war Germany's dire economic times, a "catch."

Karl's personal life was also about to take a turn he could not have anticipated. His memoir is silent about his life as a young man. His children say that he made peace with his father and always showed him great respect. His imperfect family was important to him. Not one to hold a grudge, he regularly returned to his parents' home for visits. He helped them financially when he could. His descendants also recall that before the 1930s Karl dated non-Jewish girls. That freedom disappeared along with the Weimar Republic, as Nazi influence over German culture spread.

Marion explains:

> All of a sudden, our father realized that he couldn't easily go out with non-Jewish girls. He had a lot of non-Jewish girlfriends, so he knew he had better look for a Jewish bride. He had a blind date arranged. Then he came on business to Recklinghausen, a small town in western Germany where my mother's family lived. When an upstanding Jewish person maybe looking for a wife visited the town, my grandfather and grandmother would host them for lunch. My mother's father was a little bit like the unofficial Mayor for the Jewish community. So, our father stopped there for lunch before meeting his date, and he saw my mother. It was love at first sight, and that was the end of blind dates.

■   ■   ■

Ilse's upbringing could hardly have been more different from Karl's. Born in Recklinghausen on February 9, 1914, she was twelve years younger, just six months old when World War I began. She was ten when Hitler gained absolute control over the Nazi Party. She very likely saw the aftermath of the Putsch and witnessed its horrible toll. She grew up the only child of a well-to-do merchant, Willi Hirschberg, who managed the Jewish-owned department store *Gebrüder Alberg*, Alberg Brothers. Ilse's mother, Fanny, was the store's buyer of women's apparel. Fanny traveled frequently to Berlin, where she studied the latest fashions and bought for the store, perhaps at times taking Ilse with her.

The Hirschbergs were highly assimilated, and they identified with the liberal Judaism that had gained broad support among German Jews. They were leaders of Recklinghausen's Jewish community, which numbered over three hundred. Willi served as head of the synagogue's board of directors. Although Ilse was an only child, Fanny came from what sounds today like an impossibly large family of twenty-one children. The family members visited each other often and met for Jewish holidays. Ilse was a happy, outgoing young woman, strong-willed, resourceful, surrounded by friends and relatives, and known for her beauty.

Marion remembers her mother mentioning her own father, who had served in World War I. Marion says she is "not sure in what capacity" her grandfather served:

> I have to assume that my maternal grandparents kept
> up to date on politics of the late '20s, early '30s. After

all, they were lay leaders of the Jewish community in Recklinghausen, my grandfather the manager of the town's largest department store, my grandmother a frequent visitor to Berlin and part of a large family that came together often and were likely very aware of what was happening. That said, they were probably not political activists, but certainly kept informed through the filter of the well-being and safety of the Jewish community and the future of their only child. My mother often mentioned the many non-Jewish friends she had in school and how painful it was to suddenly see the growing division and unraveling of those peaceful and "tolerant" times.

Karl's business trip to Recklinghausen in 1933 upended both his and Ilse's previous plans. Her parents respected Karl as a fair, upstanding businessman; otherwise, they would not have invited him to their home to join the family's midday dinner where he would meet their beautiful young daughter. But they hadn't considered him marriage material. He was older, his background was different, and he seemed perhaps a bit too much a man-about-town. Nor was Ilse looking for a suitor. According to Marion, "My father always had a quiet authority. He was a presence, very dignified. For starters, he was extremely good looking and always dressed in style and immaculately. Perhaps he was more outgoing at that time, when the future looked so promising."

"What I do know about our father," says Steven, "is that he was a dandy, an excellent dancer, a horseman. He was also handsome and (hate to even say this) not what some would call stereotypically Jewish in looks or behavior. That probably insulated him on the mean streets."

Marion remembers that her mother "was interested in someone else. She was about to run off to marry a wonderful man. But for my mother, too, at that meeting, it was love at first sight. Her family at first was not pleased with her choice. He came from such a different background." Ilse's family were observant Jews, but more casually than Karl's.

On February 16, 1934, six months after they met, Ilse and Karl were married in Recklinghausen's only synagogue. Karl was thirty-two, Ilse twenty. They began what promised to be a fairy-tale life. They honeymooned and skied in fashionable Arosa, Switzerland, a German-speaking mountain resort town. A New Year's Eve photo from that time shows them in evening clothes, seated at a small table, leaning toward each other and smiling broadly, their feet touching. Karl wears a crisp tuxedo, his hair glossy with Brilliantine like American celebrities Howard Hughes and Clark Gable. Ilse, her dark hair drawn back in a chic knot, wears a simple form-fitting sheath reaching almost to her ankles.

After their honeymoon, Karl continued working for United Silk, a business valued and protected by the Nazis. Ilse set up their apartment in Düsseldorf, a beautiful area of high rolling plains between Recklinghausen and Fulda; she was known as a wonderful cook. They continued to help Karl's parents financially, enjoyed the symphony, and bought a cuddly Scotch terrier, "Teddy." They brought Teddy with them on long rides in the countryside in their big Mercedes convertible. It was a good life.

■ ■ ■

As the newlyweds began their life together, the German people were adopting a new self-image. After years of upheaval and suffering, they had a stable government that boasted about German superiority and put people to work. Finally, Germans could envision a better future. Hitler's followers talked about the "Third Reich," a historically incorrect reference to the beginning of a third German Empire, but a hopeful image that Germans identified with. Some referred to Nazi governance as the "Thousand Year Reich."

One of Hitler's priorities was launching an increasingly complex system of control and enforcement throughout Germany. Within months of becoming chancellor on January 30, 1933, he formed the *Gestapo*, the official Nazi secret police, under the control of Hermann Göring. Göring dismissed many municipal police chiefs, replacing them with high-ranking leaders from the SA. Joseph Goebbels, director of Propaganda and Public Enlightenment, restricted Germans' access to news.

The black-shirted *SS* or *Schutzstaffel*, "protective echelon," was the Nazi paramilitary rival to the SA. Founded in 1925, the SS had grown exponentially in numbers and strength under Heinrich Himmler. On the "Night of the Long Knives," in June 1934, the SS, in collusion with the German army, assassinated at least eighty SA leaders across the country, leaving the SS as Hitler's personal army, reporting directly to him. The SA was reorganized under Hitler's tighter control and reduced to street enforcers who continued to arrest and intimidate Jews. They terrorized the streets, plastering boycott or *"Jude"* signs on Jewish stores, preventing Jews from attending public schools and universities, and patrolling Jewish businesses to prevent Aryans from entering.

Mein Kampf was Germany's bestselling book in 1933. That year, Hitler received about 1.2 million Reichsmarks (RM) in royalties at a time when the average annual income of a teacher was about RM 4,800. Later, the book would be given to newlywed couples and every soldier fighting on the fronts, bought and paid for by local communities—with the profits helping Hitler to pay his many debts.

When President Hindenburg died in August of 1934, the Nazi-controlled Reichstag swiftly passed a law combining the offices of president and chancellor, transferring all authority to Chancellor Adolf Hitler. In the wake of Hitler's successful takeover of the government, the German army swore an oath of unconditional obedience to Hitler, who preferred the ambiguous, nationalistic title *Führer*, derived from a High German language root meaning "leader." The title was new, flexible, and did not carry the baggage of the more limiting titles "president" and "chancellor." For sixteen years, Hitler had struggled to build, mold, expand, and command the Nazi Party; by 1934, he had transformed the violent, disorganized movement into an iron-fisted dictatorship.

Almost immediately after Hitler attained power—with an order that would come to be inseparably identified with the Führer—construction on prison camps for "corrective treatment" of his many enemies began. The black-shirted enforcers of Hitler's SS operated the Dachau, Heuberg, and Sachsenhausen camps, opened in 1933 as small, harsh prisons for political prisoners. Hitler's explicit mandate to SS chief Heinrich Himmler was brutality.

Within two years of Dachau's opening, twenty-seven thousand people, including trade unionists, Social Democrats, Communists, and Jehovah's Witnesses, were in "protective custody." Camps emerged like spring mushrooms, established by local police, the SA, and the SS, with or without central authorization; dozens of prisons in Berlin soon held hundreds of inmates. By August 1934, hundreds of Jews had already been imprisoned across the Reich.

There was a crucial difference between these Nazi camps and traditional prisons: Prisons held criminals duly tried and convicted by courts for breaking German laws. Hitler's camps, in contrast, functioned as political prisons for individuals and groups, without trial, a sentence, or legal recourse. The Nazis sent their enemies directly to camps where prisoners languished for an indefinite period. Every citizen would have been justified in worrying that he or she was not an adequately enthusiastic Nazi supporter. Germany had devolved into a brutal totalitarian police state.

■   ■   ■

Karl and Ilse charted a careful path through the chaos. As Hitler consolidated his grip on the nation, they would have encountered new sources of danger in the streets. In 1926, Hitler had organized young German followers into the *Hitlerjugend*, "Hitler Youth," calling them "our future." The Hitler Youth has been described as something like America's Boy and Girl Scouts, but, in reality, the Hitler Youth brainwashed Aryan boys and girls ages ten to eighteen to become aggressive, militaristic, fanatical Nazis. Meetings began with an altered version of the Lord's Prayer, with Hitler the new god who demanded absolute loyalty: "*Adolf Hitler,*

Sie sind unser grosser Führer. Dein Name lässt den Feind erzittern, Dein Wille allein is Gesetz auf Erden...." "Adolf Hitler, you are our great Führer. Thy name makes the enemy tremble. Thy Third Reich come. Thy will alone is law on earth. Let us hear daily thy voice and order us by thy leadership, for we will obey to the end, even with our lives. We praise thee! Heil Hitler!"

Church-run primary schools were abolished. Children began school with the morning greeting, "Heil Hitler." Women's groups in small towns embroidered tapestries depicting Hitler Youth boys, the SA, and the League of German Girls in formations in the shape of the Christian cross. Some Hitler Youth mocked their own parents who seemed too moderate and out of step with the times. By 1940, Hitler Youth membership had skyrocketed to include 80 percent of young Germans, and Nazi-based movements spread to other countries, including the Netherlands.

As 1935 followed on the heels of 1934, all around Ilse and Karl, life was changing almost daily for Germany's Jews, growing increasingly dangerous. Hitler Youth joined SA Stormtroopers in raucous nights of book burning, destroying the wide range of books banned by the Reich, including anything by or about Jews. In seventy cities across Germany, looting and destruction of Jewish property often accompanied the nearly one hundred book burnings. In Berlin in 1933, seventy thousand people marched in a torchlight procession to one such book burning. Hermann Göring, Reich aviation minister, pontificated to the young Hitler followers at a number of the wild nighttime events, shouting that "Hitler performs God's miracles." Groups of Hitler Youth roamed Germany's streets, plastering boycott signs on Jewish businesses, breaking windows of Jewish shops, and beating Jews old and young.

A stream of new laws eliminated Jews from Germany's professional and cultural life and allowed non-Jewish Germans to take over Jewish businesses. Bands of Nazi groups, including the Brownshirts and Hitler Youth, beat Jews on the streets or arrested and sent them to camps for no cause. Thousands of Jews suddenly found themselves impoverished.

Emigration increased in lockstep with the harshness of Nazi pressure. Jews fled around the globe, wherever they found countries willing and able to accommodate them; in the five years from 1933 to 1938, nearly one in four of Germany's 523,000 Jews emigrated, most of them to the United States and Palestine, others to Shanghai, South America, and Africa, notably Kenya. A few founded a colony in Uganda.

As Nazis burned books, deplored and desecrated modern art, and banned many movies, German artists, authors, painters, musicians, and scientists (including Albert Einstein, conductor Bruno Walter, and members of Hamburg's respected Warburg Institute) left Germany. Within two years of the start of Hitler's dictatorship, more than eighty thousand people emigrated from Germany, most of them Jewish. Anne Frank's family was among the more than five thousand Germans who fled to the Netherlands shortly after Hitler gained power.

Recently, speaking about the emotional upheaval their parents may have experienced when leaving their homeland, Steven and Marion were asked how long their family had lived in Germany. Both hesitated, as if caught by surprise; apparently the question made no sense. They had answered innumerable questions for me about their family during the Holocaust, but to them, the answer to this one seemed obvious.

Marion: "Hundreds of years."

Steven: "Always."

Karl and Ilse had hoped that their assimilated lifestyle, his work for a German business, and their non-Jewish appearance would allow them to "pass" for Aryan at work and on the streets. Also, because he worked for an Aryan business, Karl had been able to follow the advice of the *Hilfsverein der Deutschen Juden*, the German-Jewish Community Association, established in 1901 to help Jews escape Eastern European pogroms. In the 1930s, it again supported Jews hoping to flee, this time from Germany, but advised, "Keep your position for as long as you can."

■   ■   ■

By 1935, Hitler had grown impatient with scattershot measures pressuring Jews to leave the Reich. At the Seventh Nazi Party Congress in Nuremberg on September 15, in an uncharacteristically short ten-minute speech, he announced what would become known as the Nuremberg Laws, sweeping measures creating a foundation for current and future racial persecution. The *Reichsbürgergesetz*, the "Law of the Reich Citizen," deprived Jews of German citizenship and made them "subjects of the state." That day, Jews lost their standing as Germans and fell beyond the protection of law. Citizenship, Hitler intoned, was the privilege only of those Aryans who proved they were willing to "loyally serve the German people and the Reich." A second Nuremburg law forbade intermarriage between Jews and Aryans. To further protect Hitler's concept of pure German bloodlines, Aryan women under age forty-five could no longer work as household help for Jews. Hitler may have had a particularly sensitive reason for promulgating that law; there were persistent rumors that his grandmother, a domestic worker, had become pregnant out of wedlock by her employer—or even worse, whispers implied, by an itinerant Jewish peddler.

A third announcement: Hitler had created a new German flag. Since 1848, the national flag's three horizontal bands of black, red, and gold had flown over the nation; Hitler replaced that flag with the Nazi Party's familiar banner, its blood-red background emblazoned with a hooked black cross, a swastika, on a white circle. In Hitler's fiery speech, he referred to an incident in the United States that had triggered the change. During that summer of 1935, American protesters, including "Jews and Communists," had torn a Nazi flag from the stern of a German vessel, the *Bremen*, docked in New York's harbor. Members of that protest group had thrown the flag into the Hudson River, calling it "a black flag of piracy."

The Jewish magistrate who tried the protesters' case had released the accused because of insufficient evidence. In his verbal statement, Magistrate Brodsky had perhaps inappropriately taken it upon himself to imagine the frame of mind of the accused. The *New York Times* printed his entire statement, in which he stressed that Americans enjoy freedom of speech and the right to assemble. Brodsky said that the accused saw the Nazi flag as an emblem of the "war on religious freedom...the enslavement of women and workers...the suppression of the blessed trinity of free speech, freedom of the press and lawful assembly, the degradation of culture, an international menace threatening freedom; a revolt against civilization—in brief, if I may borrow a biological concept, an atavistic throwback to pre-medieval, if not barbaric, social and political conditions." Berlin made a formal complaint to President Roosevelt, who responded with a formal apology.

At the rally that followed the Reichstag session, a crowd numbering around seven hundred thousand applauded Hitler's announcement of the new antisemitic laws and another of equally ominous import—the reinstatement of compulsory military service. With this announcement, Hitler flagrantly "liberated" Germany from the strictures of the despised Treaty of Versailles that forbade Germany from rebuilding its military above a prescribed limit of one hundred thousand men. "What one German nation has vainly hoped for during centuries has been achieved at last.... The German people can be happy with this regained strength after such terrible suffering and long unconsciousness...Germany is healthy again." Hitler arranged for radios to be inexpensive enough that citizens across the country could tune in to his speeches in their homes.

In reality, almost all the fighting in World War I had taken place on French and Belgian soil. Germany's factories and military establishments, many of them located in eastern Germany, had escaped the war largely unscathed. Even before Hitler rose to power, President Hindenburg, a war hero, had begun rebuilding Germany's military might.

The *New York Times* ran a front-page story about Hitler's speech, giving the full text of his address and news about the annual Reichstag Congress and frenetic Nazi rally that followed it: "National Socialist Germany definitely [has] flung down the gauntlet before the feet of Western liberal opinion tonight when the Reichstag, assembled for a special session here in connection with the 'Party Day of Freedom,' decreed a series of laws that put Jews beyond the legal and social pale of the German nation, and in token of this act proclaimed the swastika banner to be the sole flag of the German Reich. With this action, in the words of Reichstag President Goering, begins the next step of 'National Socialist upbuilding.'"

The article noted that, to some observers of Hitler's Reichstag speech, it seemed "symbolic that after a beautiful day a steady downpour of rain started just as the Reichstag let out." The article concluded with the report that, after wild cheering from the six hundred Reichstag delegates and the assembled crowds that should have left Hitler elated, "Hitler returned to his hotel with a "drawn and unsmiling face." I thought it an odd observation for a journalist, seeming to foreshadow Germany's impending provocations—Hitler's breaches of the Treaty of Versailles.

That day, a bulletin in London's *Daily Telegraph* reported that a Berlin dispatch had alerted the British government that "virtually the whole German fleet of U-boats [submarines] would engage in naval maneuvers commencing Sept. 17 for the first time since the First World War."

In that same momentous year, 1935, Gebrüder Alberg, the department store that Ilse's father managed and where her mother also worked, was Aryanized, part of the forced takeover of Jewish businesses across Germany by non-Jews at fire-sale prices. Like thousands of other German Jews, Ilse's once flourishing family had lost their work and their citizenship.

Over the course of nearly six years, 1933 through early 1938, countless hundreds of laws, regulations, orders, decrees, rules, and clarifications rained down on the Reich's more than five hundred thousand Jews, which in March 1938 included the nearly two hundred thousand Jews in Austria. Pernicious decrees in 1938 required

Jewish passports to be stamped with a large red *J* and, in 1939, forced Jews to add the middle names "Sara" or "Israel" to all legal documents, making them easily identifiable targets. Over those years, the Nazis' policies of hatred and greed began their deadly escalation from crippling taxes and repressive laws pressuring Jews to leave Germany to property confiscations, imprisonment, and murder. Hitler had threatened as much in his Nuremberg speech: "If international Jewish agitation should continue....if the attempt at legal regulation fails again, the problem will have to be transferred from law to the National Socialist Party for a final solution."

CHAPTER 3

Running
1935–1937

After fifteen years of troubled peace, Hitler was leading his devoted followers down the path of war—but the world was not ready to face that reality. As early as 1934, Winston Churchill, then a member of Parliament, had alerted the British to the increasing German air menace and the likelihood of German aggression, but the war-weary nation had ignored his warning.

Among Hitler's first negotiations with foreign leaders were his meetings with Italy's Fascist prime minister, Benito Mussolini. They would meet six times between June 1934 and May 1939, their meetings marked by shouting matches and pounding fists that rattled the table and worried aides of both leaders. The Nazi and Fascist dictators agreed on their mutual scorn for what they decried as the stuffy, class-conscious English. They forged a political and military understanding, aligning their intentions for expansion into Austria,

France, and North Africa. Mussolini allowed the SA and the SS to train with his own paramilitary brigade, the Blackshirts. Hitler had already modeled his failed Munich Putsch on the 1922 "March on Rome" that led to Mussolini's appointment as prime minister. Mussolini would later replicate many of Hitler's antisemitic policies. From their earliest meeting, Mussolini enthusiastically described the relationship between the two countries as the "Axis" around which Europe would one day revolve.

In early 1935, Hitler directed a campaign of intimidation to assure passage of a League of Nations–mandated plebiscite and return the contested coal-rich Saar Territory to Germany. A League of Nations plebiscite commissioner later termed the campaign, which included espionage and kidnapping, a "reign of terror." Even the Nazis were surprised by the 90 percent vote for unification with Germany.

When in that same year Hitler announced his determination to reinstate compulsory military conscription, that flagrant violation of the Treaty of Versailles tested international resolve to oppose him, to resist his Kampf. Encountering no response of consequence to the ominous new draft laws, Germany accelerated its efforts to rebuild the Wehrmacht, its military.

The following year, on March 6, 1936, in disregard of another Versailles Treaty clause that the Allies had once viewed as crucial, Hitler ordered more than twenty thousand German troops into the Rhineland, a region bordering the Netherlands, Belgium, France, and Switzerland. Slightly smaller than the state of New Jersey, the demilitarized area had offered those neighboring nations a buffer against German expansion. That easily acquired territory suddenly opened a clear pathway for Germany to attack its neighbors. The

Allies—including Britain, Belgium, France, Italy, Japan, Russia, and the United States—had suffered over ten million deaths to win World War I, and the European countries had demanded protection from German invasion. Germany had lost nearly two and a half million war dead, but it suffered no losses retaking the Rhineland. Equally important to Hitler was that, once again, he had tested the Allies' resolve and found it weak.

What had happened to the ferocity of the World War I Allies? Remilitarizing the Rhineland was a slap in their faces. Why didn't they intervene and block Germany's early advances when they could have done so with relative ease? Why not protest loudly and confront the growing war on Jews? Hitler had made clear his intention to unify Germans living in other lands, even at the cost of war, and his persecution of Jews was no secret.

The reality that Hitler understood was that many British people believed World War I's treaty strictures were overly harsh. Their mood was isolationist; Britain had not aggressively rearmed after World War I. And France, well-armed but on the verge of a general election, was not prepared to act without Britain. After the Rhineland remilitarization, Britain's foreign secretary did meet with the German ambassador, to whom he presented toothless "proposals" for withdrawal. The World War I Allies did not know then that Hitler was secretly rearming. It is not known today what Karl's and Ilse's parents thought about Hitler's ominous military exploits. But they had seen war. And Karl was of an age to serve in the military, Ilse at a time to think about marriage and a family. They had cause to be deeply worried.

Hitler's gambles paid off, and in 1936 Germany felt free to turn to preparations for the Summer Olympic Games in August in

Berlin. Germans would win 101 medals over those sixteen days, the United States a distant second with 57. The games closed with a dazzling "light dome" formed by 152 antiaircraft searchlights borrowed from the Luftwaffe and aimed skyward, creating the spectacular illusion of a wall of light. At the same time, unknown to the visiting dignitaries and cheering crowds, forced labor was constructing Sachsenhausen concentration camp just twenty-three miles away.

■   ■   ■

At the 1935 Party Congress in Nuremberg, the Nazis had raucously applauded Hitler's fierce declaration of war on Jews, accepting his war of eugenics, a race war, as if that concept was a reasonable tenet of law. Hitler pursued his obsession with the same intensity he had demonstrated during his campaign to free Germany from Treaty of Versailles restrictions and his military aggression. By 1936, Jews had been cast out of the German civil service. German schools limited enrollment of Jewish students to 1.5 percent. Nazis were stunned to realize that nearly 75 percent of the sixty thousand school-aged Jewish children claimed legal exemptions from that law, notably those whose fathers had served during the First World War. New laws that followed the Nazis' first expulsion attempt would keep 100 percent of Jewish youth from school. Increasingly after 1936, newspaper articles, movies, newsreels, radio bulletins, and even loudspeakers blaring in marketplaces and on street corners echoed with the avalanche of new laws, reports of Germany's military advances, and speeches by Hitler laced with hatred of the Jewish people.

Life for Jews had become surreal. Jews were "denounced" by their neighbors to German police or to the Gestapo and arrested for random infractions of Nazi rules, or for no reason at all. A frequent accusation to the Gestapo about Jews concerned *Rassenschande*, "race defilement," Jews having sexual relations with Aryans. Landlords with whom Jews had longstanding and cordial relationships evicted them from their businesses and homes. One Jewish woman who survived the Holocaust, Alice Resseguie, described her family's experience in the town of Trier: "During the boycott of Jewish businesses, our business fell off, but some customers came after hours, or called in orders, before our phone was tapped. Brown Shirt troopers burst in one day and searched for Communist material and closed the store. Then they stationed themselves in front of the building. Suddenly the landlord wanted us out. We should move our store. My father had served in the Kaiser's Imperial 69th Infantry Regiment, but now, no one would trade with Jews. We feared everything." Alice's earthy mother told the family, "Hitler is going to shit on us," and she insisted on quickly getting their daughters out of the country.

Bands of Hitler Youth, police, Brownshirts, and ordinary people on the street and in churches sang the militant, nationalistic *"Horst Wessel"* song, raising their arms in the Nazi salute: "Raise the flag! The ranks tightly closed! The SA marches with calm, steady step...."

Around 1935, Karl and Ilse Hess pivoted from their lifetime of fitting in, keeping a low profile, and, more recently, just hanging on, to devising plans to leave Germany. The accepting German culture they had grown up in had turned hostile and chaotic. In the past, they had found avenues for safety and success, as Jews in Europe had done for centuries, but those were gone. The Hesses debated their options, talked with friends, agonized over their narrowing choices. Should they leave Germany? How could they accomplish that? Where could they go, and how would they live? What would happen to their families left behind? The Hilfsverein, the Jewish Community Association, had abandoned its ambivalent position. Its message to Jews after 1935 was "GO!"

■　　■　　■

Jewish unemployment continued to rise, especially in finance, banking, cattle dealing, and large department stores, among the first businesses to be Aryanized. Between 1933 and 1938, some two-thirds of the approximately one hundred thousand Jewish-owned businesses in Germany were either Aryanized or forced out of business.

As emigration numbers increased and Germany's military buildup put stress on the country's economy, restrictions on what Jews could take with them tightened. Individuals leaving the country in 1933 were entitled to take 200 Reichsmarks (RM 200). Later it was RM 50, and, in 1937, RM 10. Additionally, a May 18, 1934, law introduced the *Reichsfluchtsteuer*, a "flight tax," amounting to 25 percent of one's income or assets for those with middle class incomes. New laws required Jews applying for emigration to deposit what remained of their assets after the draconian taxation into "blocked" accounts. Those accounts came with strict oversight, allowing very limited withdrawals, barely enough to cover minimal daily living expenses. Immigration officials around the world understood that the Jews had essentially been stripped of their assets, and they accordingly devalued the assets listed on Jews' immigration applications. Middle class emigration became difficult; lower class emigration was all but impossible. Countries around the world closed their doors to the large numbers of fleeing, impoverished Jews, leaving them trapped where they were no longer wanted. A number of countries ratcheted up their entry requirements. Americans, passionately isolationist, increasingly scrutinized all immigration. The country dreaded entanglement in another European war, and some U.S. State Department officials were openly antisemitic. The United States' weak economy whipsawed between recovery from the Depression and recession; in some states, one in five people walked the streets looking for work.

■   ■   ■

Karl and Ilse urged their parents to leave Germany while they still could. Karl's parents, Josef and Rosalie, were eager to go. Their cattle business had been Aryanized. Their children had no future in German lands. Rosalie, Josef, Karl's brother, and one of his sisters began making plans to immigrate to the United States, contacting relatives in Manhattan. They would travel through neutral Portugal, where refugees thronged the streets waiting for their visas to be approved. Karl's other sister immigrated to Sweden. Karl and Ilse helped them financially.

Karl and Ilse also encouraged Ilse's parents, Fanny and Willi Hirschberg, to flee with them to Amsterdam, but they would not leave Germany. Their rabbi, Selig Auerbach, made the difficult choice to flee Recklinghausen to immigrate to the United States, while the Hirschbergs made the even more agonizing judgment not to leave Recklinghausen, but to remain there and continue supporting the town's Jewish community.

Karl and Ilse's decision to immigrate only as far as Amsterdam may seem, on its surface, inconsistent with their determination to flee Germany. Why send Karl's family to safety in America, but stay behind in Europe themselves? In fact, in 1937, the Nazis were envisioning Jewish emigration from Germany, not genocide. Also, Karl had been offered a good job, waiting for him just across the border, only about a four-hour train ride from Ilse's family, with whom they could remain close. Most compelling—in half-wishful, half–historically driven reasoning—they believed that Hitler would not be so rapacious as to attack a country that was already and repeatedly declaring its neutral intentions. Surely the Nazis would leave the Netherlands in peace, as Germany had done in 1914. But the Hess family would learn that no one, not even most Nazis, could look over the horizon, and predict what Hitler might do.

■　　　■　　　■

The Netherlands had a mixed history of tolerance toward Jews. In the Middle Ages, the Dutch sent bands of crusaders to the Holy Land to kill Jews and Arabs, and in 1350 they blamed Jews for the Plague and expelled them from Amsterdam. Yet in the late 1500s, the Amsterdam city council allowed Jewish refugees from Spain's Inquisition to settle within the city's walls. By the early eighteenth century, the Jewish community in Amsterdam numbered over ten thousand, the largest in Europe, and Jews found shelter in a new part of Amsterdam, islands in a recently drained marshland that became known as the Jewish Quarter. While some

Jews were still drawn to that traditional neighborhood, in more recent times they had spread throughout the city. Amsterdam had granted Jews equal rights in 1796, though discrimination embedded in Dutch society restrained their economic progress. When industrialization and modernization had coursed through Europe, the new prosperity brought some Dutch Jews security and increasing wealth, though many others remained impoverished. Amsterdam's Jews helped to build the city's booming diamond and textile industries, creating a new prosperous Jewish social class bent on progress.

Yet resistance to the influx of German Jews surfaced in the mid-1930s, and some of it came not from antisemites or Dutch conservatives but from Dutch Jews. In the late 1930s, the economy of the Netherlands was still struggling under the impact of the worldwide Depression. Dutch Jews held a small but significant hard-won role in the government and economy. They worried that the thousands of impoverished Jewish refugees would burden the economy and, even more frightening, trigger waves of antisemitism.

Also troubling to some of the Netherlands' Jewish community, German Jews tended to be more liberal than Dutch Jews, many of whom were Orthodox. Many Dutch Jews traced their roots back centuries to Sephardic Jews who fled the Spanish Inquisition. German Jews tended to be more liberal or, like the Hesses, only loosely observant. The influx from Germany presented an economic burden, a political threat, and a culture clash among Jews. The Dutch Jews' response to the mass immigration had been relatively generous, but from the record of migrations worldwide, history would have predicted a backlash.

Notwithstanding the vein of antisemitism running through the culture and the Netherlands' ambiguous past, its history flowed in a positive direction, with the Dutch welcoming enough to Jews in 1937 to attract Karl, Ilse, and thousands of others over the next three increasingly perilous years in Germany.

Either Karl's job with United Silk was Aryanized, or he saw trouble coming and arranged to emigrate ahead of it. As Steven points out, "United Silk was a multinational company. My father's boss said, 'Karl, here's what we're going to do. We have a manager in Amsterdam. We will bring him back and assign Holland to you as the manager. You will take over that office.' Why did they stay so close to Germany? Remember, the Holocaust had not been invented. Not in the Nazis' minds either. 'Judenfrei' ["Free of Jews"] was the goal. Jews go! Whatever they owned, stayed."

It was no simple matter for Jews to leave Germany—much less to take their assets with them. Karl's Mercedes may have been a company car, or it may have been confiscated by the Nazis. He packed his bags and took a train across the border with minimum difficulty. Even so, in the best of times, uprooting from home can be disorienting and challenging; in those menacing times, the change required both decisive action and plans inside of plans.

The Hesses sent money to a relative in America as part of a contingency plan should Amsterdam not work out. Ilse's valuable jewelry had been left with friends in Switzerland to prevent Nazi theft. Karl, age thirty-five, left Germany in May of 1937 and found a third-floor apartment at Albrecht Dürerstraat 17. Their new home was not in the Jewish Quarter, but on a busy thoroughfare in a middle class neighborhood, near tram lines and a lovely park, not far from the historic city center.

For Ilse, then twenty-three, the move would be neither straightforward nor easy. Her complicated tasks comprised a long list: arrange for her Swiss friend to bring the jewelry to her in Germany; find trusted caretakers for precious belongings she could not take to Amsterdam, including linens, porcelains, and several oil paintings and miniatures; dispose of things they no longer wanted or could not keep; obtain an exit visa; and pack and schedule for luggage to be inspected and shipped to Amsterdam. After heartbreaking moments of farewell to friends and family and the places that she loved, she would travel alone by train to her new home.

If she could get an exit visa. Steven tells the story:

> Our father was already in Holland and Mom was going through the process of getting a Nazi exit visa. She was instructed to report to a local official office (I do not remember or never knew if this was a police office or some other bureaucracy.) My mother took along their non-Jewish accountant and personal close friend since this was going to be a "where's the money?" interview. Mom told me she put on a customary elegant outfit complete with hat and feather, which was the fashion of the times. Jewelry, obviously not involved. How stupid would that have been? The German official kept insisting that Mom and Dad clearly had wealth. The accountant (a close friend and not being a Jew, totally OK with the official) finally, indicating our elegant and beautiful mother, whispered to the German inquisitor: "Take a look at her, she spends every dime her husband makes!" Problem solved. We've laughed over that.

Following that approval came another hurdle—the tricky luggage inspection conducted in Jews' homes as packing took place. Unlike nearly all Jewish refugees, because of the job transfer, the Hesses received permission to take non-valuables with them—clothing, linens, dishes, pots, and pans. While Karl's job transfer within a German company allowed his family to depart with their household goods, no Jew was allowed to leave with anything of real value. Ilse asked non-Jewish friends to keep their chest of silver tableware and those of their parents, three full sets of silver.

Steven explains how his parents "unlike nearly all Jewish refugees had permission to take their non-valuables to Holland."

My father had a corporate transfer so that came with permission to take household goods other than things of value. My mother regaled me (again, she was beautiful, and young then) with the story that a local cop was assigned to come to their Düsseldorf flat each day to make sure only household goods were being packed. Our mother told me, her exact words in her German accent. "Shteeven, I played him like such a fish."

"What does that mean?" I asked.

Mom had said to the cop: "Herr so and so, *Möchten Sie eine Tasse Kaffee oder etwas zu essen?*" "Would you like a cup of coffee or something to eat?" While my mother was playing the cop "like such a fish," she was hiding silver pieces, etc. in napkins and towels. Her exact German-accented English comment to me was the following, with a matronly grin: "I knew he wasn't looking at my packing." Another good laugh.

Still the challenges of the move were far from over for Ilse. She had yet to come up with a plan for the most difficult and dangerous task: bringing her fine jewelry, the value of which was far greater than vanity, pleasure, or ordinary financial security. For Jews attempting to flee, valuables, including jewelry, antiques, and fine art—items that could easily be exchanged—could buy them a measure of safety. Karl and Ilse had invested in several pieces of artwork and exquisite, expensive jewelry. The most valuable was a sparkling broach that held three large and thirty small perfect diamonds. The estimated value in 1943 was ƒ60,000 (guilders) (in excess of $500,000 in 2022).

Marion recounts,

> My mother was called on to grow up all at once. She had left her jewelry for safekeeping with a friend in Switzerland, who brought it to her just before my mother planned to leave. My mother never wore makeup and always dressed fashionably, but respectably. She told me that to cross the border and leave Germany, she dressed in a tacky outfit that included a red jacket with black velvet lapels. She put on mesh stockings, lots of make-up, and simply pinned the jewelry onto her lapels. Mother laughed. In her exact words (how could you make this up?), she added: "I looked like a 10-mark hooker." Obviously, everyone thought that the jewelry was fake.

Resourceful and courageous, Ilse slipped past the rigorous Nazi emigration controls, hiding in plain sight jewelry that would help save their lives.

CHAPTER 4

"At First Nothing Unusual Happened"
1937–1941

A msterdam has been called "the Venice of the North." Its low-lying terrain of islands, marshes, bridges, and canals lies just inland of the North Sea. The North Sea Canal flows fifteen miles from the sea, bringing ships from around the world including, in the 1930s, from the Netherlands' extensive colonial possessions. On the canal's southern bank lies the picturesque old city, its intricate network of canals organized in tight parallel rows that fan outward from the North Sea Canal, then splay in random patterns of land and sea, reflecting Amsterdam's history.

"Netherlands" means "lower lands" in Dutch and, indeed, the country is mostly low and flat. About half of the nation is near or below sea level. Its average elevation is 98 feet; its highest is 1,059 feet. For centuries, the Dutch have allocated a large portion of their national budget to controlling the reach of the restless sea, at times losing their battle to powerful, deadly winter storms. A British tourist guidebook from the turn of the twentieth century described the landscape: "Holland is so intersected with canals, that to a person looking down upon it from a balloon, it would have the appearance of a network extending from one end of the country to the other." The soil in many regions tends toward mud, hence the origin of the distinctive Dutch *klompen* (wooden shoes traditionally worn by farmers).

Facing the North Sea, bordered by Germany to the east and Belgium to the south, the Netherlands provided nearby shelter for Jews fleeing the Nazis; but as the number of refugees, many of them impoverished, increased, countries around the world began to tighten their borders, and avenues of escape from the Netherlands diminished sharply.

Autumn, when the Hesses reached Amsterdam, is generally the Netherlands' wettest season, though in that low-lying coastal city it can rain all year. Rain or shine, many people in Amsterdam, from business executives and diplomats to shopkeepers and families, have long preferred *fiets*, "bikes," to cars, giving the historic city an accessible, friendly atmosphere. At times, even in the newer sections of Amsterdam, North Sea currents could cause deep support structures under the city to sway slightly; Karl and Ilse may have felt the solid ground under their feet tremble slightly.

Karl and Ilse's new apartment was located near the old city, several canals away from the ordered center, in a more modern neighborhood. When they arrived, Karl acquired a new company car, a Ford, and began his job managing the United Silk office in Amsterdam. Ilse later told Steven that it was the only Ford in Amsterdam. As he explains, "Fords were admired because it was an American brand, though probably made in Germany."

Over the next few years, Karl would add Dutch to the three languages he already spoke fluently—German, English, and French. From his religious studies, he also understood some Hebrew. Ilse, too, quickly picked up the Dutch language.

Once again, life seemed hopeful, sometimes even beautiful. The seafaring Dutch had extensive international business and cultural ties. Amsterdam was a sophisticated world capital, rich with music, theater, and magnificent art museums. Karl and Ilse purchased several oil and watercolor paintings to decorate their new apartment. They likely attended the symphony, discovered favorite cafés, and watched the latest films in the cinema. Reconnecting with old friends who had also escaped and meeting new people, they soon enjoyed a wide social circle, Jewish and non-Jewish. They continued to observe three central Jewish holidays, Passover, Rosh Hashanah (New Year), and Yom Kippur (the Day of Atonement) while assimilating into their new surroundings.

Their lives became richer on January 14, 1938, with the birth of twins, Marion and Stefan. The Hesses hired a live-in nanny, Marretje Pasterkamp, who hailed from Urk, a nearby island whose occupants prided themselves on their unique historic traditions and were deeply religious Christians. As buds swelled on the trees along the streets and canals that spring and birdsong echoed through the city, the family loved car trips to the coast, tucking the twins into the cozy, leather-trimmed car blanket they had brought from Germany. "The danger of the Nazi regime came closer and closer," Ilse explained, "but it—we really didn't make any decisions because, with two babies and a secure job, we just stayed on in Holland. And then our son, Steven, was a very weak child. We didn't dare to undertake anything drastic."

In early 1938, Ilse's parents were fortunate to be granted a one-day pass to visit Karl and Ilse and hold their new grandchildren. The joyful, tearful, long-remembered visit poignantly reminded the family of the menace just hours away. According to Steven, "Our father had rented an apartment for our mother's parents in Holland, but they refused to move to Amsterdam because they saw that as abandoning the Jewish community in Recklinghausen."

■   ■   ■

While the Hesses were building their new life in Amsterdam, German forces were in motion. On March 12, 1938, Germany invaded Austria. For twenty years, the Austrian Republic, formed after the World War I breakup of the Austro-Hungarian Empire, had attempted to provide equality for its population of 6.7 million, a diverse mix of ethnic and political groups, including some two hundred thousand Jews.

Austria, the birthplace of Adolf Hitler, had never been part of Germany. That Pan-German dream had taken root among the nationalistic Austrian Nazis who persevered through years of imprisonment while taking direction and funding from Germany. Their underground Nazi Party cells incited unrest and laid plans for the longed-for *Anschluss*, the joining of the two German-speaking countries. As German tanks and troops crossed into Austria that March prepared for battle, they were greeted by cheering crowds and blizzards of flowers instead of bombs or bullets. German planes dropped little pink leaflets declaring the Germans' friendship with the Austrians. Austria was annexed as part of the German Reich. Once again, Hitler had accomplished an occupation through a barrage of threats and a strong military presence without firing a shot in combat. However, Nazi troops, the SS, and the Gestapo combed Vienna hunting for known resisters, Communists, and other potential enemies, arresting or killing them outright. Within a few weeks, two thousand Viennese Jews were arrested and sent to concentration camps, marking the first major expulsion and murder of Jews.

That fall, for the third time in two years, Hitler tested the world's willingness to go to war, threatening to occupy the Sudetenland, a German-speaking region of western Czechoslovakia bordering Germany. Britain's prime minister, Neville Chamberlain, rose to the challenge and flew to Germany several times to meet with Hitler and explore his intentions, one gentleman to another. In an ironic conclusion to those meetings, Chamberlain returned to report that Hitler had looked directly into his eyes and given him a meaningful double-handed handshake, swearing never to move beyond that single military occupation. Chamberlain found the German occupation reasonable and urged the Allies to accede to Hitler's demands.

Britain, France, Germany, and Italy, without consulting the Czechs, responded to the imminent invasion by signing the Munich Agreement on September 30, 1938, granting the disputed territory to Germany. At Chamberlain's request, he and Hitler signed a second paper, agreeing to settle future differences through consultation, not force. With a naivete that still astounds scholars, Chamberlain famously proclaimed, "Peace for our time." The next day, German troops occupied the Sudetenland, taking possession of 66 percent of Czechoslovakia's coal, 70 percent of its iron and steel, and 70 percent of its electric power. One hundred fifteen thousand Czechs smashed their windows, and ransacked their contents. Emboldened by the violence, ordinary Austrians and Germans Aryanized thousands of apartments owned by Jews, forcing—sometimes literally throwing—residents into the streets. Around five hundred Jews were murdered or driven to suicide. The SS and the Gestapo arrested thirty thousand Jewish men and sent them to Buchenwald, Dachau, and Sachsenhausen. Most were later released, many in poor shape; many families were forced to pay large ransoms and provide proof of anticipated emigration to save their family members. Following just days after Hitler's first mass deportation of Jews, the carefully orchestrated event was was the Reich's ominous first mass arrest of German Jews.

On that night of November 9, in some regions of Germany, temperatures fell below freezing. In Recklinghausen, cold, drizzling rain bit through the coats that people hastily threw on to escape the violence. Many rushed to their synagogue, only to discover an uncontrolled fire destroying the building that had been erected in 1904 to accommodate the growing Jewish population. The adjoining Jewish school also burned, and its teacher was thrown from the window. Fred Katz, a family friend of the Hesses who had been in Karl and Ilse's wedding as the flower boy and was in Recklinghausen that night, described the scene in his memoir:

> My life changed forever in the early morning hours of November 10, 1938[,] when storm troopers awakened us to take my father to prison. I can still see my mother in her long nightgown standing in agony watching them take him away. This was Kristallnacht. The Recklinghausen synagogue, Jewish school, and community center

burned. All Jewish places of business were destroyed, their windows broken. The German word Kristall, means "crystal," thus Crystal Night refers to the shards of glass that shimmered like crystal on the streets and sidewalks throughout Germany and Austria. My father later told me that in the local prison, many of the police officers were dismayed to see prominent Jewish citizens incarcerated, although they had committed no offense. Many of these policemen facilitated the delivery of food and other necessities to the Jewish men. Teacher Jacobs was a paragon of leadership there, as was our rabbi who lived to come to the US. Some of the Jewish men were never again freed before their deaths in gas chambers.

Karl and Ilse must have been terrified for their parents' safety when they heard the news. "The following day," Marion explains, "my parents would learn more. The synagogue was destroyed and my grandfather, together with other leaders of the synagogue, went there to see what they could do—tragically little or nothing. He and others were arrested for their presence, put in jail for several days, then released. The 'synagogue' was moved to my grandparents' house where some rooms were allocated for the services. At first, it was furnished very modestly. In short order, my grandparents embellished and enhanced it."

Today some Jews prefer to use the English "Crystal Night," rejecting the German term describing the sparkling shards of glass left behind after the assault. *Judenaktion*, "Jewish Action," and November Pogrom were terms used by the Nazi perpetrators. By any name, the prolonged riot was another step towards "cleansing" the Reich of Germany's Jews—the Nazis' obsession.

World leaders condemned the Nazis' vicious attacks, but by that time Hitler was inured to diplomats' loud protests and empty threats. As he had expected, none of his critics opened their doors to desperate Jews trying to flee. Once again, the world seemed to provide him with a mandate to push ahead with his brutal persecution.

Alert to any means for extorting Jewish property, Hitler then added another layer of misery to the damage he had caused. Responding to grievances of non-Jewish Germans about destruction of their own property, the government levied extortionary taxes on Jews to pay for all properties harmed during the violence. The burden on Jews already struggling to emigrate silenced complaining Aryans, though little of that "tax" money ever reached the businesses. Instead, that transfer of wealth provided a windfall for Germany's government coffers.

■   ■   ■

On March 20, 1939, Germany again declared its intention to expand, threatening to send its military into Memelland, a small, prosperous Baltic port claimed by both Lithuania and Germany. Ice-free year round, the city had strategic and economic value. Lithuania capitulated within twenty-four hours. The annexation of Memelland—after the Saar plebiscite, the Rhineland militarization, the Austrian Anschluss, and the Sudetenland occupation—was Hitler's fifth campaign to regain pre–World War I territory. His fifth roll of the dice gave him his fifth victory.

During the four years after Germany declared itself free of treaty strictures, the Germans made significant gains of territory, resources, and population through belligerent political maneuvers backed by its powerful military, spreading their rabid antisemitism beyond German borders. Ruthlessly, but with extraordinary cunning, Hitler had accomplished all of those gains without combat or casualties. Memelland had been the last of the heavily German-speaking lands Hitler sought to reclaim from the despised Treaty of Versailles, except for one—and preparations were underway to take that territory, too.

Over the tense summer of 1939, Germany notified Poland that it must relinquish its World War I acquisition, the Baltic Free City of Danzig (now Gdańsk), and provide Germany an access corridor to it. To his own military advisors, however, Hitler spoke of Danzig only as a credible excuse to invade Poland. Hitler was making another large bet. With his demand to enter Polish territory, he was acting on his promises to the German people, to give them Lebensraum, "living space."

Acknowledging that Poland's allies Britain and France might be drawn into the war, Hitler alerted his generals to the potential need to occupy the Low Countries for their airfields and strategic Atlantic location. That was nearly a year before Germany would in fact invade the Netherlands.

Chastened by its complete misreading of Hitler's intentions in the Sudetenland and its passivity in the face of Germany's continuing aggression, Britain finally shifted from back-footed, ineffectual diplomacy to decisive engagement with France and Poland. In a flurry of last-minute maneuvering, on April 6, 1939, Britain agreed to an Anglo-Polish military alliance, parallel in intent to the Franco-Polish military alliance that had been in effect since the early 1920s. Throughout a frenzied summer, Britain pressed Poland to refuse German demands—and promised to defend the threatened nation with its full military might. The three countries, the Allies, formed an ill-prepared front line of nations determined to stop the German juggernaut.

Tension mounted. The British, anticipating that they, too, were slated for a German invasion, began to rebuild their neglected military and develop top-secret coastal evacuation plans. Citizens sandbagged buildings in London, carried gas masks, and formed groups that scanned the skies for German invaders. The French strengthened core defenses, including the Maginot Line, a 280-mile-long array of border fortresses, bunkers, minefields, and gun batteries that extended as far north as France's borders with Luxembourg and Belgium. There, the Line stopped. France depended on those friendly countries' defenses for protection from an attack in the north. Germany, in turn, reinforced its more extensive 380-mile-long Siegfried Line, studded with more than eighteen thousand bunkers, tunnels, and tank traps extending along its borders with France, Belgium, Luxembourg, and the Netherlands to the North Sea.

Reading Dutch newspapers and listening to war news, Karl and Ilse would have had reason to feel both comforted and concerned. The Netherlands had unequivocally declared its neutrality. Its history as a noncombatant nation had been solidly established in World War I. But the Hesses were worried. They had experienced Nazi aggression, and they knew Hitler respected no treaties. For him, national boundaries were just more lines on a map.

During that feverish summer of 1939, Germany tightened its agreements with Central and Eastern European countries, including

Romania, Slovakian territory, and Hungary—and formalized the Pact of Steel with Italy. British, German, and Soviet diplomats traveled to each other's capitals, crossing paths as they jockeyed for political advantage.

On August 23, suave German foreign minister Joachim von Ribbentrop flew to Moscow and concluded the Molotov-Ribbentrop Pact, shocking the Allies with the Soviet Union's reversal of its World War I loyalties. The Soviet Union and Germany announced the new military alliance and commercial agreement that guaranteed German access to badly needed natural resources. A secret addendum to the pact divided Poland between the two countries, adding a spark to the political tinderbox that would explode into the Second World War.

Pact in hand, on September 1, 1939, Germany invaded Poland from the west. Two weeks later, the Soviets struck from the east. That thundering German blitzkrieg by air, land, and sea stunned and incapacitated Polish defenses. On day one, in Danzig Bay, the Luftwaffe attacked Polish warships in the first air-naval battle of World War II. Poland surrendered in less than a month, having sustained huge losses. Some sixty-eight thousand Poles died. Germany and the Soviet Union took more than a half-million prisoners.

Germany's conquest encompassed much of western Poland, including most of its industrialized regions and some two million Jews, while the Soviet Union occupied eastern Poland and, later, Lithuania. Almost immediately, Germany commenced ethnic cleansing that included terrorizing, murdering, and expelling Poles to the Soviet portion of the country. *Einsatzgruppen* (specially formed mobile killing units formed of Security Police and the SS intelligence service) shot and killed Polish leaders, intellectuals, and

Jews outright. The German goal of clearing the country of most of its *Untermenschen*, "subhumans," had begun, with the intent of reducing the remaining Polish people to peasants laboring for their German masters. When Poland surrendered on September 27, German citizens, aided by members of the Hitler Youth, were already moving into ransacked Polish homes and farms. Poland's two million Jews were already being murdered in the streets and, after a few months, would be herded into ghettos.

Some historians speculate that Hitler believed Poland's allies would remain passive after the invasion and did not expect they would come to its defense. If so, he miscalculated. By May 1940, Britain's King George had already called 2.5 million conscripts "to the colors," making a total of 4.5 million conscripts in various stages of training. The British rounded up and confined German and Austrian refugees.

On September 3, two days after the invasion of Poland began, Britain and France declared war on Germany. The first contingent of the British Expeditionary Force departed from England for northern France the next day. By the end of the month, 152,000 British soldiers, some 21,000 vehicles, and 36,000 tons of ammunition had reached the French-Belgian border, as war engulfed Western Europe and its worldwide possessions.

The Treaty of Versailles forbade Germany from maintaining submarines, but by 1939, in defiance of the treaty, Germany had secretly built fifty-seven *Unterseeboote* (U-boats), among the most modern submarines in the world, and they achieved great initial success against the British. Forty-six German U-boats, traveling in "wolf packs," proved lethally effective in damaging Allied commercial shipping. Armed German merchant ships also plied the

North Sea past the Netherlands, the English Channel, and seas around the world, laying mines and sinking or capturing more than fifty British vessels in less than two years. Battle instructions to German naval commanders included the provocation "Fighting methods will never fail to be employed merely because of international regulations." Beginning with the Allies' declaration of war, the Battle of the Atlantic would become the longest continuous military campaign of World War II.

Germany countered Britain's declaration of war by creating a defensive barrier against its island enemy. In April 1940, Germany invaded Denmark and Norway. Denmark fell within days, and by May 10, Britain's army, Royal Navy, and Royal Air Force had engaged in major battles in Norway. But ten days later, the British were in rapid retreat, and German forces pushed them south, back across the North Sea.

Though Hitler had ordered his generals to prepare for the possibility, he had not really believed that Britain would go to war over Germany's invasion of Poland. But the British stood by their ally, and as a consequence, Germany needed Dutch airfields and control of coastal shipping. Nine months after Allied and Axis nations formed their opposing alliances, neutral Netherlands would become collateral damage of Germany's invasion of Poland—some six hundred miles away—and the treaty entanglements of larger, more powerful nations.

■   ■   ■

Karl and Ilse had crossed into the Netherlands before the war, before the Dutch saw a need to manage the floodtide of refugees, and before spies and foreign agents began filtering into the country. Times had changed. Of the nearly 160,000 Jews residing in the Netherlands in 1940 about 15 percent, some 25,000, were "foreign," mostly German Jews. In October 1939, with funding from the Dutch-Jewish community, the Netherlands had built a refugee camp near Westerbork, a small town on its northeast border with Germany. Seven months after its completion, German troops flowed past the 119-acre camp and the 750 refugees there to invade the stunned Dutch. The German invasion must have terrified the Jews who had sought refuge in the Netherlands, but they could not have guessed the use to which the Germans would put the Westerbork camp.

After the May 10, 1940, invasion of the Netherlands, Belgium, and Luxembourg, German forces continued south, streaming into northern France. The supposedly impregnable French defenses did not hold. German troops advanced through the Low Countries and into northern France, largely bypassing the Maginot Line. By mid-June 1940, France's defenses had collapsed, its military retreating south along with millions of terrified French, Luxembourgian, Belgian, and Dutch civilians in what would become known as *L'exode*, "the exodus." British forces pulled out of Dunkirk and other French and Belgian coastal areas. On June 22, France surrendered, leaving millions of French and foreign Jews at the mercy of the Germans.

During the French debacle, angry British Parliament members lambasted Prime Minister Neville Chamberlain, calling for his resignation:

"You have missed the bus."

"You have sat here too long for any good you are doing."

"Depart, I say!"

Unable to maintain political support, Chamberlain resigned. Newly appointed British prime minister Winston Churchill made five trips to France, staying just ahead of the fighting, gauging the situation, talking to French leaders, trying unsuccessfully to bolster their resolve. On his return, he conveyed his somber assessment to Parliament, recalled in his memoir: "At no time in the last war were we in greater peril than now."

■   ■   ■

In occupied Amsterdam, Karl and Ilse kept a low profile and avoided contact with the Germans and the collaborating Dutch police as best they could, but it was impossible to ignore their presence. They were everywhere. Exuberant German soldiers, proud of their victories, marched in formation through the cobblestone streets, their heartfelt songs of war, like "*Wir Fahren Gegen Engeland!*" ("We're Going to England!") echoed in the streets and played, endlessly, on the radio.

> *Give me your hand!…*
> *For we go to England, England!*

In the United States, *Life* magazine's lead story of July 1, 1940, recounted France's defeat: "Helpless Humiliation Comes to the Everyday People of France." For the next fifteen months, however, from July 10, 1940, through October 31, 1941, a furious air war, the Battle of Britain, thwarted Hitler's vision of an easy victory over the British. The Hesses must have shuddered at the roar of

German fighter planes taking off from nearby Schiphol Airport, heading for England. On September 7, 1940, unable to destroy the Royal Air Force (RAF), the Luftwaffe launched the largest bombing campaign yet waged in war, the Blitz, involving 300 bombers escorted by 600 fighters.

The Blitz operated mostly from Belgium and France, but at times also from Amsterdam. Over eight months, it resulted in more than 40,000 British deaths in more than fifty cities, but the assault cost both the British and Germans major damage. Britain's Royal Air Force lost 1,250 aircraft. Germany lost more than 1,700 and suffered 2,600 casualties.

During that time, Hitler considered his vulnerabilities. To deter the United States from entering the war, on the anniversary of Poland's surrender, September 27, 1940, Germany, Italy, and Japan signed the Tripartite Pact, creating what would be known as the Axis alliance. Hitler pressured Japan to attack British interests in Asia, further straining Britain's hard-pressed defenses.

Luftwaffe aircraft roared over Amsterdam. Schiphol Airport, renamed *Fliegerhorst 561* (Air Base 561), served as Germany's air command and control center for the entire northern half of the Netherlands. Immediately after the invasion, the Germans rebuilt the heavily damaged airport, adding more taxiways, runways, and antiaircraft flak positions. They installed camouflaged surfaces, decoy planes, and dummy airfields to deflect attacks. Schiphol endured British attacks in May, June, and August 1940, sending Amsterdam's residents, probably including the Hesses, running to cellars and air-raid shelters or drawing their blackout curtains, hoping the city itself would not become a target. In the beginning of the bombing campaigns, Jews were among the last citizens given space in the shelters. Later, they were completely excluded.

■　　■　　■

German leaders understood that the Dutch required a "velvet glove" occupation, vastly different from the rampant terror being inflicted on Poland. The Netherlands' population comprised an unknowable mix of avid members of the Dutch Nazi Party, *Nationaal-Socialistische Beweging* (NSB), who had welcomed the occupying troops; Dutch collaborators aiding the invaders; anti-Nazi resisters; freedom fighters who supported the Allies; Jews and other refugees; those who sympathized with Jews; and others who simply wanted to survive. Germany hoped to pacify this complex population rather than inflame a rebellion, so they instituted control through gradual political maneuvers backed by brute force.

Soon, however, even initially apathetic citizens found themselves frustrated by the increasing German repression. Germany abolished all "unacceptable" Dutch institutions and organizations and banned national celebrations of Dutch heroes. Concerts, theater, and movies reflected only German culture and ideology. Throughout the Reich and occupied Western Europe, Nazis controlled the airwaves. There was no uncensored news. The cosmopolitan Dutch heard only Nazi-approved radio. *Eine Sondermeldung aus dem Führer Hauptquartier*, "A special message from the Führer's headquarters," interrupted programs with decrees, filtered news, and announcements of German military victories. After failing to defeat the British by air or sea, German radio abandoned the now humiliating "We're Going to England" song. Instead, listeners across Europe heard droning broadcasts extolling German heroes and successes and demonizing the Germans' enemies.

Although tanks and armored divisions did not dominate daily life in Amsterdam, Wehrmacht soldiers demanded absolute control and enforced German orders. German trucks marauded through neighborhoods. Stepping in formation, making their presence felt, troops marched through the city, their boots clanging on the cobblestones. They often sang haunting popular tunes such as "Lili Marleen," which also played over and over on the radio:

> *Outside the barracks*
> *By the corner light…*
> *I'll wait for you, the whole night through*
> *For you, Lili Marleen…*

■   ■   ■

While managing the Dutch with a façade of politeness and leniency, the German occupiers demanded uncompromising obedience. Although the invasion had been brutally military, the occupation itself was considered a "civil occupation," that is, the government was left intact, taking orders from the Germans. Initially, Germany hoped that the Netherlands, like Austria, could be incorporated into the German Reich. One Dutch family, the Wilders, who had some Jewish background, were watching a patrol pass their neighborhood when they noticed the harsh treatment a soldier received after he momentarily fell out of step. The mother of that family said, "If that's what they do to their own, imagine what they will do to us."

Her son, Lolke, seven years old, took in the scene silently, but later recalled how his mother's words made him tremble. As Karl wrote, "We were trapped. At first nothing unusual happened to give us cause for concern. The Germans were satisfied to pick up and lock up those Jews they had on their list."

■   ■   ■

Karl's statement may sound surprising. The Germans had wasted no time in laying the lethal groundwork for their war on Jews in the Netherlands. Almost immediately after the occupation, Karl's position with United Silk had been Aryanized: commandeered and given to a non-Jew. He had lost not only his job, but also his company car. Hitler appointed Arthur Seyss-Inquart, a loyal Austrian Nazi and a virulent antisemite, as *Reichskommissar* (Nazi Germany's governor) of the German-occupied Netherlands. Separately, Heinrich Himmler, *Reichsführer* (the highest rank of the SS), dispatched Hanns Albin Rauter, one of his subordinates, to spearhead the Netherlands' war on Jews. Adolf Eichmann, *SS-Obersturmbannführer* (a paramilitary rank that made him, for a time, second to Himmler, who oversaw Germany's "Jewish problem"), visited Amsterdam requesting an accurate count of the Netherlands' Jews and supervising antisemitic plans. From the earliest days of their May 1940 occupation, the Germans had been active and dangerous.

But the Germans spun their web over Dutch Jews slowly and with care. In fall 1940, as cold winds blew through the city heralding the change of seasons, German administrators "requested" that the Dutch civil service identify which of its employees were Jews. Out of confusion or terror, or a tradition of obedience, most of the two hundred thousand Dutch civil employees complied; a few months later all twenty-five hundred Jewish employees were fired. On January 10, 1941, with an order that initially seemed innocuous, all Jews in the Netherlands were required to register with the Dutch Census Office, another simple step that would soon allow the Germans to spring a deadly trap. However, it was understandable that Karl saw no reason for panic even as late as early 1941. Large numbers of Jews under German control had been arrested and sent to concentration and labor camps where many would die, but Germany's mass killing centers had not yet been established.

The Germans' cat-and-mouse game allowed the Dutch, including Jews, to believe they retained some level of independence. Later described as "pinpricks" compared with other German demands, early German orders lulled most people in the conquered nation into complacency while, step by step, Germany tightened its grip on the country and isolated its Jews.

Regardless of the Germans' pervasive military presence, Amsterdam was not completely pacified. The streets could turn volatile without warning. In February 1941, a German-Jewish refugee, an owner of popular ice cream parlor Koco, sprayed German police with caustic ammonia, mistakenly believing them to be Dutch Nazis. German troops descended on the shop. The owner was arrested, tortured, and killed; in further retribution, 425 Jewish men were randomly seized off the streets and deported to Buchenwald, most of them later murdered at Mauthausen. A few weeks later, Dutch resisters ambushed a German police patrol in the Jewish Quarter. Germans blamed the Jews, and again rounded up random Jewish men and deported them to prison camps.

The daylight raids, commonly called "razzias" by the Jews, appalled many Dutch. In sympathy, on February 25, 1941, Dutch Communists and Socialists organized a one-day strike. A large number of Dutch, estimated to be as many as three hundred thousand, supported the strike, shutting down the city of Amsterdam. The next day, the unrest spread to neighboring towns. This first large public protest against the Germans in occupied Europe would be the only mass demonstration organized by non-Jews in Europe protesting the deportations and killing of Jews. Anticipating brutal retaliation, Jewish leaders, while grateful for the support of Dutch citizens, implored them to desist. German troops used rifles and hand grenades to quell the strike. Nine people died, fifty were injured, and two hundred were arrested, some of whom would die in concentration camps.

The consequences of that uprising were seismic. Enraged by the unrest, German administrators ordered the formation of a Jewish Council, *Joodsche Raad*, to be led by Abraham Asscher, a respected Dutch-Jewish leader and owner of one of the largest diamond-cutting businesses in Europe, and David Cohen, professor and prominent Zionist. Henceforth, the Council would communicate German orders to Amsterdam's Jews to report for "labor" in "the East"; if the Council refused, the Jews would suffer deportation to Mauthausen. Insidiously, the Germans also ordered the Council to implement the orders.

With this radical change, the Germans removed themselves from the explosive role of directly policing, punishing, and arresting Jews and forced Jews, facing the barrels of German guns, to participate in selecting and then notifying Jews to appear at a collection point at the specified date and time. While the Council did not enforce the Germans' deportation orders, under threat of far worse treatment for the Jews and their own deportation, they complied and created lists of Jews to be "called" and then sent out the dreaded notifications. Terrorized, most Jews—those who had not found avenues for escape or places to hide—complied with those call notices. Did the Council save Jews from brutal roundups or simply smooth the process? Was the Council a powerful agent of collaboration? Its involvement in the processes of murder became a flashpoint of mounting controversy among Amsterdam's Jews, as it did in other occupied cities where Councils functioned.

Karl described his family's situation during those times with restraint, precision, and anger: "With more or less excitement, the years 1940 and 1941 passed." "Then came the Jewish laws. They were exactly the same as those that had been enacted in Germany itself. Everything was forbidden to Jews. Only a few stores were kept open for Jews from three to five in the afternoon. There one could buy what the others had left—which was nothing."

"Jewish Laws" included in Nazi Decree No. 138, effective September 15, 1942, empowered Nazi *Generalkommissar für das Sicherheitswesen*, "General Commissioner for Security," and *Höhere SS-und Polizeiführer* (Leader of the SS and Police) Hanns Rauter to take all measures necessary to create and enforce new laws. With this expansive mantle of dictatorial power, he immediately issued the "Proclamation on the Movement of Jews," barring Jews from all recreation or pleasure. The restrictions excluded Jews from:

- public parks and zoos;
- cafes, restaurants, hotels, and boardinghouses;
- wagon-lits (sleeping cars) and buffet cars on trains;
- theaters, cabarets, and cinemas;

- sports grounds, bathing beaches, indoor and outdoor swimming pools;
- art exhibits and concerts; and
- public libraries, reading rooms, and museums.

■   ■   ■

On June 15, 1941, Karl's parents, together with his sister Meta and her family, had set sail from Portugal en route to the United States. His sister Elsbeth made her way to Sweden, and younger brother Jules to Palestine. That part of the Hesses' family at least, was safe—a ray of light in their dark world, giving them hope that one day they, too, would be free. Yet that prospect seemed ever more distant. Karl and Ilse also feared for Ilse's parents and large extended family contending with Nazis patrolling Recklinghausen's once peaceful streets. For Karl and Ilse, the peril in Amsterdam was building like cold wind before violent summer storms. Now, even routine activities—taking the twins for a walk, shopping for groceries—could cost them their lives.

■   ■   ■

Four hundred miles to the east, new threats to Europe's Jews were in the making. On July 31, Hermann Göring, Marshall of the Empire (*Reichsmarschall des Grossdeutschen Reiches*), authorized Reinhard Heydrich, director of Reich Security Main Office (*Reichssicherheitshauptamt*) and the Security Service (*Sicherheitsdienst des Reichsführers-SS*), to submit a plan for the "total solution of the Jewish question" in all lands under German control.

CHAPTER 5

The Jewish Star
1941–1942

A sharp, deadly escalation in Germany's persecution of Amsterdam's Jews coincided with the German order for Jews to form the Jewish Council in the summer of 1941. Under threat of arrest and reprisals, the Council was forced to announce and implement a deluge of German orders, from petty to disastrous.

Throughout summer 1941 and into 1942, the Germans stripped Jews of their scant remaining freedoms, impoverished them, and isolated them from Dutch culture. Signs declaring, "*Voor Joden verboden*," "Jews Forbidden," appeared everywhere, from neighborhood parks to greengrocers and the corner café.

Jewish children were barred from attending public schools, then from attending any school. Jews surrendered their radios, losing a lifeline of information in their isolation. Jewish professionals, including attorneys, doctors, pharmacists, and midwives, could work only for Jewish clients. Jews could not hold seats on the stock exchange. Dutch orchestras were "asked" to Aryanize their members and their music; even works by composers who had converted to Christianity, including Mahler and Mendelssohn, were forbidden.

Jews could no longer travel in cars, a restriction of only moderate impact: Jews' cars, like the Hesses' Ford, had already been confiscated. No longer permitted on the city's trains and trollies, Jews walked to work, to shop for food...everywhere.

Late in the summer of 1940, Netherlands Generalkommissar for political affairs and publicity Fritz Schmidt shut down three Jewish papers, obliterating the last vestiges of the Jewish free press. "I intend to allow only one Jewish paper," he informed the Jewish Council, then ordered them to select an editor for *Het Joodsche Weekblad*, "The Jewish Weekly," with the clear understanding that all staff appointments and all communication to Jews must meet with his approval. The puppet newspaper appeared for the first time on April 11, 1941, under the editorship of a German nominee. Karl and Ilse could still enjoy phonograph records, one of the few forms of culture and relaxation the Germans seemed not to find threatening.

The list of Rauter's demands was long and thorough, as the Germans stripped Jews of their professions and the normal activities and pleasures of daily life. As Steven remembers, "We spent most days inside. Of course, I have no context, but my memory of being in the apartment all the time is strong. We were at the 'going to the playground age,' but there was no playground for us." The Germans were increasingly marginalizing Amsterdam's Jews. Yet Generalkommisar Rauter had even worse planned for them.

The Hesses' anguish deepened in August 1941 when Ilse's father, Willi, died of a heart attack. "That was a special tragedy," Steven points out. "Our mother's father died from the stress of the relentless attacks on the Jewish community in Germany. He was fifty-four. He met us only once."

Ilse did not receive the telegram carrying the sad news of her father's sudden death. She learned of it later, through friends. As Marion explains, "Friends told her that her mother was sitting shiva surrounded by the diminished local Jewish community, but totally bereft that her only loving daughter did not appear or even call. I don't know whether it was even allowed at that time to return to Germany for such a visit. It was always one of my mother's saddest memories when she spoke about her life."

Before Willi's death, the Hirschbergs had taken in several Jewish families whose homes had been Aryanized. Fanny was not alone in that time of despair, but the Germans' war on Jews had taken away her work, her husband, and her daughter. Friends were leaving. Friends disappeared. She was more vulnerable than ever.

Around 1941, Karl and Ilse had hired Leo Fischer, a well-regarded German-Jewish photographer, to take pictures of the twins, possibly to send to the children's grandparents, or simply for themselves. For the photos, Marretje, who was no longer permitted to work for a Jewish family, dressed the twins in traditional Urker clothing—for fun, but also on the chance that at some point the photos could be used to identify the children as non-Jewish Dutch. The pictures were charming, the twins bright-eyed, slightly impish, and adorable. But there was another, darker side to the story. Fischer was a member of the Dutch Underground Resistance, and he also took photos for false documents. Karl and Ilse acquired false IDs, which Fischer may have made for them, as he did for many Jews. Two years after he delivered the twins' photos, the German *Grüne Polizei*, "Green Police" (so-called because of their dark green uniforms), arrested him, transported Fischer and seventeen other prisoners to a deserted, windswept North Sea beach, and shot them dead.

Steven explains how the photos were saved, along with other treasured possessions: "My parents gave a suitcase of 'stuff' to our nanny for safekeeping. I had always believed it held linens and napkins and the like. But the nanny had our silver, or a lot of it, in that suitcase under her bed. Two napkin rings and a silver ashtray have been on my dresser for years. Never gave them a lot of thought until recently. They were in that suitcase our nanny guarded those many years."

■   ■   ■

Karl and Ilse were preparing for the worst, but most people around them were woefully unready for the calamity to come. "The Dutch Jews—as well as, by the way, most [of] the Dutch in general—were filled with a ridiculous optimism," Karl wrote in his memoir. "They believed the war would be over in a few weeks."

From their earliest days, the Nazis showed no tolerance for opposition from any group, including Aryans. In 1933, two hundred thousand German citizens, Aryans, had demonstrated in Berlin against the new Nazi regime. Shortly after that rare protest against the Nazis, opposition was banned and severely punished. Jehovah's Witnesses, a Christian group that refused to pay homage to Hitler or support his wars, were among the first people Hitler sent to concentration camps. The words "Heil Hitler" never passed their lips. The Nazis incarcerated some ten thousand German Jehovah's Witnesses and murdered nearly three hundred for refusing military service.

In the Netherlands, the Germans' so-called "velvet glove" was in tatters, though its remnants were still useful to the Germans in pacifying the largely compliant nine million Dutch. Dutch cinemas acquiesced to an order to screen *Der Ewige Jude*, "The Eternal Jew," an antisemitic Nazi propaganda film. Disney movies, which Hitler at one time enjoyed, were prohibited for their American free spirit. The list of banned materials, from music, art, and films to books, magazines, and newspapers was extensive; they immediately disappeared from shops. The Dutch had learned that open opposition brought immediate violent repercussions. Dutch Resistance groups fought the Germans courageously, but they were relatively small. Neither the Dutch government nor the population rose in protest of the antisemitic repression.

More ominous for Jews than the passive compliance of most was the active collaboration by some Dutch. In one incident in February 1941, forty members of the Dutch Nazi Party's paramilitary group marched through Amsterdam's Jewish Quarter randomly attacking residents. In the melee that followed, a Dutch Nazi was mortally wounded. Six hundred German Grüne Polizei converged on the area, randomly seized 427 young Jewish men off the streets—including one returning from grocery shopping and three brothers who had just picked up their unemployment checks—and interned them at Schoorl military camp on the coast. The police released about thirteen suspected of having tuberculosis, then deported the rest to Buchenwald. Most were later murdered at

Mauthausen or poisoned in carbon monoxide gassing experiments in Austria.

Amsterdam's Jews faced one brutal incident after another. In June 1941, Germans blamed a plot to bomb Wehrmacht headquarters in Amsterdam's southern region on the Jews. Although Dutch Resistance had been responsible, Germans arrested and deported three hundred young Jewish apprentices, along with anyone else in that age group they encountered during their roundup. The Germans strove to make their reprisals as painful as possible.

The most damaging act of Dutch collaboration was the "List of Family Names of Persons of Jewish Blood," produced by the *Rijksinspectie van de Bevolkingsregisters* (Dutch civil service) in March 1942 and presented to German leadership in a photo op, with devastating consequences. Marion explains:

> Critically important in rounding up Jews was the work of Dutch civil servant J. L. Lentz, head of the Population Registration Office in The Hague. Lentz developed a population registration system, along with an identity card, which would effectively cover the entire population of the Netherlands. The German occupation authorities adapted Lentz's work to create a central register of Jews with links between that register and municipal registration offices. The registration record, identity cards, and Lentz's 1942 report on the location of Jews in the Netherlands, culminated in so-called "dot maps" showing population density of Jews by district. Those were used in the creation of transport lists by the Nazi

SS. Ultimately, Nazis used these overlapping systems of identification with great efficiency.

■   ■   ■

WAR—on a massive scale! On Sunday, June 22, 1941, riding a tidal wave of military victories, the German Wehrmacht and a phalanx of allies—nearly three million troops—turned against its supposed ally the Soviet Union in a campaign code-named Operation Barbarossa, which would bring deadly consequences to Jews across Europe. The combined armies and the Luftwaffe smashed through Soviet-occupied Poland and Ukraine and pushed into the Soviet Union. The largest invasion force ever assembled advanced at the astonishing rate of fifty miles a day. Initially, Stalin met the massive attack with disbelief, duped by the worthless German treaty, just as Chamberlain had been tricked four years earlier. Inexplicably ignoring warnings about the invasion from both Churchill and Roosevelt, Stalin delayed his response while he verified the information, losing military advantage as Germany pummeled western Russia. The invaders' scorched-earth tactics allowed them to penetrate deep into Soviet territory, exceeding even their own optimistic predictions. German troops reduced much of Stalingrad to rubble, and some entered the city itself; Army Group North surrounded Leningrad (now Saint Petersburg) in a siege designed to starve the city into submission. When the invasion forces came within striking distance of Moscow, they halted for reprovisioning.

Of the occupied Western European countries that supported the invasion, the Netherlands sent the largest contingent of soldiers—twenty-five thousand conscripted men and volunteers. Dutch soldiers fought in the SS *Vrijwilligerslegioen Nederland* (SS Volunteer Legion Netherlands) and the 12th Panzer Division alongside Finnish, Norwegian, and other volunteer fighters. The war for the Soviet Union's vast agricultural lands, reserves of oil, and other resources seemed to jubilant Germans an unmitigated victory, fulfilling Hitler's imperialist Kampf far beyond his original dream and promise to the German people. The Soviet population, like that of Poland, was slated to become enslaved workers. With this apparent victory, the resounding thump of German boots echoed in European capitals from Paris to Oslo and east past Minsk to the outskirts of Moscow. It seemed that nothing could stop the Germans.

The victors promptly celebrated their progress, flattering themselves that they had planned well and fought fiercely. They had overwhelmed Soviet defenses with a fury convincing Germans that total victory over the Soviet Union was at hand, a feat that not even Napoleon had accomplished; more than eight hundred thousand Soviets had been killed and six million Soviet soldiers wounded or captured. Russian and Polish prisoners, many of them Jewish, worked as slave labor in factories across the occupied Soviet Union and Poland, and in Germany. Jews toiled in Krefeld, Germany, in the United Silk factory where Karl had once been a manager. In 1941, the large corporation was producing more parachute silk and submerged netting used to entrap enemy submarines than nylon stockings and velvet ribbons. Announcements of the eastern victory blared from Nazi loudspeakers throughout Germany and its occupied lands. It is easy to imagine that, upon hearing those reports,

Karl and Ilse were probably thrown into a state of hopelessness, seeing no end to their plight.

Germany's victory had been costly, and it was incomplete. Many Soviet industrial centers had escaped attack. The Allies resupplied the Soviet military with convoys through the Arctic Sea. Barbarossa would become known as the deadliest military operation in history. German forces suffered nearly 775,000 casualties and expended enormous resources to fight their former ally. Soviet prisoners of war filled existing German POW camps past capacity. Unknown numbers were slaughtered outright, and millions would die in German prisons and hastily constructed labor camps. Responding to the pressures of their multiple victories, Germans initially converted Auschwitz, an army barracks, into a harsh camp for Soviet prisoners of war. Convicts from German prisons sent to staff the camp gave Auschwitz its early reputation for sadism and murder. Soviet POWs were among the first victims of Zyklon B poison gas experiments at the now-notorious camp.

Like a snake that swallowed more than it could digest, Germany discovered that its conquests in Poland and western Russia had become a major logistical problem. Hitler's policies lurched unevenly from pressuring Jews to emigrate to annihilating them all, but he had no coherent plan in place for the millions of Jews in these conquered lands. Killing began immediately after Operation Barbarossa forces drove into the Soviet Union. In German-occupied Ukraine, on September 29, 1941, Einsatzgruppen herded close to thirty-four thousand Jewish men, women, and children to a ravine, Babi Yar, near Kyiv, and massacred them over two days. Throughout the Soviet territory under German control, German soldiers, joined by local volunteers, marched into villages, locked Jewish residents in barns, and burned them alive.

In October 1941, Hitler approved the use of deadly trucks that could be driven from one village to the next. Guards forced Jews into the back of the mobile vans and asphyxiated them with exhaust gas fed by a pipe from the running engine, a gruesome process. Two months later, more than a thousand Jews from Krefeld and Duisburg, the region of Germany where Karl and Ilse had lived, and thousands more from Vienna and other occupied cities, were deported in freezing temperatures to a railway station outside Riga, Latvia, and summarily shot and killed. From June 1941 to December 1941, German Einsatzgruppen death squads killed some half-million Jews.

The close-range killing of innocent civilians—men and women of all ages—proved to be too much even for battle-hardened German soldiers. Field commanders began to report that the murders demoralized their units. But the large increase of Central and Eastern European Jews under German control inflamed rather than diminished Hitler's hatred.

He issued a secret order that October, with lethal consequences for Jews in German-occupied territory from the Soviet Union to the Netherlands: "In view of the approaching final solution to the Jewish situation, emigration of Jews with German citizenship is forbidden." In reality, the Germans had already forbidden almost all Jewish emigration from occupied lands, and the Hesses had lost that possibility when Dutch guards blocked their escape to Britain.

But Hitler's order formalized the Nazis' goal of murdering Europe's Jews and launched Operation Reinhard, the first large-scale, state-ordered genocidal killing of noncombatants in history.

The secretive plan included construction of four additional killing centers in German-occupied Poland. With no facilities for holding prisoners over time, the death camps were an innovation designed solely for the efficient, systematic murder of large groups of civilians and Soviet prisoners of war. In December 1941, killing center Kulmhof (Chelmno) began murdering Jews with exhaust fumes of specially designed trucks immediately after their arrival. At Auschwitz in September 1941, Germans tested a new method of murder—Zyklon B gas, a lethal pesticide. Inconsistent historical accounts place the first mass murders at Auschwitz some time around early 1942. Over the next year, Auschwitz would expand its geographic size and killing capacity dramatically with the construction of Auschwitz II-Birkenau. Four additional killing centers in Poland using gas chambers—Belzec, Sobibor, Treblinka, and Majdanek—became operational by mid-1942, putting the systematic murder of millions of Jews within German control.

Dissatisfied with unorganized progress on "the Jewish question," Hitler ordered *SS Obergruppenführer* Reinhard Heydrich, director of the Reich Security Main Office, to form a comprehensive plan for exterminating Europe's Jews. Heydrich called a January 20, 1942, meeting of government department leaders in the comfortable Berlin suburb of Wannsee. The fifteen attendees, eight of whom held academic doctorates, heard Heydrich's report on Germany's progress in murdering Jews.

Germany had already eliminated 700,000 Jews from lands under its control and established ghettos in many large occupied cities. Plans to accelerate the mass murder were underway. Heydrich distributed a tally, prepared by Eichmann, of Jews remaining in Europe, those in territories under German control were listed in

Column A, and those in countries as remote as Ireland and Portugal in Column B. Of the 11,000,000 Jews in German-allied lands, 160,800 resided in the Netherlands, more than in any country except France. Like the Germans in Amsterdam, the cultured, highly educated Wannsee group did not use the words "kill" or "murder," but instead conversed in coded terms less burdened with savage implications, such as "eliminate," "evacuate," and "Judenfrei." In that rarified atmosphere, the German hierarchy clarified its position and its processes for killing Jews, and took firm control of them.

The Wannsee Conference was significant for all Europe's Jews, and it directly impacted the Hesses' already precarious situation. Because Hitler had prohibited further Jewish emigration, Heydrich proposed that all Jews in German or German-allied lands be deported to camps where they would be worked to death. Heydrich blithely told the group that the surviving remnants, the strongest of their race, should be "treated accordingly." He talked about a "final solution of the Jewish question." That phrase resonated with the group, whose members went on to repeat it often in their work, and it soon became embedded in the Nazi lexicon. Eichmann would later report that after the formal proceedings, over cognac, "the gentlemen…were discussing the subject quite bluntly.… They spoke about methods of killing, about liquidation, about extermination."

During that momentous time, Hitler could reasonably have believed that he had prevailed in both of his wars—the war on Jews and the war for Lebensraum. The British food supply was threatened. Churchill pleaded with President Roosevelt to send battleships, destroyers, planes—anything to strengthen the flagging British military—and to declare war on Germany.

The United States sent Britain and the Soviet Union badly needed war matériel, but the American people were staunchly opposed to joining Europe's war. In spring 1941, the wildly popular American aviation hero Charles Lindbergh, head of the isolationist America First Committee, addressed a standing-room-only crowd of about twenty-five thousand at an anti-war rally in Philadelphia. He exhorted America to stay out of the war. In Congress, in a heated oration, Senator Burton K. Wheeler of Montana warned that if America joined the fight against Germany, "Our boys will be returned in caskets."

In December 1941, however, Germany's stability would be challenged in a way that its leaders had anticipated and planned for, but that spun out of their control. In 1940, Hitler had celebrated Japan's signing the Axis's defensive Tripartite Pact. If the United States considered entering the European war, he reasoned, Germany's Pacific ally, Japan, would engage America by attacking its Pacific possessions.

Hitler viewed Americans as something akin to rambunctious children, racial "mongrels," a nation wealthy in resources but unprepared for war and, to its detriment, strongly politically influenced by Jews. He believed that the United States would not fight in both Europe and Asia. On November 26, 1941, when a large Japanese fleet set sail for Hawaii, he was confident. On December 7, when Japan surprised the world by attacking Pearl Harbor, wreaking havoc on the United States fleet stationed in Hawaii, he was delighted. And when the United States declared war on Germany's ally Japan on December 8, and subsequently lowered its draft age to eighteen, he may have congratulated himself. His years of planning had reached the projected outcome. Believing that the United States was growing stronger and that war with America was inevitable, on December 11, Hitler announced Germany's declaration of war. The same day, America declared war on Germany. The flames of war ignited by Germany's invasion of Poland had exploded into World War II.

■　　■　　■

As Germany's long reach stretched into the Soviet Union, Hitler's war on Jews shifted from a holding pattern of persecution and isolation to deportation and mass murder, shattering the tenuous stability of the Hesses' lives. In early 1942, unaware of the true horrors of German brutality further east, Amsterdam's Jewish Council obeyed German orders to organize medical exams for unemployed Jewish men, identifying those healthy enough for work in labor camps. When the Council attempted to delay the exams, the Germans proceeded without Council involvement. Over six months, Germans sent seventy-five hundred of those "useless people," as the Nazis described the unemployed, to thirty-seven harsh labor camps in the Netherlands.

■　　■　　■

Commissar Rauter's expansive titles—Generalkommissar für das Sicherheitswesen and Höhere SS-und Polizeiführer—reflected the dictatorial power he wielded over the Netherlands. In April 1942, evening newspapers across the Netherlands published his latest decree, ordering all Jews over six years old to wear a "saucer-sized" yellow star over their left breast whenever they were in public. The Nazis' star, a caricature of the Star of David, was a six-pointed yellow star outlined in black containing the word "*Jood*," Dutch for "Jew," written in stylized faux-Hebrew lettering.

In his memoir, Karl described the conditions they were forced to live under: "We had to be at home by eight o'clock in the evening; we had to wear Jewish stars on all our clothing, and we had to keep with us identification cards with a 'J' (Jew) stamped on them." "At the beginning of 1942, the Germans ordered a 'Joodsche Raad' (Jewish Council) to be organized. This organization was supposed to act as the representative of the Jews for the Germans; the Germans did not want to have anything to do with the individual Jew.... This was the opening phase of the deportation."

Germans did not invent the Jewish star, emblem of German cruelty. That symbol of Nazi contempt and identification, stigmatizing Jews, had been in use in Europe at various times for centuries, distinguishing Jews from the dominant Christian culture. In 1215, the Catholic Church's Fourth Lateran Council—in addition to forbidding prelates from engaging in duels or taking part in "trials by ordeal"—mandated distinctive garb for Jews, a precursor to the yellow star. That same Church Council banned Jews from public office, forbade Christian servants from working in Jewish households, and assessed a compulsory tax on Jews. Those antisemitic precedents, like the star, fell conveniently into eager Nazi hands.

In the early days of the regulation, many Dutch people also wore stars as an act of solidarity. One newspaper observed, "Truly stars in the streets are as numerous as buttercups in May." The Catholic Church in the Netherlands publicly condemned the Nazi order. Beginning shortly after the occupation, thousands of Protestants, the largest Dutch religious group, heard sermons from the pulpits decrying Nazi discrimination as being "in direct conflict with the concept of Christian charity." The Jewish Council registered protests. In response, the commissar's office simply issued 569,000 stars for the Council to distribute to Amsterdam's Jews.

As Marion explains, though the twins' beloved nanny "could no longer work for us," she "still visited us at times, and brought some food. She could take us to the playground because children under six did not have to wear Jewish stars."

Council president Abraham Asscher was not as distressed about the stars as he would later become. He and many other Jews tragically misjudged the Germans' deadly plans. They believed the danger would soon pass—perhaps like a ferocious winter storm—like the many trials Jews had weathered over the centuries.

■   ■   ■

By mid-1942, the Germans' plan for deporting Dutch Jews to deadly concentration camps was firmly in place, following the pattern already long underway in the Reich itself. The Nazis' hidden agenda became clearer with orders for Jews in outlying towns and villages to move to designated Amsterdam neighborhoods. Most of the rural Jewish families billeted in the heavily Jewish Rivierenbuurt neighborhood—which became a virtual ghetto without walls—not far from the Hesses' apartment. Also foreboding were orders prohibiting Jews from travel outside the city. With these orders, both hiding in the countryside and fleeing the Netherlands became even more difficult. Jews were required to carry at all times an identification card stamped with a *J*; to affix a star, drawn in black on white paper, to their doors; and to be home by 8:00 in the evening. The Jewish Council was advised to refrain from "spreading alarm."

Seeking an easily accessible central location at which to hold Jews before their deportation, the Germans settled on the *Hollandsche Schouwburg*, a large Grecian-style theater built in 1892. Over the years, the popular theater venue had staged hundreds of events, including the highly praised play by Jewish writer Herman Heijermans, *The Good Hope*, a name that now reeked of irony.

The Schouwburg's function under the Germans could hardly have been more different. Germans renamed the venue the *Joodsche Schouwburg*, the "Jewish Theater," declaring it the only theater where Jews could perform or attend concerts. The next year, the Germans gutted it, shoved the rows of seats from a vastly different time against the walls, and prepared the building to temporarily hold a thousand or more Jews per week.

From the Schouwburg, Jews would be loaded onto trains bound for the Westerbork transit camp, on the Netherlands' northeast border with Germany. Large numbers of Jews would be housed in barracks in Westerbork for a few days, weeks, or longer, awaiting final deportation. In summer 1942, Eichmann confidently informed the German Foreign Office that the "arrangements" had been completed. The "operation" was running smoothly, and by the end of the year he expected forty thousand Jews to be "evacuated" from the Netherlands for "labor service" in Auschwitz.

Karl explained in his memoir how German Jews were taken first. "In July 1942, the Jews were informed that all men, eighteen to forty years of age, and their families had to go to Germany for the industrial effort. It is not clear who made the decision at the time that German Jews were to be 'called' first. It is my personal opinion that this was the way the Dutch Jews tried to throw a calf to the crocodile, in the hopeful attempt to be spared themselves. The calls to this unfortunate group came within one week, by mail." This "call" was a summons ordering them to report for deportation.

While German Jews were an easy target, most without much influence, Dutch Jews, too, were called in the rounds. When regular mass deportations began, young Jews received special delivery call-up notices, beginning July 5, to report to "special work-camps in Germany, where your family will also be accommodated." A seventeen-year-old girl who received a notice during her graduation ceremony from the Jewish Lyceum asked what she should do. "Don't go!" one teacher exclaimed, but most of the frightened faculty remained silent, heads bowed.

One might imagine that this early stage of the deportations would have alerted the Dutch people to the impending disaster for Jews. Residents of a cultured international metropolis, they would have heard the Germans' confident declaration that Vienna would soon be Judenfrei. Yet the German deception worked. Even some young Jews who were called appeared at the transit camp cheerfully, ready for work, singing Hebrew songs, though others came with deep misgivings. Some simply did not show up. That week, teenager Margot Frank received her call for transport to a labor camp; the Frank family, including thirteen-year-old Anne, refugees from Germany, went into hiding. Those that did go never returned.

On July 14, German Grüne Polizei, aided by Dutch police, conducted raids in all parts of the city and delivered seven hundred Jews to German Security Police headquarters instead of the

Schouwburg. They were to be held as hostages until four thousand Jews who had been called for deportation presented themselves at the Schouwburg. (The four thousand did not show up; the seven hundred died in Mauthausen.) The same day, the first weekly train loaded with Jews left Amsterdam for Westerbork transit camp. The next day, more than a thousand detainees were deported from Westerbork to Auschwitz-Birkenau.

■   ■   ■

Undeterred by the occupation, the Hesses had gone ahead with their plan to move to a larger apartment at Albrecht Dürerstraat 17 that would better accommodate them and their two-year-old twins. Had they delayed, the move might not have been possible. Article 3 of a September 1941 proclamation required Jews to obtain a permit before changing their residence.

Their new home overlooked the end of the trolley lines, which, by 1942, Jews could no longer use without a special pass. From their third-floor window, Karl and Ilse had a clear view of the trolleys' movements below. In his memoir, Karl described what they saw:

> Whoever had received such a call had to be at the end stop of the trolley which made this run only at one o'clock at night; that was, with his family and his knapsack, the contents of which were written out. The nights before our call, we spent standing at the window. The city was veiled in darkness. Ghostlike figures walked out of their houses by the faint light of flashlights. One could hear the crying of little children and the tearful farewells

of the old ones who had to stay back. By half past one, the trolley was crowded.

Living hardly thirty yards from the end stop, we watched this whole drama, filled not only with the thoughts of those unfortunate ones, but also imagining ourselves being forced to walk this last road with our children. The trolley would start and the squeaking of the steel wheels taking the curves went right through our bones. Once again, good friends and acquaintances were on their way to the unknown.

Then it came. "We received our call one Friday evening at half past five," Karl wrote. "I knew at that moment that our own fight for life had started."

CHAPTER 6

The Jews Must Go
1942–JULY 23, 1943

On the coldest day ever measured in the Netherlands—January 27, 1942—the temperature plummeted to seventeen degrees Fahrenheit below zero. In that winter of 1941–1942, the second coldest on record, the average temperature hovered around twenty-three degrees Fahrenheit. Leaves had long ago fallen from now barren trees, and most birds had flown to warmer lands. Undeterred by the weather or the occupation, the Dutch rode their bicycles through Amsterdam's icy streets and skated on frozen canals and rinks created in open spaces around the city. Karl and Ilse were not permitted to own bicycles, nor were their days spent on sport. They were consumed with worry and plans for their family's survival.

All around them, Germans beat Jews on the streets for reasons that could not be predicted, arresting Jews as reprisal for real or imagined acts of disobedience or disrespect, separating families, deporting some to harsh labor camps, and worse. Rumors of mass killing centers in "the East" terrorized Jews throughout German-occupied lands. German-approved newspapers, radios, and loudspeakers on street corners trumpeted Hitler's post-Wannsee proclamation: "The Jew must get out of Europe.... The world over, he is the chief agitator against us.... All I say is that he must go away. If in the process he is bruised, I cannot help it. If he does not leave voluntarily, I see no solution other than extermination."

Employing his typical mendacious doublespeak, Hitler had put a deceptive gloss on his intentions. Some months earlier, he had secretly forbidden all Jewish emigration. It was no longer possible for Jews to "go away." Emigration had already slowed to a trickle as countries around the world closed their doors to the flood of impoverished Jews desperate to flee. Germany's wars in Poland and the Soviet Union had exponentially increased the Germans' "Jewish problem." At the time Hitler made that sinister speech, he had already shifted his intentions from expelling the Jews to exterminating them.

With the threat of worse treatment to come reverberating through the Jewish community, in 1942, Karl and Ilse, like thousands of Jews in the Netherlands, debated the unthinkable: asking non-Jewish friends or even strangers to take in their children. Some Dutch people were willing to hide Jews out of compassion, others for the cost-of-living expenses, and still others for a profit. Some twenty-five thousand children and adults, Jews and other German targets in the Netherlands, went into hiding in this way. Through the Dutch Underground, the Hesses paid for a hiding place for the twins in the countryside and planned to pass as non-Jews in a small town nearby.

But after wrestling with the implications of that painful choice, Karl and Ilse instead made a commitment that they hoped could be their guiding light through trials they would face—come what may, they would keep their family together. Ilse remembered, "We were prepared to go underground, but even this was difficult because we would have had to be separated. . . . It was impossible for people to hide two small children together with grownups, because you cannot keep children quiet. At that time they were maybe four years old, so we would have to be separated. My husband, working at the Schouwburg, saw daily hundreds of children caught without their parents, and we figured the better solution would be to die together than to be separated."

With that agonizing decision made, the Hesses turned to other strategies for survival under the Nazis. They had obtained false identity cards. They packed all but a few basic belongings and approached non-Jewish friends to ask them to keep their oil paintings, silver, linens, and most of their clothes—whatever could be stored in closets and under beds. Ilse also packed up a few family photos, including a precious photograph of her mother. Maybe that's why, today, Marion can say, "I have a photo my mother saved, of my grandmother, Fanny. She's sitting in what I think was her living room. It's large and bright and full of plants. On the wall are six miniatures, beautiful paintings, a poignant reminder of what once was, but then was brutally taken away."

In early July 1942, the Germans issued the first general summons for deportations, and Karl and Ilse's plans went awry. They had received their call at 5:30 one Friday evening, and were required to report to the Germans at 8:00 the next morning. Karl remembered, "I had to report to the Germans…to pick up our 'travel certificate.' It was all done 'legally,' meaning that the Jew was deported even with official certificates. This evident ploy turned into a ridiculous farce. We had two hours left in which to arrange something because at eight o'clock [that evening] there was curfew."

Karl's anger is palpable in his controlled description of events, and his fury extended to the Dutch Jews who made up the Jewish Council. He believed they had provided the Nazis with names of German-Jewish refugees, hoping that group would be called first, that the war would end, and that Dutch Jews would be spared the horrors of deportation. In the short time remaining before the 8:00 p.m. curfew, biting back his anger toward the Council, Karl raced to the office of Abraham Asscher, whom the Hesses had known for years as customers and friendly acquaintances. Explaining his precarious situation, Karl leaned heavily on his personal relationship with Asscher, copresident of the Jewish Council, proposing that Asscher make Karl his secretary, charged with the duties of an interpreter. Asscher acquiesced.

"This," Karl explained, "was, of course, a phony kind of position which had never existed before and would never exist in the future. With a letter stating this, I went to the German authority called Zentralstelle für Jüdische Auswanderung (Central Administration for Jewish Emigration) and saw the head of that group, the Hauptsturm-führer Aus Der Fuenten. He put a note on my call card—based on that letter—to the effect that the start of my work service had been postponed for six weeks. This way I had won the first round. Once more we could take a deep breath and consider what could be done next."

The Hesses had won a battle, but the German war on Jews in the Netherlands had just begun. German-Jewish refugees had been the first names provided by the Jewish Council, but the next week Dutch Jews' names filled call lists. And those lists were only one source of worry for the Hesses. Germans employed an array of tactics to keep trains filled with victims and departing on schedule. Like jungle predators, German Grüne Polizei and Dutch police roamed the streets on foot and in vans. They had quotas to fill and carried lists. Victims often hid or ran, the pursuits tearing down streets, across rooftops, between chimneys, into the homes of friends. If a targeted victim managed to escape, police conducted random sweeps, picking up Jews, even children, wherever they found them. Most Jews in hiding changed addresses frequently; many were parents separated from their children. Lolke Wilders, a non-Jewish child of seven, was playing soccer with friends in his quiet, mostly Jewish neighborhood when a van pulled up near them. In an interview years later, Lolke vividly recalled police jumping out, asking no questions, grabbing all of the children, and shoving them inside. The police drove the terrified children to the Schouwburg, where they were processed and sent to Auschwitz. Most were immediately gassed, but a few, including Lolke with his blond hair and blue eyes, were selected for medical experiments. After this disaster, the Wilders family went into hiding, one son in the basement of a nearby Catholic church, the others with families in small rural towns.

Dutch police routinely aided Germans in planning and assisting with the roundups. In one instance of such cooperation, Dutch police records from 1942 include the contents of Telegram 4, sent on July 25, warning German police to take notice of Jews carrying luggage. A telegram on August 5 requested a daily list of Jewish suicides. Dutch police guided the Germans through the unfamiliar city streets and helped by interpreting for them. Most Germans did not speak or understand Dutch. It remains perplexing how many police collaborated to the extent that they did, after living in harmony with Jews for so much of Dutch history. Some sympathized and helped Jews, but, more generally, police capitulated to German commands and went to extraordinary lengths to trap them.

No one knew who might collaborate. Private Dutch citizens sometimes took it upon themselves to report Jews' infractions of German regulations, on occasion even infractions involving German police. One who frequently did so, Dahmen von Buchholz, bragged on May 19 that he had "shopped" two German police for talking to a Jew in public. An auxiliary [collaborating volunteer] police officer took to noting in his diary his daily capture of Jews: "Caught eight Jews tonight. Later, with G. and DeV caught a further twenty-four Jews in Weesper Street." "Jew-hunt tonight, a very successful evening."

One group of collaborating bounty hunters, the Henneicke Column, specialized in reporting Jews in hiding; they received payment of ƒ7.5 (approximately $70.00 in 2022) for each Jew, including children, that they brought to German authorities. By 1943, that payment rate would increase by nearly 500 percent. Another collaborator listed his occupation on a tax form as "Jew catcher." More than ever, the Hesses needed to stay quiet and out of sight, making themselves invisible to the glaring German searchlight.

By June 1942, more than one million European Jews had been massacred. The World Jewish Congress charged that about one-sixth of the pre-war Jewish population of Europe, estimated at six to seven million, had been murdered in less than three years and that Jews deported to central Poland from Germany, Austria, Czechoslovakia, and the Netherlands were being killed at an average rate of one thousand per day. Four thousand Jewish youth aged twelve to fifteen had been taken from the Warsaw ghetto to work as forced labor on German farms as the war increasingly ravaged the Jewish population, regardless of age.

On Monday, June 29, 1942, every Dutch newspaper in the country ran the Germans' draconian announcement that all Dutch Jews would be deported to labor camps. A July 15 Amsterdam Dutch police telegram sent "to all stations," reported, "Between midnight and 2 a.m. on July 15, 16, and 19, three tramcars…will be diverted to Central Station for the transport of Jews."

On July 16, five trains transported some forty-seven hundred Jews from the Netherlands through Westerbork to Auschwitz, where almost all of them died. Early reports of the mass killings were met with skepticism or outright disbelief by the American and British governments. Slowly, reporting of the well-guarded secret gained credibility, but even the most shocking reports did not begin to describe the scope of the Germans' murder operation.

■   ■   ■

In 1942, Germany's power seemed unassailable. To buttress its defenses against the Allies, Germany began construction of the "Atlantic Wall," an enormous undertaking consisting of 6,000 concrete structures, most of them bombproof bunkers, extending from northern Norway along the shores of the Low Countries and then south along the entire Atlantic coastline of France. More than 510 concrete bunkers lined the Netherlands' coast. Building those formidable defenses was a major endeavor and a heavy burden for a country that, three years earlier, had possessed almost no gold or foreign reserves. In early 1939, Germany's economy had teetered near collapse as Hitler poured resources into the military. Before the occupation, the Netherlands had been among several nations threatening to freeze German assets—perhaps making those nations even more attractive military targets.

As Hitler had planned—and as he needed to happen—the war bolstered Germany's economy and the Nazis' popular support. Forced labor improved factory output. More significant, in every country Hitler invaded, specialized Nazi detachments sped to take possession of valuable resources, from factories to oil fields and from art to the contents of national treasuries. Germany stole $193 million in gold from the government of the Netherlands (worth close to $4 billion in 2022). The Germans targeted Dutch national treasures, including rings set with as many as twenty-five diamonds and embossed gold from the Dutch possession of Lombok in the South China Sea.

The Germans also absconded with $223 million in gold (worth over $4.6 billion in 2022) from Belgium. By the end of 1939, the German government catapulted from debtor nation to creditor with amassed gold reserves of $71 million ($1.5 billion in 2022). The Germans shipped much of their bounty to the Kaiseroda salt mine north of Frankfurt, where precious artwork and other prizes of war were secretly stored and heavily guarded. Germany's wars were also aided by business arrangements with international corporations, a number of them American.

■   ■   ■

As the Germans' grip on Dutch Jews tightened, Karl and Ilse continued to strategize. They struggled to keep their family safe as the "collection" and "evacuation" operations gained momentum and efficiency in 1942. Sensing danger in every German order, many Jews who received summons refused to gather at the designated trolleys or trains, a show of defiance to the German behemoth. Some went into hiding. Increasingly, Germans resorted to dragging Jews from their homes, pulling them from their beds at night, allowing no time for their victims to gather essentials. Karl and Ilse were caught up in one of these raids, probably in the early summer of 1942, as the mass deportations were beginning but before the Jewish Council recruited large numbers of Jewish volunteers to staff the deportation site.

Karl described how they escaped that time:

One afternoon, our whole street was occupied and all the Jews were taken out of their houses. Among them, Ilse and me. When I asked a German soldier—a huge fat hulk of a man—what was to happen to our children, he barked that the children had to stay in the house. "You and your wife, march-off-down the stairs!" You can imagine the horror we felt at the thought of having to leave our children alone in the apartment [the twins were four years old at the time] and being deported. In the street, all the Jews were standing in line, their backs to the row of houses. I asked a German guard if I could talk to the officer in command of this action ("Aktion"). The guard yelled at me and said that he would shoot anybody who dared move from his place. I said, "Go ahead, shoot," and calmly walked another fifty yards to where the officer stood. I asked him if it was his intention to have small children left alone in the apartment. He had watched the scene with the guard and said, "You have guts—send your wife back up to the children."

So I was taken alone. I waited until the truck was filled and sat down next to the chauffer [sic]. The truck took us to an assembly point, from where the deportation was supposed to start. Getting off, I slipped to the side that was not watched by the Germans; they did not expect a Jew would dare to just run away. That night I spent in an office of the Jewish Council, and in the morning I was home again.

Karl and Ilse realized that their precarious safety, resting solely on Karl's thinly disguised concocted position as Asscher's interpreter, could not last. Karl had escaped arrest, but he feared that the Germans were aggressively pursuing him. "Often," he remembered, "I sneaked out of the house at four in the morning and kept myself hidden in the bushes. Sometimes I hid in the beams of our house, or I slept away from our apartment, in hiding with Gentile friends."

And then, a possible reprieve: the Jewish Council published a notice asking for workers to assist in the daily operations of the Jewish Schouwburg. Karl immediately volunteered and was chosen from among hundreds of other applicants, either because of his facility with languages or on account of his relationship with Asscher, or both.

Each Schouwburg worker received a white armband, inscribed by the Germans with identifying numbers, to wear on his right arm. Karl's new position was demanding and not of his own choosing, but it was the choice forced upon Amsterdam's Jews, and it offered the family breathing space in a suffocating world, a respite from the terrors of the night. "As part of my routine," Karl explained, "I left my house at six-thirty in the evening and by seven o'clock, I was at my place of work. The shift was always twelve hours with no break. The theater was guarded by the SS and the Dutch SD (Sicherheitsdiensts [sic]—security service). In general, the whole deportation was carried out by the Dutch SD—people who acted as helpers, spies and bloodhounds of the Germans."

As group leader of the night shift, Karl supervised a team of twelve to sixteen workers. At 7:30, a van delivered huge buckets of food prepared by a local Jewish restaurant. Karl and his team lugged the buckets into the Schouwburg, passed out plates, and fed the dazed, terrorized prisoners. As Karl detailed in his memoir,

> Usually at nine thirty, the nightly round-up was started and at ten o'clock sharp the first truck would arrive with the arrested Jews. I had arranged the work in such a manner that the same three people would always go to the trucks. These men had the needed tact and cal[m] when helping the unfortunate ones out of the truck. We helped carry the luggage of the people into the building

and received the little children who, mostly crying, had been taken from their beds, not comprehending what was going on. For the next hours, one truck after another would come rolling in. This inhuman work would take until about half past two in the morning. It is beyond description—how many tears of despair were shed there, what countless superhuman attempts were made to escape the claws of the persecutors at the very last moment.

As the night deepened, around 2:30 a.m., Karl's team bent to their work, dragging some three hundred mattresses into the large hall so that the terrified prisoners could rest, and perhaps even sleep. The mattresses were dirty and lice-ridden. The hall echoed with every cough and nightmare. There was no privacy and no peace for the captives at the Schouwburg. "There they would be laying [sic] with their belongings," Karl remembered, "the women on the right, the men on the left. On the floors of the upper hallways would be lying the ones for whom we had no mattresses. Sometimes we had a thousand Jews a night in this prison. I can well say that I, and the others, did our utmost to help each and every one, even if sometimes that was no more than with a comforting word."

When the Schouwburg's lights were turned out, Karl made hourly rounds, checking that everyone was settled. If a person needed medical help, it was provided when possible. As Karl walked through the sleeping area, he tried to quiet prisoners unable to sleep, whose noise disturbed "those who, thank God, could forget their misery for a few hours."

Between 2:30 and 7:00 on Friday afternoons, the Schouwburg was full, or nearly so. Then prisoners would once again be loaded onto trucks, but this time driven to a solitary railroad spur in a lonely warehouse area of Amsterdam's Eastern Docklands, the Borneokade, where the train to Westerbork awaited them. Two women in Karl's group walked through the train with a typewriter, transcribing messages from departing Jews to their friends and relatives. Early in the Dutch deportation process, some Jews did not understand that they were going to their deaths. Karl believed that by winter 1942, no one remained ignorant or in denial. Few, however, had his direct personal experience of the departing trains. Schouwburg staff understood, perhaps sooner than many Jews, that deported Jews were not traveling for "labor" in "the East," as the Germans proclaimed. The workers had unique contact with weekly mass deportations of young and old, strong and feeble, and witnessed train after train returning empty. That experience would be seared into Karl's memory: "Due to my work in the Schouwburg, I am one of the few surviving witnesses of those horrible deportations and mass expulsions of old people who were dragged out of the Amsterdam old age home....How often we had to intone the "Sch'ma" [Shema] when one of these people, advanced in years or sick, died in our arms." He remembered, "I was at the train when four hundred and fifty orphans arrived....Those poor little children were all excited because they thought they were going on an outing. Only a few realized they were being deported." According to Karl, "On Tuesday nights, the transports went to Vught, another Dutch concentration camp. The train left at two thirty a.m. We went with the people to the station. Pitch-dark, often raining, and above us the humming of the English bombers. Little children crying. The

awhile, when the Germans found out, we just lied and
said that this was the grandmother who had wanted to
see her grandchild once more.

Karl and Süskind later turned their small effort into a larger
operation and, over the course of a year, smuggled some eleven hundred young Jewish children and many adults out of the Schouwburg
through the *Kindergarten* building, a few steps across the narrow
street. Gentile friends living in the countryside provided sanctuary
for some escapees, but the Germans continued to prowl the local
neighborhoods. Newly freed prisoners who remained in familiar
surroundings were caught again and deported.

Even when the tram was "barricaded by SD and Green Police,"
Karl recalled, "…even there, we succeeded in letting people escape,
partly through utter daring, partly under the protection of winter
darkness. We ourselves [the Jewish Council workers] always had
one foot in a transport, but we kept at it. The fact that I had a wife
and children at home, and that many of my colleagues had already
been shipped off with these punitive transports, did not keep me
from continuing my work for this great human cause. It was a
tremendous satisfaction to save another fellow Jew from the hands
of the tyrants."

Karl never revealed his name to those he saved. He implored
them never to discuss their escape, but they did. The German
guards began to hear rumors and attempted to identify the culprits
and staunch the flow. They never discovered how the rescues were
accomplished, and Karl continued to work in the Schouwburg for
a full year. Frequently, he slept less than four hours a day. During
terrible raids that blocked off entire sections of the city, he worked

for grueling days and nights without a break. The stress brought on acute insomnia.

During long nights that sometimes stretched into two or more days, while Karl was working at the Schouwburg, Ilse remained home with Marion and Stefan. When Karl asked colleagues to go there and request that Ilse send food for him, they invariably came back and told him that he had a brave wife who was not distressed by the bell ringing at 3:00 in the morning and had even offered them coffee.

■   ■   ■

During 1942 and 1943, as Karl worked in the Schouwburg, the war raged in the air and at sea. During the Battle of the Atlantic, from August 1942 to May 1943, German U-boats sank some six hundred Allied merchant ships, many of them oil tankers, jeopardizing Britain's supplies of food and munitions.

By February 1942, the British bombing campaign had become less focused; it now targeted both industrial and civilian areas. That year, the United States flew more than five thousand aircraft across the English Channel and the North Sea to bomb German targets along the French, Belgian, and Dutch coasts and into Germany itself. The millions of Europeans who endured the trauma of German domination then suffered the additional ordeal of Allied bombers roaring overhead. Fear permeated the lives of all Dutch, who could never predict what might befall them. On July 4, 1942, American Independence Day, American and British crews from Britain made a daylight raid against four German airfields in the Netherlands, one in IJmuiden, less than thirty miles from

Amsterdam. Intense antiaircraft fire downed two planes. The raid was the first in which American airmen flew in American-built bombers against a German target. Some months later, British bombs hit an eastern section of Amsterdam, creating a firestorm that consumed much of the city center. For the Netherlands' Jews, the double horror of the bombings was knowing that the Allies might kill them in the process of saving them.

One of Steven's early memories is of the blackout: "The Nazis insisted that all people have black curtains at their windows so no light could be viewed by Allied bombers. One night, flashing lights and noise at the edge of the curtains drew my curiosity. I pulled the curtain back and our mother rushed over and yanked me away. She said, 'You can't do this.' I later wondered whether it was her fear of glass exploding or the violation of regulations that got her so frantic. Perhaps both."

■   ■   ■

In early July 1943, Karl noticed an exceptionally large number of trucks loaded with Jews arriving at once at the Schouwburg. Realizing that a large raid was ongoing and terrified that his family was in jeopardy, he rode in the crew van to their apartment, bundled Ilse and the twins into the van, and attempted to reach an area beyond the roundup:

> On the way we were stopped. The van was confiscated, the driver arrested. On a brutally hot day in July 1943, Ilse, the children and I were standing at a street corner and seized by the Germans. No luggage, no food. Thus we stood for

two hours. Again and again, I tried to influence the guard with the most fantastic lies that he should let us go, but to no avail. On the contrary, he wanted to put the whole family and me in jail because I had attempted to smuggle us through the blockade. For us, that would have meant direct transportation to Poland as punishment. We were loaded into a truck and my identification papers were handed to the driver. After the truck had started, I happened to recognize him. He was an executive sergeant of the "Green Police." I told him a story that, against orders, my family had gone into the street, and I happened to meet them. I, myself, had a pass for that day and was working. The trick worked. He stopped the truck, returned my papers to me and let us get off. On the way home, Stefan could not walk anymore and, on top of it all, we were stopped about eight more times by police patrols. They did not arrest us, though, since we were within the blockade. Only one Dutch SD man wanted to seize us anyway, despite the fact that he knew me and was aware that I worked in the Schouwburg. Just as we were approaching our house, out came the SS who had gone there to pick us up. They had found the apartment empty, thanks to our escape attempt, and thought we had already been picked up. This way, we once more escaped immediate deportation.

Steven has vivid memories of that night:

I guess Marion and I were five years old the night we tried to escape. We were taken down to the street. I remember very clearly it was a green pickup truck. To this day I think it was a Ford. We were put in the back under a tarpaulin. Our parents had arranged for us to try to reach the border. At one point we heard voices and we were told to get out of the truck. We were herded to a small collection area. I can still visualize it. I was frightened. Dad spoke to the driver. But this was one of several strokes of fortune that we encountered. My father knew the driver and talked to him. He let us off in the middle of the night, and we returned to the apartment. I remember that walk, being pulled and dragged along. I had flat feet. I remember complaining that I couldn't walk anymore.

Again they had escaped capture, but the danger surrounding them was unrelenting. During the night of July 23, 1943, Karl and Ilse's doorbell rang at 2:00 in the morning. The German Green Police ordered the family out.

A year earlier, the Jewish Council, along with several "indispensable" Dutch war industries, had negotiated with the Germans to exempt a number of their members and employees from deportation; seventeen thousand Jews had acquired these passes, and they wanted to believe that they had won a measure of safety. In a strange bureaucratic stab at honesty, each exemption (called the "Bolle" stamp, after the name of the Jewish Council secretary), was ominously marked with the words *Bis auf weiteres*—"until further notice." That "further notice" came due in the form of a July raid, when the passes proved worthless. The Germans had never intended to honor them. They had simply used the passes as a ploy to pacify the Council and maintain that helpful organization, as Karl would soon learn:

> I showed them my pass, but, as we found out later, during this night all those who had a pass were being picked up. Under the pretext that our passes were supposed to be checked at the Schouwburg, we were taken along. We had to get our poor little ones out of bed and had hardly ten minutes to get ready. I, myself, was completely calm, because I was absolutely sure that we would either be released or that I would smuggle my family and myself out of the Schouwburg. My dear wife was less confident. Despite the fact that I did not think it necessary, she took at least some luggage along and that proved to be our luck.

Ilse explained how the Jewish Council "selected my husband and many others, coworkers [to work at the Schouwburg], because they all spoke fluently Dutch and German. And since the Germans came day and night, and some of the prisoners there spoke only Dutch or only spoke German, they needed these people just as helpers. But even though it happened very often that we were torn from our home, landed on trucks going to the Gestapo office, and when they found out that the Germans needed their help in the Schouwburg, we were sent home again until there was no help any more."

Marion recalls the night they were picked up. "I was about five years old. I remember being awakened in the middle of the night. We had a custom in our family that every night my brother and I would put out a little wooden shoe and, in the morning, it would have chocolate or candy in it. That morning, it was empty. Then I saw soldiers, and I saw my mother trying to pick up some things. I was afraid, and realized that something very different and frightening was happening."

Steven remembers, too, "There was a lot of noise. The Germans shouting orders, their huge boots loud. Our mother rushed to get us dressed quickly."

The truck transported the family to a large square, previously a stockyard. The Hesses stood in the dark with 450 other Jews, including children, all of them fearful and without food or water. Allied bombers' engines thrummed overhead. The twins played or just lay on the ground between two pieces of luggage. Karl's experience told him that if a Schouwburg worker was left behind while his family was transported to Westerbork, there was a chance—a small one—that the family would be spared deportation to Poland and instead would be sent back to Amsterdam. Karl only had to put on the white "staff" armband he had in his pocket, and he would be indistinguishable from the Schouwburg staff working there. He and Ilse debated for hours whether he should stay. Perhaps they would be lucky.

In the end, Karl found it "impossible to let my wife and children go by themselves. Ilse herself—who, to be sure, wanted nothing but the best for me—advised me to stay back. But I did not do that. I did give Ilse one last suggestion: to 'faint,' and simulate a seizure. She did. She fell to the ground, screaming. The children cried with excitement and sat next to their Mammi. Nothing worked. I asked the company commander to give me at least two days' time to get my luggage in order. I pointed to my wife who was lying on the ground, supposedly unconscious. Nothing worked.... Now we were really caught."

Karl had worked at the Schouwburg for a year, witnessing the deportation of some fifty thousand Jews, as his own family, like all Jews in Amsterdam, tried to evade capture. That night, he and his family were trapped. Loaded onto a windowless truck like goods for delivery, they struggled to stay upright as the crammed vehicle wound its way through city streets to the rail yards in the dark of night. Remaining outwardly calm, they felt desperate, "really caught," with no more tricks up their sleeves or possible avenues for escape—their only "treasure" a bottle of milk that some kind person had pressed into Ilse's hands for the children.

CHAPTER 7

Westerbork
JULY 23, 1943–SEPTEMBER 18, 1943

O ver the years," Ilse remembered, "we went through many razzias, which is the rounding up of Jews in the streets. We always managed somehow to get home again.... One day during the night—in fact at the moment I don't remember the special, the exact date—we were caught and we were sent to a central place, and from there we were shipped to Westerbork as I mentioned before, to the Dutch concentration camp."

The distance from Amsterdam to Westerbork is just under one hundred miles, a relatively short train ride. Heading northwest through rural towns, small farms, and gentle countryside, the train skirts the scenic marshes of Dwingelderveld, Europe's largest wetlands. But the Hesses' first view of their destination was anything but lovely. Constructed on a soggy, windswept plain, Westerbork was surrounded by barbed-wire fences and studded with seven guard towers staffed by German soldiers bearing rifles. It had every appearance of the prison that it was.

In 1939, when Westerbork initially opened as a refugee camp for Jews fleeing the Germans, Amsterdam's Jewish press had been indignant at the idea. Why hold Jews in confinement there, the paper demanded. Why not help them emigrate or integrate into Dutch society as Jews had done for centuries? Those suggestions went nowhere in a country whose economy had stagnated for a decade and still suffered recurring labor strikes. The Netherlands was unwilling, perhaps unable, to welcome the influx of mostly impoverished Jews. The camp was operating as the Dutch had planned when German troops roared past during the 1940 invasion. In mid-1942, three years after it opened, the Germans took control of the former safe haven and checkpoint for Jews fleeing to the Netherlands. From 1942 through 1944, some one hundred thousand prisoners would be confined there, then deported further east, mostly to their deaths in Auschwitz and Sobibor.

The Hess family arrived at the dismal prison camp on July 25, 1942, exhausted by their ordeal. Railroad tracks ran directly into the center of the nearly half-square-mile camp, but the transport stopped first at a reception area where the nearly a thousand Jewish captives disembarked. "On arrival," Karl recalled, "we had to wait for hours, with our children, in the dense crowd, until it was our turn to be registered. After registration, we passed through one room where they took the rest of our money from us. I remember this situation very vividly. An SS man stood behind a desk where an SD official sat. This official called just one word to each new prisoner who filed past him—'Money!'"

There was no choice. The prisoners had to give up everything they had. If they were found out trying to hide their valuables, the punishment barrack awaited. Rumors held that previous Westerbork commandants had been known to brutally whip or kick inmates to death. *SS-Obersturmführer* Albert Gemmeker, Westerbork's third commandant, was not personally physically violent, but held rigidly to camp rules, punishments, and deportation schedules. He sometimes ordered severe group reprisals—often the unannounced deportation of groups of random prisoners—for the misdeeds of a single prisoner, but he laughed heartily at the humor in the camp's cabaret shows, sometimes inviting the Jewish performers to his home after the show. Prisoners joked that he saw prisoners off to the extermination camps with a smile.

With his Orthodox Jewish education, Karl would probably have seen a frightening irony in the timing of their deportation; his family was confined on this pathway to death during the three-week period of mourning beginning on the Seventeenth of Tammuz, a Jewish fast day. The final day of this remembrance of ancient calamities that befell the Jews is regarded as the saddest time in the Jewish calendar, a day destined for tragedy.

Yet Westerbork was a transit camp, not a killing center; it was known as one of the more benign German camps. Still, after registration, prisoners were subjected to humiliating body searches, then sent to quarantine, from which, Karl observed, he emerged dirtier than when he entered. On one side of the camp were two hundred interconnected cottages of two rooms each, a toilet, and a hotplate for cooking. Those cottages were mostly occupied by German-Jewish refugees who had been held

there for years with no clear path forward. Long rows of barracks extended along both sides of the tracks. Each held about
seven hundred prisoners in dirty, lice-ridden, iron-frame bunk
beds stacked three beds high. A narrow hall separated men's
and women's dormitories. The sanitation was abominable. As
Karl explained in his memoir,

> All night long there was a continuous procession of
> those who suffered from diarrhea, which was a common
> camp illness. Most of the barrack-inmates wore wooden
> shoes—you can imagine the "nightly rest" where hun-
> dreds of people passed the long gangway past the beds.
> The gangway measured about thirty yards in length.
> In the washroom at the end of each dormitory, there
> was one toilet that could be used only at night. Besides
> that, in each washroom there was a long drain made
> of stone with about fifteen water faucets on each side.
> In this drain, you washed yourself, your clothes, eating
> utensils, etc. However, it was mostly used to dump the
> food leftovers and the contents of chamber pots, so that
> it was usually stopped up and unusable by the early
> morning hours.
>
> Little red houses, the latrines, were our "quiet little
> places" for the day. They were located outside the bar-
> racks and consisted of approximately twenty-four holes,
> on which one sat, or rather stooped, one rear end next
> to another. In the seven months we spent in Westerbork,
> we did not once succeed in finding a "clean seat." The

Westerbork latrines were the breeding place of sickness and disease....

In addition, the sewerage was so poor that if the wind came from the south, the stench from the latrines filled the camp and turned your stomach.

In the burning summer heat, flies buzzed everywhere, landing on every crumb of bread and every sweaty brow, tormenting the prisoners and spreading disease. In a ludicrous, unsuccessful effort to control the flies, camp authorities ordered every inmate to hand in fifty flies every day. Karl described the food at Westerbork as "disgusting slop," prepared in huge kettles and arriving cold in the barracks. However, in a peculiar aspect of this transit camp to death, Jews were allowed to receive mail and packages. Friends sent the Hesses packets of food. In addition, a friend's brother had been in the camp for four years and worked in the "potato kitchen." Quiet and unassuming, at times he was able to give the Hesses potatoes, vegetables, and milk for the children. "In this barrack," Karl remembered, "we could sometimes cook something for the children. Then, in the evening we would hurry into our own barrack, which was about a hundred and fifty yards away, with the huge cooking pot wrapped in old, filthy rags to keep the food warm. You are going to laugh about this: a few times we even prepared a gigantic potato schalet [casserole], and twice Hermann invited us for noodle schalet."

Germans did none of the camp work. All inmates were given jobs, mostly organized by members of the Jewish Council, who were forced in Westerbork, as they had been in Amsterdam, to participate in administering the camp. The Council appointed *Dienstleister*, section leaders, who had to draw up work assignments and transport lists. Through their connections with the Council, the Hesses received relatively light assignments. Karl swept a barrack twice a day, scrubbed it twice weekly, and cleaned latrines. Ilse worked as a children's "nurse" and so was able to keep Marion and Stefan nearby. When they weren't in the nursery, the children played between the barracks in sand, sometimes a foot deep, that turned to thick mud in the frequent rains. Ilse fought the dirt continuously, scrubbing the family's clothes in the often stopped-up washroom sink or in a bucket when she could find one. The clothes sometimes emerged from the scrubbing dirtier than when she had begun.

Ilse explained how she managed to take care of the twins: "My children were with us in Westerbork. And some women and I volunteered to take care of the children and we formed a little kindergarten. So we kept them busy, and we taught them whatever we could. . . . In Westerbork there were relatively quite a few children because the families were sent to Westerbork. And there was the first, I would say, selection, not in the meaning of Auschwitz, but selection made who was to be sent away. Now people—families with small children were always sent away first because for two children [sent away], they could keep two grown-ups in the camp who could work for the Germans."

Westerbork was an intentionally confusing, contradictory environment. On some days, prisoners would begin to think that if this camp was not so terribly harsh, perhaps they could survive the "labor camps." In addition to an on-site prison and the several punishment buildings, the camp had a café and beauty salon that some inmates, mostly those who had lived in the cottages since the camp was first built, could visit after their work. Children might attend a camp school. The camp hospital, staffed by Jewish doctors, treated Jews' health problems. The camp's Nazi commandant sometimes strolled through the camp, engaging in friendly conversation with his victims. In the course of my research, as I learned more about Westerbork, it occurred to me that being imprisoned there must have felt like being an inmate in a mental hospital, where the underlying dark reality was camouflaged by placid enforced routines.

Day-to-day patterns of life might have become a kind of endurable normality, but the rigid weekly schedule of deportations reminded everyone that, for the Germans, "normal" meant cruelty and murder. The first deportation transport to depart Westerbork left the camp on July 15, 1942. Trains loaded with Jews, Communists, and other targeted German victims would continue to leave with unrelenting regularity for ninety weeks, the schedule virtually uninterrupted except for the Christmas holidays.

"On Friday afternoons," Karl explained in his memoir, "the mood in the camp would start sinking lower and lower. From that moment on, the weekly transports out of the camp were being readied. On average, there were eight thousand to thirteen thousand Jews in the camp. The weekly number in the transports varied from one thousand to three thousand. From Friday to Monday there was this guessing game—who would be among those unfortunate ones?"

Karl had come to use the German word, *unglücklich*, "unfortunate" or "unlucky," as naturally as breathing. That description was only partially accurate. All of Amsterdam's Jews had attempted in one way or another to evade deportation. And all Westerbork prisoners attempted to negotiate with the Council, the guards, and each other about all aspects of the camp. Luck played its unpredictable role in the processes, but the German determination to exterminate Jews was the driving, immutable force that condemned them. Loaded trains departed from Westerbork weekly, on Tuesdays. On Monday nights or pre-dawn Tuesday mornings, "the completed transport lists arrived at the barracks." The barrack leader read the names to the terror-stricken Jews—fifty to two hundred captives in each barrack. Names on a page. Life and death sentences meted out in a mere second. The unpredictability of the prisoners' fate was torture in itself.

As Karl explained in his memoir,

> Heart pounding and temples hammering, you would wait to see if your name was next. Then, those who were called jumped from their plank beds to pack their wretched belongings. We who remained helped those in complete despair to ready their luggage. We gave or collected foodstuff or other things for the selected ones. In the greatest rush, blankets were sewn together, all pieces of clothing were put on the children, one on top of the other—always hoping that this way, one or the other thing might be salvaged. The atmosphere of these horrible nights of the transports can hardly be described. Even more miserable than the ones who were wailing and screaming seemed to be those who took their fate with total apathy.

Etty Hillesum, a Jewish diarist from Amsterdam and keen observer of her times, was confined in Westerbork during the same time as the Hess family. Once a worker in the Jewish Council's Amsterdam offices, she had quit in disappointment over the Council's participation in the deportation process, but volunteered to go to Westerbork, hoping to be helpful to Jews confined there. In the camp, on June 23, 1943, she wrote a letter to an Amsterdam friend: "We are sitting just now, Father and I, on a kind of stone drain.... In front of us, people with yellow stars are digging a moat to stop us from running away, and beyond that stretches the barbed wire. To the left...the military policeman stands high up in his little hut on posts. We are black with sand.... We shall try somehow to pull each other through." Once again, Jews had been coerced to participate in their own demise. Two weeks later, she wrote, "Today my strength failed me...I fainted right in the middle of a big barracks. This morning yet another transport of 2,500 left.... [T]hings are getting quite desperate."

She flung her last note, written on a postcard, from the moving cattle car as it journeyed to Auschwitz on September 7, 1943. Not uncommonly, farmers whose land abutted the tracks found desperate notes that deportees squeezed between slats of the moving cattle cars. The farmer who discovered Etty's final diary entry sent it to the Amsterdam address she had written on the note. She died two months later in Auschwitz.

Tuesday mornings at 7:00, the doomed Jews were required to stand in front of their barrack, ready to be loaded onto cattle cars waiting on the central track. The camp's SS commandant, who may have spoken friendly words to the deportees a day before, supervised the process, including loading large numbers of very sick prisoners. Departing prisoners waved, cried, threw last-minute letters from the open doors as the heaving engine roared to life, the iron wheels screeched, and, in an unholy symphony of belched steam and discordant noise, the train pulled out of the camp.

The unreality of life at Westerbork was brought into high relief by the Tuesday night theater performances, staged just hours after the emotional deportation—as the loss of friends, family, and acquaintances still burned in the camp inmates' minds. When the Germans took over Westerbork from the Dutch, Commandant Gemmeker had ordered "a grandiose stage" to be built for cultural events. Inmates were permitted to perform "operettas, cabarets, and musicals."

"Unbelievable as it seems," Karl wrote in his memoir, "on Tuesday evenings, after the transport had gone, there was not a seat to be had [in the theater], despite the fact that most people in the audience had, only hours before, lost a loved one or a friend. For us, too, this contradiction of emotions was not to be explained. Perhaps one can possibly explain it by the fact that everybody was happy to have gained another week's respite." "[T]he orchestra of fifty men was absolutely first rate. Every night the theatre was filled to capacity."

Karl's reactions were not so strange as he imagined. Besides enjoyment of fine music and distraction from oppression, other emotions may have been at work for Westerbork's captives. With their music, the prisoner performers made a lie of almost a decade of Nazi propaganda grinding Jews down, pushing them from normal society, branding them in every way possible as subhuman, and then threatening them with death for their mere existence. In the unlikely setting of the German prison camp, in this theater, Jews could experience a brief interlude from suffering. They could soar with the undeniable beauty of music that Jews were creating and recall times when they had thrived and were valued for their many and varied contributions to Dutch society.

Mischa Hillesum, Etty Hillesum's brother, a talented pianist and composer, had been given special permission to play at Westerbork. Louis Bannet, a Dutch Jew widely considered Europe's foremost jazz trumpeter and bandleader, performed there before being sent to Birkenau.

Jews had been leaders in Amsterdam's industries from textiles to diamonds and the law, though most had owned small businesses. Many Jews had also been acclaimed artists and writers, members of leading orchestras. The seventeenth-century Amsterdam-born Jewish philosopher Baruch Spinoza was revered as the most important Dutch philosopher of all time; his library was an important Amsterdam landmark and an early target for theft by the Germans.

Those Tuesday evening performances may have restored the Jews' inner strength—a renewal they would need in the days ahead. The grateful audience was probably not aware that the stage the musicians played on was built of wood from the destroyed synagogue of Assen, a small Dutch town a few miles from the camp.

The magic of Tuesday evenings did not last long or eliminate the fear and grief that permeated the prisoners' existence. Watching ill prisoners being loaded onto the trains was especially terrifying for Karl and Ilse. In Amsterdam, Stefan had already undergone a mastoid operation for a severe ear infection. In Westerbork, he had developed another ear infection. Karl and Ilse brought their febrile five-year-old to the sickbay, where he lay in a room with some twenty other children. They found the health care frighteningly haphazard, and they were allowed to see Stefan only one hour a day, long enough for them to see that he ate very little and was growing weaker.

"[Westerbork] was what they tell us now, after the war," Ilse would say, "[was] one of the most bearable camps, if you call it bearable that every Tuesday a train was standing in the center of the camp going east either to Auschwitz, to Theresienstadt, or to Bergen-Belsen. We all had to work, but we saw each other almost every day, and this was really a consolation."

■　　■　　■

Three weeks passed for the Hesses in Westerbork...six weeks...eight weeks. The barracks were stifling in the summer, thick with the smells of overcrowding and minimal sanitation. Etty Hillesum described the Jews living "like rats in a sewer." As fall came, the winds blew through, and temperatures plummeted. The Hesses worked frantically with Jewish Council representatives, seeking an opening, a loophole in the German regimen that their family could slip through and escape the transports east.

When deportations had begun in Amsterdam, the Council managed to negotiate forty thousand "exemptions" from deportation, to be issued to people of the Council's choosing. Karl was among the many Westerbork prisoners who besieged the Council offices—in Amsterdam and in Westerbork by mail, phone, and in person, pointing out his service in the Schouwburg, petitioning to be granted a reprieve. The Hesses waited, their concern for Stefan's health mounting and prospects for freedom occupying every thought.

But even if they could return, they knew they no longer had a home in Amsterdam. Friends had informed them that their apartment had been taken over by opportunistic Dutch and their belongings looted, probably by A. Puls & Sons "removal" company. Abraham Puls, loyal member of the Dutch Nazi Party (NSB), profited handsomely during the Holocaust by cleaning out the apartments of deported Jews, then turning over confiscated property to the Nazis' appointed liquidator, Einsatzstab Reichsleiter Rosenberg. The Hesses' home had been "Pulsed."

■   ■   ■

By 1943, as the Hesses were fighting for their safety, the Germans' war on Jews intensified. The system for rounding up, deporting, and murdering Jews ran efficiently, sometimes ahead of schedule, and city after city in the Reich and occupied countries was reporting itself Judenfrei. But Germany's military machine was not reporting the same success; it had begun to falter. Announcements of victories in the Soviet Union that had once blared from thousands of Nazi loudspeakers turned out to be premature, less certain than they had seemed. Germany had poked the Russian Bear, and it had awoken with unanticipated fury.

In early December 1941, needing to regroup, the forces carrying out what the Germans had code-named Operation Barbarossa had halted their advance deep inside Soviet territory, near Moscow and Leningrad. Their previously successful blitz invasion strategy was proving inadequate in the vast spaces of the Soviet Union. Because of the Germans' hubris about their military prowess, and because Nazis stereotyped Slavic Russian people, in the same way that they did the Poles—as inferior human beings—the German army had not prepared for a protracted war. German soldiers did not have winter uniforms, and winter 1941–42 came early. German troops froze, vehicles were mired in mud and snow, and trains for resupply were spread thin over German-occupied countries across the Continent. Ominously, despite significant losses, the Soviets had not broached the possibility of armistice or surrender.

For the Germans, there could be no turning back. Germany needed Soviet oil and grain to fight what German generals had long projected would be an inevitable, protracted war with both Britain and the United States. For several years, the United States had been sending war supplies to the Soviet Union, thwarting the Germans' dreams of a quick victory. Stalin's spies had alerted the Soviets to Japan's imminent Pearl Harbor attack. Understanding that the Japanese would not threaten the Soviet Union's eastern flank, Stalin had redeployed twenty army divisions from the east to Moscow and unleashed a pulverizing counterattack on German troops.

For the first time in its years at war, news from the front was raising concerns in Berlin. Some struggling German units were in retreat; the Germans had been compelled to shift units from Moscow to other fronts. Hitler acknowledged to Japanese ambassador Hiroshi Ōshima that he was "not yet sure" how he would defeat the United States. The bloody battle at Stalingrad (now Volgograd) had begun in December 1942, but in encounters that wove even through the city's streets, Soviet troops and citizens were fighting the Germans to a stalemate. At Leningrad, too, at terrific cost in Soviet lives, citizens and beleaguered, starving troops withstood Germany's strangling encirclement of the city, holding on through two years of fighting.

German generals had long dreaded a two-front war and warned Hitler against it, but now German forces were engaged at all points of the compass, from Norway to North Africa, from France to Moscow. From July 1942 through June 1943, Allied bombers had struck German coastal targets on the western French coast, north along the English Channel and the North Sea, and as far east at the Baltic Sea. German forces were stretched to their breaking point as Allied bombs fell across occupied countries and in their homeland.

■   ■   ■

Even as war raged across the Continent and Jews were being deported from the Reich in terrifying numbers, the Hesses were released from Westerbork. "For all these weeks, the Jewish Council in Amsterdam kept on trying to get the four of us out of the camp," Karl recounted. "On September 18, 1943, we were overjoyed to learn that we were to be a part of a small group of those who were permitted to return to Amsterdam."

Their release gave them a wisp of hope. Perhaps life under the Nazis was possible, after all.

Or perhaps not. As Ilse recalled, "After having been there [in Westerbork] for few weeks . . . we were packed on—again on a train and sent back to Amsterdam. But at that time, we did not have an apartment any more, which was looted ten minutes after we were taken away."

And there was worse to come. As Karl would write in his memoir, "At half past one at night, we lucky ones—few as they were—got together to start on their way back. Stefan was taken to the train from the hospital on a stretcher and was lying underneath all our blankets. In the morning, we were back in Amsterdam.... A few days later, a good friend warned me of a massive raid that was to take place, so that the last remaining Jews would be deported from Amsterdam."

CHAPTER 8

No Refuge
SEPTEMBER 19, 1943–OCTOBER 3, 1943

K arl and Ilse's return to Amsterdam was no joyful homecoming. The Germans continued to pursue their dual wars—territorial and racial—relentlessly. Germans were still arresting Jews with ferocious intensity, warehousing them at the Schouwburg, sending them to Westerbork, and then to uncertain fates in "the East." With no home to return to, not knowing who might still be alive in Amsterdam, Karl and Ilse had called friends in a mixed Jewish–non-Jewish marriage, hoping they were still safe. At Wannsee, over glasses of cognac, Nazi leaders had debated murdering Jews in mixed marriages, but decided to postpone that volatile task until war's end. The Hesses' friends welcomed Ilse and the children. Neighbors across the street took in Karl.

The next days proved both heartening and distressing. Despite the Jewish star on his chest still marking Karl as a target, he went often into the city center to learn what he could about troubling rumors of an imminent raid. He understood that his supposed exemption from deportation, issued by the Germans through the Jewish Council, had only been a delaying tactic, another German ruse to keep Jews from hiding or attempting to flee. However, he also carried with him his precious certificate of release from Westerbork, which, the Hesses had been told, would protect them from arrest.

With the menace of another raid hanging over the family, Ilse, too, found no relief from their ordeals. Not knowing how much time she might have before trouble erupted again, she made the most of every minute. Wearing her star, as always, and carrying her certificate of release, she, too, ventured onto Amsterdam's dangerous streets. She took their damaged belongings to tailors, laundries, and cleaners, hoping to restore the filthy, torn clothing to reasonable condition as quickly as possible, fearing that they had not seen the last of Nazi terror. Preparing as well as she could for whatever might happen, Ilse took her active five-year-olds to a Jewish cobbler to have him make them sturdy shoes, with plenty of growing room.

"Strange, what sticks in your mind," Steven told me. "The shoemaker got on his knees and put a yellow pad on the floor. He placed first one foot and then the other on it, and traced each foot with a pencil while we giggled. It tickled. He made shoes for us with thick soles and laces like on ice skates or hiking boots, with metal tabs. They were built to last forever. Our mother rubbed dust on them, so they did not look as shiny, new, and desirable as they were. Things were getting worse by the day. I think of those years as joyless, gray, boring. Too young to know the fear, but old enough to miss doing things and going places, like the beach, where we went in better times, or just going outside. I remember no activity, no laughing, and no smiles."

Karl had discovered nothing about the rumored raids. He and Ilse agonized about their next steps. At Westerbork, they had been eyewitnesses in terrifying proximity to months of deportations. No one ever returned. The vibrations of those iron wheels still reverberating in their hearts, they concluded that their only hope was to wait for Stefan to recover from his infection, for their clothes to be readied—then they would hide.

This was a daring, difficult decision. Hidden Jews who were discovered—and approximately one in three were found—were sent directly to Westerbork's punishment building. If they survived that, they were shoved onto the next train to Sobibor or Auschwitz. Earlier, Karl and Ilse had rejected the option of separating from their children and hiding as too painful for their family. Besides the emotional upheaval, that plan was fraught with other dangers—the possibility of a drawn-out war, discovery of the children's true identities, Stefan's ear infections, Marion's panic at being separated. Too much could go wrong. In hiding, they would worry constantly. And if trouble arose, they would not be able to help their beloved children.

After they made that wrenching decision, their options narrowed considerably. Deportation seemed just one small mistake away. Staying together was important, but surviving was paramount. That reality forced them to make the once-impossible choice. The Dutch Underground may have found the rural family Karl and Ilse paid to shelter the children. They could live under cover nearby. They would do whatever it took to save their family.

■   ■   ■

While Karl and Ilse were making arrangements to hide, the escalating air war continued to rock the Dutch capital. By summer 1943, the Wehrmacht's tactics had shifted dramatically in ways that the once-proud Germans could not have imagined. Eight years of German mastery over Europe's skies had devolved into a sometimes-desperate defense. In Amsterdam, bombs exploded a few miles from the city center. Because Schiphol Airport was a major base for German attacks on Britain, it had become an Allied target. Bombing raids on Schiphol had begun ten days after the 1940 invasion and then increased in intensity, pounding the airfield until late 1943, when the Allies struck a decisive blow. More than seven hundred Allied bombs cratered runways and landing areas, shattered hangars and supply sheds, making repairs impossible. German antiaircraft fire shrieked into the sky, and air-raid sirens sent citizens racing to shelters, which Jews were not permitted to enter.

The constant roar of Allied and German planes echoed through the city, punctuated by the sharp *ack-ack-ack* of their machine guns and the frightening whine of planes falling from the sky. During the war, six thousand planes would crash to the ground across the Netherlands, an average of three per day.

The American Eighth Air Force, based in Britain, had grown to a strength of 396 heavy bombers. In the summer of 1943, good weather and long sunlit days allowed that group to send missions south to France; but in mid-July its new B-17s—American-built heavily armored "Flying Fortress" bombers—attacked the Fokker aircraft plant in Amsterdam. The cloud cover over the city obscured the crews' aim, and the bombs fell on a nearby neighborhood, killing some 150 Dutch civilians. The roar of the planes when they returned a few days later must have terrorized the neighborhood, but this time they hit their target, destroying the factory.

■   ■   ■

The Hesses' release from Westerbork had offered a reprieve from deportation but no guarantee of safety. Karl and Ilse made their way cautiously through Amsterdam, with German and Dutch police all around them. Maneuvering through the city's familiar byways, they must have felt chilled by the changes that had taken place during their two months in Westerbork. Missing were many of the starred coats they had once seen on the streets. Fewer Jews remained in the city, and now most Jews they did encounter were shabbily dressed. When Jewish workers in diamond factories and small businesses—about half of pre-war Amsterdam's Jewish workers—had been thrown out of work, many turned to selling fruit, pickles, and second-hand clothing from carts in the streets.

It is not a simple task to quantify how many Jews remained in Amsterdam or the Netherlands in September 1943. By some estimates about 80,000 Jews, making up approximately 10 percent of Amsterdam's population, had resided in the city at the time of the occupation. Approximately one in three of those were refugees, like Karl and Ilse. In 1941, before the mass deportations, between 140,000 and 155,000 Jews lived in the Netherlands. An estimated 28,000, including children, had gone into hiding, but that number, too, is difficult to gauge, as Jews said goodbye to friends and family or simply disappeared.

Numbers also depend, in part, on the definition of a Jew. By German estimates, defined by "race," rather than religion or culture, the count was higher, including people with one or more Jewish grandparents, even if those individuals did not consider themselves to be Jews.

As Karl and Ilse reconnected with people they knew, the reunions brought some warmth back into their lives, but those friendships also were fraught with heartbreak—the loss of mutual friends, fears for the future, and painful memories of good times that would never return.

■   ■   ■

Life under the Germans was difficult for non-Jewish citizens as well. Food and fuel were scarce. Trainloads of food, clothing, and other property stolen from murdered and deported Jews flowed in a rampaging flood from the Netherlands into the Reich. The Dutch paid exorbitant taxes to Germany for "services." Poverty and hunger stalked the streets along with German soldiers, German Green Police, Dutch police, and collaborators eager to denounce Jews and resisters, informing the Germans about their location.

The Dutch economy was in shambles. Growing numbers of non-Jewish men had been sent to work in German factories and farms. Ever-increasing demands on Dutch industry to support Germany's war effort drove the Netherlands' economy down to half of its pre-war level. Germans controlled the rationing system that had been put in place by the Dutch government shortly before the occupation, and they repeatedly reduced the amount of food allotted. Sugar, tea, soap, candles, and other necessary items were hard to come by. People ate gluey potato cakes and pudding concocted from grey skim-milk powder. Dwindling supplies of wood for stoves forced people to wear coats indoors. During the night, some citizens cut down trees in city parks and lugged the wood home before they could be arrested. People walked or biked to the countryside to buy fresh food, then carried it back home. Rubber, needed by the German military, was impossible to find. People who still owned bikes rode on bald tires, their rims grating on the cobblestones. Jews received the same ration cards as others, but their access to grocery stores was increasingly restricted, so they could buy only the leftovers, which were sometimes adequate, sometimes nonexistent.

■　　■　　■

German war news in 1943 carried more than a hint of alarm for the Nazis. Although Germany still controlled the European continent at the start of that year, on New Year's Day the *New York Times* published a radical assessment of the rampaging world war: "Some tick of the great world clock, possibly unheard at the moment, marked a transition from the period when the Axis might have been successful, to this period, when it cannot…. The Axis tide may have a long ebbing, but it has turned." Indeed, the tide would have a long and deadly ebbing, but erosion had already undermined many of Germany's earlier triumphs.

The Battle of Stalingrad stretched to seven bloody months, from August 1942 into February 1943, turning into a disaster for Germany and the Axis allies. More than two million troops battled, often at close quarters, as both Hitler and Stalin ordered,

"*No retreat.*" "*Not a step back!*" Soviet citizens, men and women alike, joined the fight in the city's streets.

Axis forces suffered a staggering eight hundred thousand casualties in that onslaught; ninety-one thousand German troops surrendered. Taking losses of more than one million dead, wounded, missing, or captured, the Soviet Red Army repelled the German attack and pursued the retreating Wehrmacht forces. Hitler's hoped-for victory over the city named for the Soviet leader, potentially cementing German access to major Soviet industrial centers, had turned into a rout, a burning humiliation for Hitler—that would later be seen as the war's turning point.

By early September 1943, as Karl worked long days and nights at the Schouwburg and the family struggled to remain free, the Soviets opened a drive on Germany's large bases, cutting rail lines and lancing into northern Ukraine, killing eleven thousand Germans on one disastrous day for the Reich. The Soviets forged ahead on all fronts. In late September, they advanced on Ukraine's capital, Kyiv. In a speech broadcast throughout German-occupied lands, Hitler admitted withdrawing some fighting groups from the Eastern Front, uncharacteristically noting recent Soviet successes and superiority in men, matériel, and reserves. But he termed Germany's troop withdrawals part of its "elastic strategy." As Europe entered its fourth year of world war, in a talk transmitted worldwide from Quebec, Churchill promised an invasion of France.

The most devastating of Hitler's military setbacks in 1943 were from Allied bombing raids on the German homeland. In late July, in one of the most damaging of these raids, code-named Operation Gomorrah, the Allies firebombed Hamburg. That devastating tactic created what was described as a "firestorm," which severely damaged German armaments production there and killed thirty-seven thousand civilians. In cities and industrial sites across Germany, the British Royal Air Force (RAF) dropped phosphorus bombs that rendered firefighting practically useless.

Axis forces also suffered major losses on other fronts. Allied forces wiped out gains in North Africa won by celebrated German general Erwin Rommel, the "Desert Fox," and the war front moved across the Mediterranean into Italy. Allied military forces poured into Sicily, Southern Italy, and Italian-occupied southeastern France. On September 8, Italy announced an armistice with the Allies. A defiant Hitler reacted immediately, dispatching German paratroopers to rescue his closest ally, Mussolini, and establishing a joint base of operations in Northern and Central Italy to continue the battle.

As its war machine reeled from setbacks, cracks began to appear in the internal support for the Nazi regime in Germany, which had once seemed rock solid. Food shortages, which Hitler had promised his followers would never happen, ravaged the German populace. In spite of food stocks appropriated from occupied lands, meat, fats, vegetable oils, butter, and eggs were sharply rationed. Morale suffered as Germans were ordered to accept the "struggle"—it was "you or me." Gestapo eavesdroppers on the streets reported people who expressed pessimism about the war. Voicing a negative opinion could get you arrested. Authorities intercepted personal letters, tapped telephones, and punished anyone who dared to dissent.

■   ■   ■

While the military was suffering reversals across Europe and western Russia, roundups, death camps, and killing fields continued to operate with deadly efficiency. A lethal spiderweb of rail lines transported Jews to the largest of Germany's death camps, Auschwitz-Birkenau in Poland, the cattle cars sometimes traversing more than a thousand miles from squalid holding camps as distant as the Pyrenees and the Soviet Union.

Night and day, ovens burned and acrid smoke rose from the chimneys in death camp crematoriums. By spring 1943, nothing had stopped the massive killing operation. The ferocity of the Warsaw ghetto uprisings in April that year had shocked the Germans and offered Jews who might have heard about them an example of courage and resistance. That Pyrrhic victory had briefly delayed the deportations and cost Germany over one hundred killed and wounded soldiers, but they did not prevent the ghetto's destruction.

■   ■   ■

In Amsterdam, asking questions and listening to friends and Council leaders, Karl and Ilse learned of a ploy that might offer their family, if not freedom, at least an alternative to Auschwitz. In February 1943, a tiny loophole had opened in the rigid concentration camp system in which the Jewish population was designated for death. Some months earlier, Nazi Minister of Foreign Affairs Joachim von Ribbentrop had noticed that Amsterdam harbored Jews from around the world, especially from South America. At the same time, Germany's mounting military losses meant that large numbers of its soldiers were imprisoned in other countries.

Ribbentrop wanted to bring them home. His idea seemed simple. To kill Jewish citizens of neutral foreign countries would be at a minimum inflammatory, if not an act of war. He proposed to select a few prominent South American Jews in the Netherlands and *not* send them east. Instead, they would be held in a special camp in Germany, for possible prisoner exchanges or even to ransom for trucks or other war matériel—bargaining chips in the game of war. The mandate for this singular camp would be that camp personnel inflict "no disabilities whatsoever" on the inmates.

In April 1943, "Bergen-Belsen" appeared for the first time in the files of the SS Economic-Administration Main Office, Section D, headed by Heinrich Himmler. The proposed new camp would be a "detention camp," unique among German concentration camps.

Bergen-Belsen would also differ from the system's only civilian internment camp, Theresienstadt. Himmler's concept of Theresienstadt as a "show camp," supposedly subject to Geneva Conventions, had been established in late 1941 to counter international reports of German cruelty and murder of the Jews. But by 1943, it, too, had become a death trap. While Theresienstadt maintained a veneer of survivability, thousands died from the harsh conditions, and thousands more were deported from there to death camps.

That April, SS leadership in Germany and the Netherlands quietly enacted orders to move forward with Bergen-Belsen; these orders were kept top secret to prevent other neutral countries from making similar claims of immunity for their Jewish citizens. The order was distasteful to Nazi officials because it forced them to recognize that just possibly some Jews were not "vermin," but instead persons valued in other places; they essentially also had to admit that Jews were useful to the Reich. Accepting this necessity, they granted Jews with Latin American passports the possibility of avoiding extermination camps.

Ribbentrop's proposal lay at the intersection or, more accurately, the collision of Hitler's two wars. After years of murdering Jews, the German military now needed them, at least those with foreign connections—and Karl and Ilse hoped they might be able to make use of this small loophole in the system and save their family from near certain death in Sobibor or Auschwitz. Like hundreds of other Jews in the Netherlands, they began to explore the convoluted process of acquiring a phony Latin American passport.

In September 1943, however, time was not on the Hess family's side. Rumors of a large roundup proved true. Eight days after their return to Amsterdam, German and Dutch police banged on the door where Ilse and the twins had found refuge and arrested everyone in the house. As Ilse remembered, "We were picked up during the night and sent back to Westerbork. When my husband came in the morning to pick us up, we were gone."

Steven explains:

> We had been arrested by the Nazis and taken from our home. All Jews kept a suitcase, or a backpack next to the door. The one we had, I can see it in my mind's eye, was a Swiss rucksack with a metal frame. The Jews knew the Nazis would get them. You just never knew where and you never knew when.
>
> Always the Dutch police worked alongside the Germans. In the night, they came to arrest you. There was nothing but panic. It was nothing like, "Just give me a moment." It didn't work that way. You have no time for anything. Jump out of bed. Open the door. When the time came, Jews took whatever they could carry. They packed,

thinking, *If your house was going to burn down in an hour, what would you take?* The police wouldn't give you any time—*Okay, give me a moment.* No! It was bang on the door, then, *"Aus gasse!"* "GO!"

As Karl wrote in his memoir, "That night, all the Jews were dragged from their houses. Three times, I was in imminent danger of being taken and avoided arrest only by presence of mind. I tore my Jewish star off my coat and had myself thrown out of a building of the Jewish Council as an 'Aryan' by a German trooper. He yelled at me and asked me what I, as an Aryan, had to do with the Jews."

The September 29 roundup that snared Ilse, along with three to five thousand other Jews, was the last major raid in Amsterdam before that city was declared Judenfrei. Germans pulled Jews from the streets, from shops and homes—including even the homes of leading members of the Jewish Council. The absence of any solid information ahead of the rumored raid perhaps should have been a red flag, warning Karl and the Council of their danger. This raid targeted the last Jews living in the city. The Council itself had been targeted.

That night, Germans officially shut down the Council in Amsterdam, arresting its officers, members, and the five thousand Jews holding supposed exemptions. Although the Germans knew that some Jews remained hidden throughout the city—they were searching relentlessly for them—German officials announced the total liquidation of Amsterdam's Jews and declared the city Judenfrei.

When the SS and German police converged at his home that night, Professor David Cohen, joint head of the Jewish Council with Abraham Asscher, willingly volunteered to be arrested. He later admitted that sitting in the train for Westerbork, he was "elated."

He had felt guilty about his protected position while Germans deported thousands of other Jews.

After the raid, members of the Dutch Nazi Party known as "key men" received an alert to go to the houses of deported Jews and collect their keys. Further raids would follow in coming months as hidden Jews and others who had eluded capture were discovered.

The night of Ilse's arrest, chaos reigned in the Amstel Station, where the Jews had been collected. She struggled to protect the twins and keep them at her side amidst the shouting, shoving, and beatings as German Green Police and Dutch police forced thousands of trapped Jews onto trains destined for Westerbork.

"When I came home in the morning looking for Ilse," Karl remembered, "the whole house was cleaned out and my dear wife and children were once more sitting in a train for Westerbork. Like a desperado, I rammed the locked door. Then I climbed, via a neighbor's house, into the apartment which I found empty."

Karl stayed in Amsterdam for three days. He broke into the Jewish shops to retrieve their clothes that had been cleaned and repaired, as well as the children's new boots. The owners of those shops, too, had been arrested. Karl recalled,

> At night I roamed the streets like a criminal or looked for a hiding place. Our friends took care of me in a most devoted manner, trying every possible thing so I would not have to return to hell. However, after I had collected all our things—a job almost beyond human possibilities because the owners of those shops had been picked up as well—I could not stay in Amsterdam any longer. Hunted like a dog, I ran through the city, voluntarily

surrendered to the Germans to be "permitted" to go to Westerbork. This was the smallest transport ever—one Jew wanted to join his wife and children, accompanied by two "volunteers," on a local train.

In Ilse's words,

My husband volunteered to be sent back to the concentration camp. He went to [SS-Hauptsturmführer] aus der Fünten who was leader of the Dutch—of the German Gestapo [in Amsterdam] and asked him to be permitted to go to his concentration camp. [Fünten] said, in his German, that he never saw such a crazy man who would do such thing.

And in fact he called in some of his co-workers to show them what had happened, that they never had a Jew who volunteered to go to the concentration camp. He also mentioned that it would be very easy for my husband not to go because he had light blond hair, blue eyes, spoke perfect Dutch, spoke perfect German. And he just—he himself was almost puzzled. And to make a very, very sad story funny, he told my husband that he could take along whatever he wanted to—but there was nothing to take along because everything had been taken away when they plundered our apartment.

The two "volunteers" as Karl referred to them with dark humor, SS officers, commandeered first-class seats as they always did when traveling. That October evening, Karl and his Nazi captors traveled in some comfort to Westerbork.

CHAPTER 9

On the Edge
OCTOBER 3, 1943–FEBRUARY 15, 1944

The family reunited in the grim camp, exhausted, discouraged, overjoyed to be together, determined to survive—experiencing all the clashing emotions of the trauma—safe for a time, as they negotiated an increasingly unsafe world. In Westerbork, Karl learned that Ilse had withstood her deportation bravely, yet the world they both had re-entered could hardly have been more unstable. Even the dirt under their feet turned from dust to mud and then to ice as winter set in. Nothing seemed to be solid ground except for their devotion to each other.

Friendships were a double-edged comfort that made life more bearable six days of the week but on the seventh day brought heartache when the train, like a fearsome beast, rumbled past their barracks to gather up prisoners—their friends, the children's playmates, and possibly themselves—and then would return, empty, relentless, the next week, prepared to take more victims to "the East."

Walter Süskind, Karl's friend and inspiring supervisor at the Schouwburg, had arrived in Westerbork several weeks before the Hesses. He had saved many Jews, but he could not save himself or his family. The Süskinds endured a year in Westerbork before being deported to Auschwitz, where they died in September 1944. Abraham Asscher and David Cohen, the copresidents of the Jewish Council, also languished in the camp awaiting unknown fates.

During the Hesses' first imprisonment, friends had sent them food packages, but most of their friends were no longer in Amsterdam. A ghoulish camp system gave Westerbork's inmates a diet somewhat more stable than that of many non-Jewish Dutch people; when shortages occurred in Westerbork, the Germans deported more inmates. The thousands of ration cards that deported inmates left behind provided food—mostly for the Germans.

In the Netherlands and throughout Europe, war had taken a severe toll on the food supply. Germans fared better than others, as trainloads of food confiscated from occupied countries rolled into the Reich, but by 1943, when the Hesses were in Westerbork, Europeans' food intake had plummeted to 75 percent of pre-war levels, and then even lower. Dutch farmers had increased production of potatoes, grain, and oil seeds at the expense of grazing pastures, reducing the availability of meat, milk, and cheese.

As winter set in, an outbreak of infantile paralysis (polio) that was spreading across America and Europe, killing and crippling thousands, ravaged the camp. In the barracks at Westerbork, which were crammed three beds high with seven hundred weakened, vulnerable prisoners, the one miserable small stove did nothing to ward off winter's debilitating cold. It radiated heat for barely three yards. That winter, Marion complained of nausea and headache and spiked a fever, terrifying the family. "We feared that she had contracted the crippling disease [polio]. Thank God, this was not the case," Karl recalled. "Marion never did show the normal reflexes when while being examined with the little hammer." As he observed, "What we went through during that time cannot be told."

According to Karl's memoir, the camp "situation" on his return to Westerbork remained much the same. Yet the stresses on the Jews were exacting a toll. There was controversy and resentment over the Jewish Council. Some prisoners argued that the Council had served its German masters too well, enabling the deportation of Amsterdam's Jewish population to run too quickly, too smoothly.

Council supporters, like Karl, believed that the system prevented rampant brutality and that nothing could change the Germans' ultimate goal. Terms like "collaboration" and "cooperation" stung Council members, who felt that the censure fundamentally misrepresented the Jews' position in an occupied country. Council critics were vocal, but all agreed that no Jew hoped for or supported a German victory or wished for a Nazi New Order—German political domination.

Council leaders maintained that the situation demanded they decide which of the Jews' dreadful alternatives was least abhorrent and would result in the lowest loss of life. They believed that the Council offered an opening for negotiation.

Others argued that many Dutch Jews had refrained from resisting the occupation or going into hiding because they believed that the Jewish Council would, and could, fight for them. They felt that while the Dutch Constitution obligated the government to protect all citizens, the Council had usurped that role—but had done it poorly. When the Council office in Westerbork began negotiating with the Germans about deportation lists, the prisoners' anger and distrust deepened. Why had Council leaders asked for "exemptions" for seven thousand of their employees at the expense of other Jews? Why did the trains, with Dutch National Railroad employees at the control, run so smoothly? The unanswerable questions lingered as train after train carried Jews away.

In the camp, other more pressing issues burned: Where did the departing trains go? What happened to those prisoners? For a while, some Jews in Westerbork clung to German propaganda about survivable work camps. For the Hesses, that hope collapsed under the weight of their eighteen-week second imprisonment, especially after they witnessed guards loading the camp's hospital patients into cattle cars. As Karl explained in his memoir, "In January 1944, the most gruesome transport ever left Westerbork, a transport of sick people. Almost the whole hospital was deported, along with the families of the patients. It just so happened that all of us were healthy that week."

Steven later said that, when witnessing these invalids shoved onto the train, "the scales came off my parents' eyes." With new, devastating clarity, the Hesses then understood that those weak, ill patients and their families were not useful for slave labor—and that deportation meant death.

Jews' beliefs about their fate differed widely. Few people outside the Nazis' inner circle and those who participated in the murders knew the whole truth. The prisoners in Westerbork, like world leaders, had differing levels of understanding—and they would come to grasp the cruel reality of the transports and camps at very different times.

Dukie Gelber, an Amsterdam Jew who was in Westerbork during the time the Hesses were there, later recounted his childhood memories: "In 1942, when already in the east probably two million Jews were already eliminated, massacred, and we had no idea what was going on in Eastern Europe. We didn't know about Auschwitz. We never heard the name Treblinka, Sobibor, nothing. So, we didn't know."

But Etty Hillesum, the young Jewish diarist from Amsterdam whose brother played in the Westerbork concerts, did know. On July 11, 1942, two months before her family's deportation to Westerbork and then to Auschwitz, she wrote with biting irony in her diary, "The Jews here are telling each other lovely stories: they say that the Germans are burying us alive or exterminating us with gas."

Another young Amsterdam Jew who wrote in her diary about the Jews' frightening fate, Anne Frank, famously penned that all people were good at heart, but later, probably in May 1944, wrote a darker observation about the deported Jews: "We assume that most of them are murdered. The British radio speaks of their being gassed." The Frank family would arrive in Westerbork on August 8, 1944, some six months after the Hesses were deported. It's not known what the Hesses believed when they arrived at Westerbork for the second time. Because of Karl's close relationship with Asscher and others in the Jewish Council, he had surely heard the rumors. What *is* known about all the Jews' understanding of

the fate they faced is that after the first few months of deportations, no Jews volunteered for "work" in Auschwitz, Sobibor, or
Treblinka—and no one deported to those places returned.

■   ■   ■

In the United States, for much of the war, Jewish Supreme
Court justice Felix Frankfurter found reports of the mass murders
"impossible to believe." He accepted President Roosevelt's position
that "deported Jews were simply being employed on the Soviet fron-
tier building fortifications." Yet by the end of 1942, the volume and
credibility of information about the death camps was such that on
December 17, eleven Allied governments joined a public declaration that Germany was carrying out Hitler's plan of murdering all
of Europe's Jews.

Even so, in 1943, Jan Karski, a Polish Underground envoy and
eyewitness to the horrors of the Warsaw ghetto and deportations to
the Belzec extermination camp, carried the first eyewitness report
of the atrocities to British foreign secretary Anthony Eden but
was frustrated by the lack of an Allied response. Later that year,
he carried his firsthand information to President Roosevelt, who
also met him with an apparent unwillingness to act. The president
simply responded, "Tell your nation we shall win the war." For
the duration of World War II, the Allies would fail to intervene.

Marion points out, "Jan Karski was a courageous, unsung
hero of the Holocaust, a Polish Catholic who witnessed first-hand
the horrific tragedy befalling the Jews in Poland. Like the canary
in the coal mine, he wanted to warn Allied Leaders of what was

happening before their eyes. Through contacts, he was able to get personal interviews with, among others, Felix Frankfurter, President Roosevelt, and, I believe, Churchill. They all chose not to listen or take action. Karski went undercover for many years, feeling he had failed to avert the attempted extinction of the Jewish race."

Even while imprisoned in Westerbork, Karl and Ilse pursued every rumor about camps in "the East" and explored every avenue for release. One possibility, especially, seemed in keeping with Nazi greed, and therefore encouraging.

In 1943, the Germans again dangled another "exemption," this one known as a "Puttkammer Stamp," before the desperate Jews. It worked something like dangling a pardon in front of a death row inmate—a way of pressuring Jews to bargain for an escape from the German murder machine. In order to extort Jews' last remaining hidden resources, the cruel deception amounted to the threat: "Your money or your life—and the lives of your family."

In 1941, Erich August Puttkammer, a banking lawyer for the Eichmann-supervised Rotterdam Banking Association, had set up an office in Amsterdam where he offered his desperate Jewish "customers" the possibility of a *Sperre*, a pass, exempting them from deportation to "the East." The minimum payment for this presumed life-saving document was ƒ30,000 (guilders) per person, roughly equal to $18,000 in 1943 (some $300,000 in 2022). Since the Germans had already stolen most of his customers' cash, he also accepted gold, jewelry, diamonds, paintings—any tangible assets the Germans deemed valuable. Over four years, the scheme would extort some ƒ10 million from the Jews.

Ilse explained how the Hesses bought their "exemption":

> After our arrest we found out that Jews destined for
> deportation to Auschwitz could obtain an exemp-
> tion if they had a so-called "Puttkammer-Stempel"
> [Puttkammer-Stamp] on their papers. In order to save
> us from a transport to Auschwitz, we asked our Dutch
> friends to hand over my brooch to Mr. Puttkammer
> in return for which he marked our papers with the
> previously mentioned stamp. The entire transaction
> was done through—with the knowledge and approval
> of the occupation forces . . . who thus came into pos-
> session of the jewelry and diamonds of imprisoned
> Jews. . . .
>
> On August 3, 1943, I had the brooch released to Mr.
> Puttkammer and received a receipt from him in which
> he described the brooch as having three large and about
> thirty small diamonds, in insured value of about 60,000
> guilders [twice the minimum value demanded for the
> "Stempel"] and confirming the "provisional exemption
> from work deportation."

According to Steven, "My parents managed to get my mother's luxurious pin to Puttkammer and received a "Puttkammer
Stempel" (rubber stamp) exempting us from arrest. But it was a
huge ruse. It delayed the deportation for some weeks (the Nazis
had to honor them for a certain time enough time to fool enough
Jews, so they presumably delayed picking Puttkammer list Jews
for deportation)."

Talking with friends and Council members, working with all their energy to save their family, Karl and Ilse also purchased counterfeit Paraguayan passports. By 1943, Jews had begun obtaining the phony South American passports in the hope that they would be designated what Ribbentrop had called *Austausch Juden*, "exchange Jews." That devil's bargain meant that some imprisoned Jews might be deported to Bergen-Belsen instead of to Auschwitz. From there, a hostage might be traded, like a sack of grain, for German POWs held in increasing numbers in other countries, or for war matériel, especially trucks.

The Hesses' fake passports were the product of a six-member group of Polish diplomats and Jewish activists, known later as the Kados Group, working in Switzerland to get forged documents to trapped Jews. The Paraguayan passports, unlike other counterfeit Latin American passports, held a special value in 1944: neutral Paraguay, pressured by Poland and the Holy See, temporarily recognized their validity. Recipients paid handsomely for the precious documents, produced at some personal risk to the group in Switzerland. International politics and dark money flowing around the world, with the collusion of both the Germans and the Allies, presented the Hesses with a potentially life-saving opportunity, and they leapt at it.

Marion explains, "This was not a profit-making, exploitative activity, but various agents and go-betweens had to be paid. The three main drivers of this scheme were in fact well-known, reputable Jewish leaders who used part of the payment to help Jews in the ghettos with similar passports. Clearly, they charged a high price because the supply of these passports was limited, and the consulate in Bern, Switzerland, was always under siege and in danger of being shut down. Konstanty Rokicki, the one in the consulate who actually forged all the passports, died a pauper."

Few options remained for the Hess family to fight deportation to Auschwitz or Sobibor, camps dreaded by all Jews, so they staked their dwindling resources, and their lives, on desperate schemes and German promises.

■   ■   ■

While the murderous war on Jews proceeded unchecked, by December 1943 many world leaders were predicting a German military collapse. British code breakers were able to intercept virtually every message the Germans sent. In November of that year, the Tehran Conference saw the first face-to-face meeting of Allied leaders Roosevelt, Stalin, and Churchill. They were beginning to envision a post-war world. Stalin prodded the Western leaders for a cross-Channel invasion. Roosevelt committed to May 1944. In this pivotal meeting, Stalin grasped that the United States and Britain had left primary responsibility for attacking Germany from the east to the Soviet Union. To Stalin that meant that the Soviets would control the lands that they conquered; they had every incentive to push west as far and as fast as possible, claiming territory as they went.

The contrast between Germany's unimpeded war on Jews and its military reversals could not have been starker. In September, Italy surrendered to the Allies, and the next month the Italians declared war on their former ally. The Wehrmacht was losing ground to the Soviets almost daily. Sabotage, assassinations, and daring guerrilla operations erupted in conquered regions, undermining the

Germans' grip on Central and Southeastern Europe. French resistance, once negligible, gained momentum and posed a credible threat. In Denmark, dock workers spied on troops in the harbors and passed information to the Danish Resistance and the British. Forced laborers on the massive defensive Atlantic Wall smuggled valuable information about its vulnerabilities to the British. In Norway, the Wehrmacht erected street barricades in anticipation of an uprising. Over six months in 1943, growing partisan activity in Greece provoked Germany to ravage more than a thousand Greek villages.

In the Netherlands, too, Germany's once vice-like grip was showing signs of strain. Harsh conditions throughout the country, deportation of young Dutchmen for work in German industry, and exorbitant "taxes" paid to the German occupiers created widespread anger. In May 1943, suspecting disloyalty among members of the former Dutch army, the Wehrmacht ordered all Dutch soldiers to be interned. Infuriated citizens—who had not risen in protest over deportation of the Jews—went on strike and began a campaign of passive resistance, jamming phone lines, obstructing roads, and hiding Dutch soldiers. A spiral of resistance and mass reprisals forced hundreds of thousands of Dutch to "submerge," to go into hiding. But for the Hesses—and nearly ninety thousand other Jews deported from the Netherlands—that resistance had come too late.

Queen Wilhelmina, in her annual Christmas broadcast to the Dutch people from Britain that year, was not as optimistic as Allied leaders at the Teheran Conference: "This is still a dark Christmas.... There are many signs of approaching victory, [but] there will be one last struggle. Then the brave, untiring fighters for liberty and justice will have beaten the enemy of all that is sacred to us."

The Allies threatened to hold the Germans responsible for war crimes after the war, but no Allied bomber changed course by as little as five miles to destroy the railroad tracks to the camps. That lack of response to the mass murders sent a clear signal to Hitler that the Allies would not intervene, exactly as Chamberlain's gullibility about the Sudetenland had signaled some five years before.

■   ■   ■

Even in countries under Germany's control, resistance to the murder of Jews had been possible. In Belgium, the secretaries general refused to pass anti-Jewish measures, and Belgian citizens, particularly Catholic priests and nuns, hid large numbers of Jews. Denmark's King Christian X openly objected to German deportation plans, and over two months in the fall of 1943, Danish Resistance ferried seventy-two hundred Jews across a marshy strait to neutral Sweden.

By the end of the year, twenty-one ghettos in Poland had risen in revolt; many who escaped joined local partisan groups. That year, 1943, also saw three death-camp uprisings—in Auschwitz, Treblinka, and Sobibor—and another, in Auschwitz, would erupt in the following year. The most successful of these occurred in Sobibor, the second most frequent destination from Westerbork. Some 260,000 Jews had already been murdered there by November 1943, when an armed prisoner revolt killed several SS supervisors and Ukrainian guards, allowing about 300 prisoners to flee. Guards killed many of the escapees and remaining prisoners, then dismantled the camp. Like the Warsaw ghetto uprisings, the Sobibor Jews' Pyrrhic victory was costly.

More than 34,000 Jews had been deported from Westerbork to Sobibor before that death camp closed. The Hesses probably would not have heard about these instances of resistance and rebellion. For Jews that did know, the rebellions may have offered a sense of pride, but scant hope. Mass extermination, in Auschwitz-Birkenau and other camps, starvation, and harsh forced labor continued relentlessly.

■　　■　　■

In Westerbork, after watching the deportation of children and hospitalized Jews, the Hesses understood that families were being deported so that only adults useful for labor would remain. They needed to get away from Westerbork as soon as possible, but believed that deportation to Theresienstadt, previously seen as a refuge, now meant being one short stop from Auschwitz. Even in the transit camp, the Jewish Council continued to negotiate with the Germans and maintained some very limited influence over individual Jews' fate. In February, the Hesses' unremitting efforts to negotiate with the Council seemed to align with a measure of luck that offered an alternative to Auschwitz for the Hess family.

As Karl explained in his memoir, "There was then only one way for us to get into a transport that was not going to the east, as fast as possible. We, ourselves, tried everything to get to Bergen-Belsen with the transport that was to leave on February 15, 1944....On the night of February 14/15, our names were called. We were to go on the transport to Bergen-Belsen on February 15, 1944."

Marion points out, "It seems that well-off Jews spent a lot of effort 'feeding the beast' in order to gain a chance to stay alive or not face the worst circumstances. I wonder if, at the end, any of that made a real difference. In our case, it seems the foreign passports were the key to us not being exterminated in a death camp."

Steven's thoughts are along the same lines:

> Puttkammer was trusted by the Nazis, who hoped this system would lead them to hidden Jewish assets not surrendered to the bank. The promise of protection proved to be a scam. Nearly everyone with a Puttkammer Sperre was later deported. Our parents had three potential "get out of jail" cards:
>
> 1. Our father's employment with the Jewish Council;
> 2. Our mother's purchase of the ultimately worthless Puttkammer Sperre stamp, a scam; and
> 3. Their purchase out of Switzerland of a phony passport declaring us Paraguayan citizens.
>
> The Nazis were not impressed by any of these ploys, but they probably bought us time and got us onto one of the occasional Belsen transports. That turned out to be our ONLY slim chance of survival. The vast majority of those holding any of these documents were murdered with the rest.

Ilse remembered how Karl decided to try to have their names included on the list of those to be sent to Bergen-Belsen:

> My husband knew one of these camp Elders, and he asked him whether he could do anything for us. He

said, "I cannot do anything. You will have to leave. The only thing I might be able to do instead [of your going] on the train to Theresienstadt . . . or Auschwitz, it might be possible for me to get you on the train to Bergen-Belsen." Now at that time, very little was known of Bergen-Belsen. . . . Bergen-Belsen was near Hanover in Germany. My husband thought for a little while. Since we knew that Theresienstadt was one of the camps offered as reward to a lot of Jews, but all of a sudden he also realized that it would be far away from any place we knew, and since we knew Germany very well, he just out—without even thinking, maybe only realizing—without even realizing what he was saying, he said, "[We] want to go to Bergen-Belsen." . . . had he chosen Theresienstadt . . . [we] would not be sitting here to tell the tale. . . .

Between July 15, 1942, and September 13, 1944, the Germans deported approximately one hundred thousand Jews from Westerbork to deadly concentration camps, mostly to Sobibor, before it shut down, and to Auschwitz. For four years, Karl and Ilse had done everything they could to escape, to hide, and to avoid deportation and protect their family, but in early 1944, they remained one stroke of a pen, or click of a typewriter, away from Auschwitz.

That winter, their efforts won them a reprieve from the gas chamber. Late in the day on February 15, 1944, the Germans loaded the Hess family onto a train heading for Bergen-Belsen, the twins wearing thick layers of clothing and their new heavy boots to keep them warm through the dark, cold, winter night that lay ahead.

CHAPTER 10

Bergen-Belsen
FEBRUARY 15, 1944–AUGUST 1944

ocked from the outside, the train bearing the Hess family to Bergen-Belsen passed through rolling hills and landscapes that once had been familiar to them. Now, the bomb-damaged towns seemed unreal, ghostly, with heaps of frost-encrusted rubble everywhere and only slivers of light showing around blackout shades in the buildings left standing. The twins were probably dozing as Karl and Ilse stared out the window, aghast, to see Hanover, the formerly thriving regional capital, in ruins.

The train had departed Westerbork mid-afternoon. Of the ninety-three transports that left the transit camp over nearly three years, only nine went to Bergen-Belsen. The Hesses didn't know whether to consider themselves lucky or simply trapped in another level of hell. They had purchased fake passports and lost a fortune in jewelry buying bogus exemptions. They had watched murder in the streets, lost friends and family, and struggled for four years to survive. They understood that this transport was a gamble, a roll of the dice. After nearly eleven hours of travel, at 2:30 in the morning, each passenger received a quarter of a loaf of bread.

On a normal journey, in normal times, the 175-mile trip might have taken a few hours. But military trains, many of them heading to the Eastern Front, took priority; some tracks may have been bombed, compelling the train to detour. The hours wore on, frightening, and feeling endless to the exhausted family as they traveled toward an ominous future as prisoners in a German camp.

Before dawn the train slowed as it entered a deep pine forest, then ground to a halt on a sidetrack near the town of Celle in Northern Germany. Rifle-bearing SS guards surrounded the train. Dragged from their seats onto the loading platform, the eight hundred Jewish prisoners emerged, blinded by flashing lights. Many screamed in fear and pain as snarling dogs attacked stragglers and guards shouted orders, brandished truncheons, and beat the Jews, pushing the dazed prisoners the three miles to the camp. Old and young, strong and feeble, mothers carrying children—everyone walked in the dark, cold night. Their reception at this "privileged" camp did nothing to allay their growing terror.

Karl had been designated transport leader, probably by Westerbork camp's Jewish commander, Kurt Schlesinger, or by Abraham Asscher, a member of the camp's Elders' Council, though all decisions may have been made or overruled by the SS. As leader, he stayed behind with thirty volunteers handling the luggage. When he did approach Bergen-Belsen, he saw it as a "maze of barbed wire." Electric fences surrounded the entire camp, dividing it into various subcamps that changed along with Germany's evolving needs. Spotlights on the perimeter fence and throughout the camp lit the entire area and the road that ran through the center of the camp. SS guards with machine guns watched the camp night and day from nineteen guard towers, 250 yards apart. Pine forests rose on low hills nearby, but the camp was built on flat terrain. The forest that once thrived there had been clearcut; no shrub, no blade of grass relieved the bleakness of the camp's cold, hard ground.

Although the German foreign affairs office had initiated the concept of a "detention camp" for exchange prisoners, its implementation had been transferred to the concentration camp system under Heinrich Himmler. That decision meant the SS administered Bergen-Belsen—a reality that impacted every aspect of the camp's operation. To establish the concentration camp, the year before the Hesses arrived the SS had taken over half of a prisoner-of-war (POW) camp on the site, a mile from the largest military training ground in the Reich. More than eighteen thousand Soviet prisoners of war had died of starvation and typhus in the camp in the winter of 1941–42. In 1943, it was in such filthy, dilapidated condition that squads of prisoners from three concentration camps had been sent to rebuild it, and then to build the new *Sternlager*, the "Star camp," the largest of several subcamps inside Bergen-Belsen's barbed wire.

The Sternlager was the Hesses' destination. Something of an experiment, it was an orphan in the German concentration camp system—under orders, Sternlager prisoners were not to be harmed in any way that could impair their usefulness as hostages. The prisoners toiled at assigned work but were to remain in reasonable health. Furthermore, this camp held families. Men and women occupied separate barracks, but they could visit each evening. Children slept with their mothers but roamed the camp during the

In the mornings during quarantine, guards ordered the prisoners outside in the cold; a few stayed behind and cleaned the cluttered barracks with branches. The prisoners found no inside toilets in the Sternlager. There were only three or four latrines for the entire camp, at a distance from their barracks. Latrines consisted of long, narrow pits with a rough, dirty board cut with thirty or forty holes for so-called seats running the length of the pits. Even before the camp swelled in numbers, the latrines reeked and were dreadfully inadequate and unhealthy. Having already spent months in the unsanitary Westerbork transit camp, many prisoners suffered from dysentery. Bathing, too, was difficult. Inmates were rarely allowed to use the group shower, staffed by male guards. Two long concrete sinks, with faucets facing both sides, served the entire camp. Sometimes water streamed from the faucets; other times they were dry. Lice crawled in every crevice, everywhere in the camp. These lice had twisted crosses on their shells; some prisoners called them *Boche* lice—a derisive slang term for Germans derived from the French word for "head" or "cabbage."

During the Hesses' fifth week in camp, in mid-March, guards herded the prisoners to the eighteen barracks housing exchange prisoners. Like a version of the Tower of Babel, the barracks held Jews from Germany, the Netherlands, Yugoslavia, Albania, North Africa, France, and Salonika in Greece. Bunks rose three beds high. With no fuel, the stove at one end of the barrack stood cold and useless, another reminder to the Jews of their despised and vulnerable situation in that "privileged" camp. Ilse described her first impressions: "To start off, to give a description of Bergen-Belsen, it was a nightmare. We had to sleep in the barracks two together on a single wooden cot, but not the American cot size. There was hardly any food. Each day, we got one centimeter of bread and one bowl of turnip soup, and in the morning, we got some warm, brownish water. . . . I remember that I never drank it. I used it to wash my children with." That was the Bergen-Belsen version of "coffee."

As Marion explained to me, "All prisoners wore their cup on a piece of string attached to their clothing or around their necks. If you lost your cup, you didn't eat."

The prisoners' new routine required everyone, including children and the sick, to wake at quarter to five and appear in one hour on the dirt field adjoining the barracks for *Appell*, roll call. Men and women lined up separately. Only older women charged with watching the children or prisoners with a proven temperature over 103 degrees could stay in the barracks. On the Appell grounds the Jews assembled in rows, standing military-straight as an SS guard shouted names. If numbers did not tally, roll call was repeated. The intentionally cruel ordeal sometimes dragged on for three or four hours, regardless of weather, as the weakest prisoners dropped to the ground and all of them suffered. Guards carrying whips walked past the assembled Jews and lashed anyone out of line, talking, or not standing rigidly.

Marion and Stefan, then six years old, sat at Ilse's feet or wandered nearby, silent and fearful. Karl and Ilse warned them to remain as unobtrusive as possible, blend into the background, and never attract attention. They told the children never to talk about the camp; if eavesdroppers or guards overheard them, it could trigger a brutal reprisal.

The same cruel system of using Jewish "Elders" to make decisions and work assignments for prisoners—under control of the

SS—that had been imposed first through Amsterdam's Jewish Council and again in Westerbork's Jewish Administration put prisoners in the role of managing slave-like work assignments and the fate of their fellow Jews. A prisoner's chance of survival was heavily influenced by the complex system of privileges and special functions and jobs in camps—pitting prisoner against prisoner, Jew against Jew, as they vied for positions that could mean the difference between life and death, relieving the SS from that contentious role.

As they were throughout Germany and German-occupied lands, Sternlager Jews were forced into the painful position of cooperating with their captors and managing the conditions of their own imprisonment. The Jewish Council in Amsterdam no longer existed, but the SS had immediately formed a *Jüdischer Ältestenrat* (Elder Council) in the Sternlager with orders that the Council deal with work assignments, disputes among prisoners, requests for medicines and other supplies—all the issues of daily life. Communication between prisoners and their jailors began with the Council. The Germans had no wish to entangle themselves in the details of enforcing the concentration camp regime in the Jews' lives.

Josef Weiss, *Judenältester* (leader of the Sternlager's Jewish Elder Council), had, like the Hesses, fled Germany for the Netherlands, and then spent twenty months at Westerbork. The tasks of the Council were hateful—assigning fellow prisoners harsh tasks and communicating bad news—but Weiss was well respected by the Jews as well as by the SS. In fact, he was considered by many Jews a *mensch*, a wise and good-hearted leader. He served as the pivot point, enforcing SS demands while doing his best to make camp life bearable.

Work assignments announced during Appell, which could change from day to day, were demanding and unpleasant, but initially not intended as killing labor. The assignments varied from kitchen duty to sorting buttons for soldiers' underwear and chopping wood in the nearby forest. One group sorted silk cocoons, probably preparing them for the United Silk Corporation, Karl's former employer, to use for parachute cloth. With intentional cruelty, the weakest prisoners, often rabbis and those wearing eyeglasses, were given rigorous work in the woods, with the Council powerless to change SS orders. Ilse remembered, "Most men had to dig ditches. No one knew for what until much later that the ditches were supposed to be for the German SS, to go into hiding as soon as they heard an airplane."

Karl's first assignment was in the shoe building, outside the Sternlager's barbed-wire gates:

I, myself, worked with the "shoe commando" [a group work assignment]. This unit of about five hundred and fifty men left the camp at six o'clock and marched to different work barracks located outside the camp. There was a circus tent filled with, believe it or not, eight hundred thousand old shoes which had been collected by the Hitler Youth from all over Germany, and which we Jews now had to take apart so they could be used over for different purposes. About one hundred of us sat in an ice-cold horse stable. Each received a shoe knife with which he had to rip apart the shoes just above the sole. It was disgusting work. Aside from the fact that the shoes were stinking and partly decomposed, the physical effort was great. The shoes were wet and the knives were dull. The dust settled in the lungs and our physical strength diminished visibly. The minimum output per day was one hundred pairs. If you did not achieve that, you were either beaten or you had to stand at the camp fence during noon recess instead of eating. For repeaters, there was the bunker as punishment, i.e. that you were locked up in a subterranean cellar for a few days and nights without warm food.

Ten minutes before noon, when the section leader blew his whistle outside the shoe building, the 550 men in Karl's work group ran out to assemble. When the order was called—"*Vordermann und Seitenrichtung*," the Wehrmacht command to line up in formation—the Dutch in the group yelled, "*Voddeman en Zijkinrichting.*" That sounded to the Germans like a repeat of their command; in fact, in Dutch, it meant, "Ragpickers and pissoir [a public urinal]." At exactly noon, the commander shouted, "Dismissed!" giving the prisoners exactly thirty-five minutes to eat lunch before they lined up again on the Appell ground.

With some irony, Karl recounted, "The ground shook from all these starving people running away and rushing into their barracks, each hoping to be the first to catch a pail of cabbage soup. The last one hardly had five minutes' time to just lap down the food without a spoon and immediately to run back to the parade ground. Of course, we never had time to wash our hands before eating. They were pitch black and stinking, covered with welts."

Ilse's first work assignment allowed her to remain close to the twins. Work inside the barracks was typically reserved for women older than fifty-five, or mothers with four children or more, but she pleaded with the camp's Jewish Elders and also with the SS to accommodate her. She succeeded in acquiring an assignment that kept her scrubbing the barracks and scouring wooden stools outside, whatever the weather—and, when possible, watching over young children running around the barracks.

But staying close to Marion and Stefan came with a cost for Ilse. As Karl explained, "Because she was strong, as well as one of the youngest [thirty years old at the time] of the women working in the camp, she had to fetch, together with a few men, the pails of food, carrying twenty-five and fifty liters, from the kitchen gate, about two hundred yards further than the barracks. We were, however, obsessed with the single idea that Ilse had to remain in camp at any price so she could look after the children now and then. They had nothing else to do but play in the dirt that lay several feet high."

That work assignment would not last. Appell meant hours of fear and terror as the SS ferreted out the younger prisoners for the hardest work. Ilse "disguised herself as an old woman," hid behind taller women, or kept Stefan and Marion clinging to her legs. But one day, those ploys failed, and the commander yelled at her, "shoe commando."

And so, like Karl, Ilse found herself cutting up old shoes to reclaim the leather. "Lots of men and women, among them myself, we had to work in tremendous shoe camps," according to Ilse. "They were far outside the [main] camp. . . . We were marched there always in rows of five. In these shoe camps, they had collected millions and millions of pairs of shoes from all over Germany and all over the concentration camps. These shoes were taken away from Jews who had died or were gassed in Auschwitz, and they were all sent to Bergen-Belsen to be recut, resliced, and resorted for the use of the German army."

With razor-sharp knives, they cut usable leather from the worn shoes and threw those strips into old helmets set out to hold them; they never knew the purpose of those leather strips, but day after day they cut up old shoes. Ilse later reported that, as with all camp work, the shoe workers had a "system" for thwarting their supposed contribution to the German war effort. "Most of the usable parts never reached the helmets. We sliced it all up as soon as we were not watched." The work was sedentary and dull but demanded some strength and care. One day, Karl's knife slipped and cut his wrist—by luck not a major injury.

Jews in the shoe camp were permitted to talk to each other under the watchful eyes and ears of the SS, who constantly barked commands and insults at the prisoners. Cautious conversations included philosophy and psalms recited by heart, but mostly they revolved around hunger and the paltry food the prisoners received. "How many potatoes did you get in the broth?"

Somewhat inexplicably, the Germans assigned Jews as bookkeepers for the shoe work, to keep an account of the number of shoes collected and cut apart. When possible, the bookkeepers recorded inflated figures for shoes fetched from the huge pile and for work finished, after which unfinished shoes were returned to the original pile. The Germans did not seem to notice that, though the books showed work done, the piles got no smaller—perhaps not grasping that prisoners under their constant watch could still find ways to defy them.

As spring arrived and the days grew longer, some squads worked every day, seventy-two hours per week. Punishment meted out for poor work was immediate and severe. When one woman nodded off for a minute, the SS commanded the entire group to stand at the fence without lunch, then return for more hours of work. Not infrequently dozens, sometimes hundreds, of the camp's Jews were forced to remain standing at the fence during lunch or at night after work for offenses as minor as marching to their work in uneven lines.

■   ■   ■

During the day only children, the sick, and the very old remained in the camp, while everyone else worked in forced labor. In the beginning at the Sternlager, the twins experienced a disjointed jumble of emotions, misery, and fear juxtaposed with fun and laughter. At one point in the first few weeks, Ilse asked an older woman to watch over the twins while she herself did her cleaning work. When Ilse finished in the evening, the woman reported that Marion and Stefan were "uninteresting children" who only enjoyed playing with lice. Insulted, Ilse suggested that the woman offer them "something better to play with." That caregiving arrangement soon ended, and the twins roamed more freely. Together almost constantly, and without their parents near, Marion and Stefan became even closer. They developed their own secret language, "Hoolefloo"—and played with the lice.

As Marion remembers, "We played with the lice because they were all over and they made a very interesting crackling sound when you killed them."

"So we would have this game," says Steven, "popping them and lining them up, in a straight, often long line."

It was a game that could have proven deadly. As Karl explained in his memoir, "Slowly the whole camp was in a condition of dissolution and decay. Typhus decided on life and death. One single infected louse was enough to transport you to the next world. And everyone had lice. The children played with lice."

Besides playing with disease-bearing lice, the twins made friends with children of Karl and Ilse's friends from Berlin, Amsterdam, and Westerbork who also were Sternlager prisoners. Stefan sometimes played with a boy about his age named Tommy. Another camp child, also named Marion, became almost inseparable from the twins; the three met frequently after Appell. They showed each other which barracks they slept in and cheered each other up in the evenings as they waited near the fence for their parents to return. Several times, as they explored the camp, they watched groups of people on the other side of the barbed wire. The children tried to speak with them, ignoring the fence and the language barrier; Stefan informed the girls that these people were from a country called Hungary, which was far away.

Playing their games, exploring the camp, the children had discovered that other groups of prisoners from distant lands were living in Bergen-Belsen. Some prisoners in the *Ungarnlager*, the "Hungarian camp," with its barracks near the Sternlager, were bright and cheerful, pleased to try to chat with the children. Their camp had opened in early July, six months after the Hesses reached Bergen-Belsen, and it required no Appell or assigned work. The Hungarians believed that ransom negotiations with the Germans for their release were underway and would soon free them all.

The children would not have known much about the drastically different subcamps that coexisted behind Bergen-Belsen's fences, or the fact that large numbers of prisoners had already come and gone. By mid-1944, when the Hesses had been in the Sternlager for some four months, Bergen-Belsen's population had more than tripled, from two thousand to seven thousand. The *Häftlingslager*, "Prisoners' camp," a harsh labor camp at the other end of the camp road from the Sternlager, held up to one thousand Poles and Russians, whose heads were shaved and who wore striped, pajama-like clothing. That camp saw some fifty Russians tunnel to freedom about the time the Hesses arrived; deadly overwork and deportation to death camps were Häftlingslager prisoners' more common fate.

Jews from neutral nations Spain, Portugal, and Argentina filled two barracks in the *Neutralenlager*, "Neutrals camp," and received better treatment than Sternlager inmates. The Belsen children could not have spoken with anyone in the "Special camp," the *Sonderlager*, where Polish Jews holding non-Polish passports or papers for Palestine were kept strictly isolated from other inmates so that they could not spread information about mass murder in "the East" and cause panic. But as the children raced around the camp, they had probably become accustomed to the banging of hammers constructing new barracks, to the impossible crowding, and to the groups of prisoners marching under guard in work groups or struggling to walk from the Celle train station.

A number of Sternlager inmates, too, had come and gone. Some 340 diamond merchants and cutters from Amsterdam and Antwerp and their families had been imprisoned in the Sternlager along with their diamond-cutting tools. Hoping to force those prisoners, many of them Jewish, to divulge where they had hidden a large store of diamonds, the Germans negotiated with them for months. The workers kept their silence until spring 1944, when most were sent to Auschwitz, leaving some fifty orphans in Bergen-Belsen. Jewish Council head Abraham Asscher, who represented one of the most important Dutch diamond enterprises, was one of the few in the industry permitted to remain in the Sternlager.

■   ■   ■

The two Marions each had a doll they carried everywhere. Stefan had a little wind-up car that he loved. The children played *krijgertje* (tag), calling to each other as they raced through camp, and they invented more games. One of those would have horrified their parents, had they known, but the children played it over and over during their first months in camp. Although (or because) their parents had warned them to stay away from the guard towers, they found the towers intriguing, not frightening. Taking turns, one would walk slowly toward the fence to see who could come the nearest before the guard shouted, "*Stehen bleiben oder ich schieße!*"—"Stop, or I'll shoot!" Then they ran away laughing.

Their childish hunt for something, anything to do, brought them close to danger in another of their games. As the camp commandant issued orders, moving barracks and creating subcamps, the twins sometimes followed behind the construction crews and found interest where there had been none. "When they were glazing windows," Steven remembers, "we would run our fingers around and take some of the glazing compound to play with like clay. Once, a guard chased us around. We ran like hell. Basically, being there meant just being alone and waiting for nothing to happen."

The children's carefree fun would not last long in the German camp, but while it did, the view of innocents frolicking on the margins of murder may have frightened Jews who saw them, adding to prisoners' heavy burdens of grief and worry. As Steven says, "How to stay out of trouble…Play? Work? Trouble was everywhere."

■   ■   ■

Trouble found the Hess family on April 8, 1944, when air-raid sirens blared through the camp. Those warnings were not uncommon, but this one was real. Karl was toiling in the shoe camp, and Ilse working at a short-term assignment cleaning the stockroom for SS uniforms, when an Allied plane strafed the barracks. A coworker told Ilse that people in the Hesses' barrack had been killed. No amount of imploring persuaded the SS to allow her to check on her children. As Steven recalls, "One day the camp was strafed by aircraft and Marion remembers she took my hand and ran so we could hide under a concrete sink. I don't think I ever thanked her for possibly saving my life. Some Allied fighter plane must have thought it was a troop camp. Bullets came flying through the barracks, and all we knew was that we were in a bad place."

Ilse remembers that she was "frantic to get back to the barrack and see what had happened to my children. So when I went, when I came back to the barrack, an old woman approached me and told me that my children are very disobedient because she told me they, when they heard the alarm, they should have stayed with them in the barrack. But my children ran out and went into hiding under both the concrete sinks. And that was their salvation, because when I came to our sleeping cot, [I saw] a sniper had hit our pillow."

At least twenty-three inmates died in that attack, and many others were wounded, some of them by ruthless SS guards who shot prisoners running in panic. Marion recalls an Allied air attack that felt at first like there was a sniper in the barracks. "Everyone was screaming and screaming. I heard all the bullets and saw the bullets and basically tried to find a place that was safe. I remember dragging my brother." The night nurse who slept three beds away from Ilse was killed. Shrapnel that shattered the roof sent deadly splinters flying through the barracks, and littered Ilse's bed.

There had not been a "sniper" in the barracks, but the strafing had been just as deadly. Oswald Pohl, head of the German concentration camp system, later reported to Himmler, "This is the first real attack on one of our camps. I assume that the Americans thought this camp was part of the barracks of the Wehrmacht training area in the immediate vicinity."

The reason for the attack was immaterial to the trapped Jews. They understood that if this had happened once, another air raid or some other sort of danger could strike them at any time. Ilse vowed to risk anything to avoid leaving the camp. Karl said, "She carried on her private war against the SS, and she really succeeded in never leaving the camp again up to the last day in Bergen-Belsen. During roll calls for work, Ilse used to hide in the latrines. Whenever she was gotten out for count out, she simply did not go to work. We accepted the possibility of being punished with bunker arrest or deprived of bread. This would have been nothing as compared to leaving the children without supervision, even for one hour."

■   ■   ■

In the summer of 1944, the situation for Jews under German control remained disastrous. Uncounted millions had been murdered, and hundreds of thousands were imprisoned across Europe. In cities that had been declared Judenfrei, including Amsterdam, Germans still discovered and arrested hidden Jews.

Militarily, Germany continued to lose ground and fought desperately to keep its remaining conquests. A Wehrmacht assignment to the Eastern Front now seemed a death sentence. Eight of ten German military deaths in World War II—more than five million soldiers—in addition to nearly two million civilian deaths, would occur in those battles. By mid-1944, the Red Army had taken Ukraine, Crimea, and parts of Finland and fought through Byelorussia (Belarus) and Lithuania. Slovakians had risen in revolt. The Polish Underground fought the Germans in Lwów (now L'viv). Germans and collaborating Soviets in Poland retaliated for a Warsaw uprising and slaughtered forty to fifty thousand civilians. Hitler rejected his Wehrmacht field marshal's proposal to withdraw from Estonia and northern Latvia and ordered them to fight on; the Soviets later captured both. That summer, Allied forces pushed farther up Italy's boot and took Florence. Soviet troops liberated the Majdanek concentration camp in eastern Poland, the first of many camps the Red Army would free.

On the Western Front, Allies dropped five thousand tons of bombs on German coastal gun batteries in advance of the June 6, 1944, D-Day invasion. Had the Germans known where the largest amphibious landing in history would occur, they could have better defended against it with their massive contingent of troops deployed further north near Calais. With a ten-to-one manpower ratio in their favor on that site, the Germans would have decimated the Allies, throwing them back into the sea. But the Allies fought past Atlantic Wall defenses in Normandy and flowed into the French interior. At the end of August, Allied troops marched into Paris, ending its four years of occupation.

Yet in June, the first of Germany's V-1 "flying bomb" rockets began smashing into London and southern England. At first they caused little damage, but by the end of the month the rate of bomb attacks increased dramatically, terrorizing citizens, causing extensive loss of life, and disrupting production. Restaurants advertised how quickly patrons could access nearby shelter. Nearly a million and a half people left London in the first months of the summer.

In the first aerial battle involving a jet-powered fighter, the German Messerschmitt Me 262, the Luftwaffe emerged victorious against a British fighter. In mid-July, for a time, Axis battalions held off a Soviet attack in Estonia. In one engagement, some 22,000 Germans repulsed 137,000 Soviet troops. On both sides, combat losses ran to the tens of thousands. In Berlin, a bomb plot to assassinate Hitler failed. He claimed his escape was a "mandate of providence." In Hitler's savage response, the plotters were hanged, their bodies suspended on meat hooks, their families killed, and nearly 4,000 alleged accomplices executed.

■   ■   ■

The Jews in Bergen-Belsen were not as insulated from outside news as the Germans might have imagined. As prisoners were transferred, so was information. Reports of German withdrawals spread like wildfire. Prisoners who worked outside the camp heard news. Ilse, in a short-term job cleaning an SS storeroom, discovered a way to learn news she could relay through what the prisoners ironically termed the JPA, "Jewish Press Agency." Working with three other women, she seized the opportunity:

> Since I was the only one who could read and speak Dutch, I saw a German newspaper and I told these women in Dutch, if they would watch out that no one would see me, I would read the newspaper and would tell them later on what happened.... And the Germans sure would not put down that they were losing the war, but in between the lines you could see that things were not going too well, which was good news to us.
>
> Looking backwards, I do not know how we really reacted to it. I only know I was a little bit afraid to share the news with these women because it would be very easy to [find] out who had worked outside the camp. But I shared it with my husband. And told him that [I thought] sooner or later we either would be killed, liberated, or just die before we would see the end of the tunnel.

Ilse had recited all options she could conceive of. But Himmler himself was beginning to consider other possibilities for the Sternlager's Jews.

CHAPTER 11

Losing Ground
AUGUST 1944–DECEMBER 1944

Genocide: "A coordinated plan of different actions aiming at the destruction of essential foundations of the life of national groups, with the aim of annihilating the groups themselves." In 1942, at Wannsee, when the Germans mounted their organized murderous campaign for a Final Solution, none of them had heard the word "genocide." It hadn't been invented. Raphael Lemkin, a Polish-Jewish lawyer who had escaped to the United States, coined that term in his 1944 book *Axis Rule in Occupied Europe*, which documented German policies. The definition above is his. Lemkin's dry, descriptive language veiled the violence and unbridled hatred embedded in the Germans' campaign against Jews, but it contained enough power of truth to quickly find its way into common use.

Karl and Ilse did not need to read Lemkin's book to understand what was happening to their family. Karl had predicted the destruction of Europe's Jews as early as 1933, when he witnessed Nazi fanaticism taking over German streets and minds—and he and Ilse were experiencing the genocide in Bergen-Belsen.

In the camp, through the merciless heat of summer and into fall, morning Appell persisted, relentlessly, intentionally pushing bone-weary prisoners beyond endurance. As Karl would explain, "[R]oll call cost thousands of lives. It took from one to four hours. The worse the weather, the longer it took. At times, the SS took pleasure in holding it twice or three times a day, very often in the evenings, and as an additional treat on Sundays. The children would lie down in the mud because they simply could not stand up any longer."

The number of dead grew larger. One morning an orderly asked Karl how many in his barracks had died in the night. The answer, "twenty-six," displeased the orderly, who told Karl that he, the orderly, would have to be satisfied because this was Sunday and he knew the next day it would "improve." From that response, Karl grasped that the Germans knew, "with mathematical precision how long it would take for a human being to perish from hardest labor and starvation."

Hunger gripped the prisoners even more painfully as rations were cut—and cut again. In late summer, a typical breakfast had shrunk to one small slice of bread, bulked up with sawdust, watery soup made from kohlrabi, a turnip-like vegetable, and the warm, brown water that the kitchen called coffee. Marion remembers, "Kohlrabi and very occasional horse meat was the main diet, which is not to say that from time to time another ingredient was added, but never ever anything good or plentiful. . . ."

Even the six-year-old twins developed their own food survival strategies. According to Steven,

> We learned things about survival, even though we were quite young. We were six, no longer the toddlers of the invasion time. We knew that when they brought out the kohlrabi slop in their *Gemellen* (large garbage cans with handles), it was better to be in front of the line than the back, by which point it might all be gone, awful as it was.
>
> But nothing was simple, especially survival. The Germans had a lot of horses. Really a lot, used as work animals and as recreation for the Nazi SS. And these horses would die from time to time, and were brought to the camp kitchen, butchered, and thrown into the Gemellen. Of course, that meat sank to the bottom. Then, you did not want to be at the front of the line because the horsemeat was at the bottom. But standing at the back of the line was no guarantee either. It could all be gone. So, the best place was near the end of the line but not too far.

The Gemellen were corrugated. Marion, Stefan, and other children learned to tip the cans a bit, lean into them, then crook their fingers and swipe up the grooves, bottom to top, collecting the smallest scraps of food, and lick their fingers.

Bread was the black-market currency among prisoners, traded for a bit of extra space on a bunk, a pair of socks. It was also a tool, as harsh as any whip, that the SS used for controlling and torturing the prisoners. One inmate, Jewish Elder Josef Weiss, used bread to negotiate with the Germans after his "bad job performance." To save his fifty comrades from group punishment, Weiss accepted a penalty of four breadless days. Karl had observed that some of the prisoners arrived at Bergen-Belsen overweight, but all Jews in the camp soon were walking skeletons: "In time, all of us looked the way the SS wanted to have us to look—ashen, filthy, our clothes torn, our backs bent. We shuffled to our places of work, but in rank and file. Already we lacked the strength to walk like normal human beings. Our feet just did not carry us any more."

By late summer, some 7,000 Jews from different countries, and holding different papers, had arrived at Bergen-Belsen, hoping to be part of a prisoner exchange. Some held South American passports, real or fake. About 1,300 had British passports, dual citizenship, or certificates permitting them to enter British Palestine. In April 1944, 222 of the 1,300 Jews holding Palestine certificates were the first prisoners to be exchanged from Bergen-Belsen, raising the hopes of other prisoners. Those dreams were dashed as prisoners continued to become more frail and no more exchanges occurred. By that summer, it was obvious to all that the camp had changed its focus—the Germans would never release them.

Hot summer days that kept the barracks broiling like ovens finally cooled with fall breezes, for a short time giving the Sternlager's inmates a small measure of relief. But nothing was comfortable or brought lasting comfort to the bone-weary, starving Jews. In their bunks, legions of lice bit them, made them itch, and exposed them to disease. Rats crawled over them. As cold weather descended on the camp, some prisoners burned their straw mattresses in the barracks stoves. Then they slept on bare, wood planks. As temperatures dropped, some burned a plank from their bunks and spaced out the remaining planks...then they burned a second plank...and a third. The rough, widely spaced boards became painful to their thin, wasted bodies, and even their time to rest was a torment.

Before the deadly Allied attack on the camp, Ilse's work kept her away from the twins for almost the entire day. She left for work in the dark and hurried back to the barrack for a precious half hour at lunchtime—most of which she spent trying to persuade the children to eat the disgusting food. She had no time to eat before rushing back to work, which often kept her until well after dark.

The accidental Allied attack changed everything for Ilse. She made extraordinary efforts never again to be placed in a labor unit outside the camp gates. Even so, she had little time to monitor the twins' activities. One day during a walk with their friend Marion, they heard two Germans shouting near the Appell yard. They saw SS in the yard kicking and beating a man, bloody and on the ground. The children held each other's hands, hardly daring to breathe as the beating went on until the man died. When the SS finally left, the children heard them say, "*Lass jemand den Dreck aufräumen.*" "Let someone else clean this mess."

In the seven months that the family had been imprisoned in Bergen-Belsen, Karl and Ilse had been relieved that Stefan was free of the painful ear infections that had plagued him in Westerbork and before. But that fall, dropping temperatures and Stefan's weakened condition triggered a recurrence. One day he spiked a high fever, and they saw that the scar from a previous ear surgery had formed a thick crust of pus. They carried him to the *Erholungslager*, the sick bay or recovery barracks.

Bergen-Belsen site maps showed a hospital in the Sternlager, but it did not exist. In reality, the camp had an Erholungslager where sick, injured, or exhausted inmates unable to work might recuperate. The facility included no medical equipment, no medicine, and no assigned doctor. It functioned with rows of cots and the care of Jewish doctors and nurses who happened to be among the prisoner population. The Jewish doctor who examined Stefan advised an immediate operation and requested camp authorities to order the necessary instruments. During the days that he awaited the equipment, the infection opened up, allowing the ear to heal. Stefan's fever dropped, and, as Karl recounted, "our little darling revived in spite of total weakness."

Stefan remembers that experience well, and with some awe: "There was absolutely no medical care. Prisoners were not meant to live. The word, miracle, is too religious for me. It was another bit of the luck that kept us alive."

The frightening experience presented Ilse with an unexpected opportunity. She found the rule restricting her visits to the sick bay to twice a week impossible to bear, so she persuaded the orderly to allow her to come more often to comfort and care for Stefan in exchange for cleaning. She begged the orderly, the SS, and the camp's Elder Council to formally assign her to clean the barracks. According to Karl,

Ilse moved heaven and earth to bring about a change. Finally, with the help of doctors, she managed to be employed as a cleaning woman in the sick bay. This way, she was always admitted to the hospital barrack. When the superior commander caught her in her new job, he fired her, scolded the doctors severely, and gave the order to employ old women exclusively. But one SS orderly, who was quite taken with Ilse's "cleaning," put in a good word for her and she got a pass from the company commander, saying that she was officially appointed in the sick bay. We were much relieved because Ilse did not have to attend roll call any more, since the sick bay personnel were allowed to remain in the barrack. For Stefan, this meant a piece of well being because Ilse was now able to take care of him. Unfortunately, we had nothing we could have given him additionally, since the patients, too, got nothing but kohlrabi soup. We saved some of our bread rations, which we exchanged for a marmalade jar filled with sugar and a few spoonfuls of oatmeal.

As Ilse said, "I hope that these listeners don't believe that the Germans were so good to the [prisoner] doctors. They only were good to some of the doctors because they used them for their own health. Typhoid fever, spotted typhoid, dysentery, and the most horrible sicknesses would rampage within the camp, and the Germans were afraid that they themselves would catch [them]."

Ilse's efforts to help Stefan probably included charming the orderly in the same way she had "fished" the cop who oversaw her packing to leave Germany. Her new permanent work assignment cleaning the Erholungslager relieved her worst fear, that she could not help her children when they met trouble or were frightened. Ilse's "private war against the SS," as Karl described her efforts to stay in the camp by hiding and not appearing for an assigned job, had been inherently dangerous. Her new cleaning job meant no more Appell and guaranteed work inside the camp gates. The twins could find her whenever they needed her.

That hard-won victory came at a cost, though. "Ilse's work in the sick bay was probably the filthiest and most disgusting that anybody can imagine," Karl explained.

> She had to clean the toilets; I prefer not to describe what they looked like. The wards were in a sickening condition. In the so-called "laboratory," there were the uncovered corpses on the one bench and the bread for distribution on the other.... Stefan and Marion could always reach their Mammi. Even they were shocked seeing Ilse in this unbelievable filth. Often the sick bay was without water and cleaning materials for days, but the mess had to be done away with.

Ilse didn't complain. In fact, according to Karl, she "saw nothing but 'sun' because she finally had a 'secure position.'" Later, the orderly permitted her to clean only the outpatients' department and physicians' room and to avoid the bloody remains of more serious procedures.

■   ■   ■

By the end of April 1944, the Sternlager held about 4,100 prisoners, most of them Dutch. Throughout 1944, the number of arriving Jews approximately balanced deaths. Of the 1,300 Sternlager prisoners who held valid Palestinian certificates (approved immigration papers), only 222 were approved as part of an exchange and left camp that year. The others, including the rest of the exchange prisoners, remained behind to endure the worsening conditions.

The Hesses' last shreds of hope for exchange had disappeared by the end of summer 1944, but the family found their strength in protecting each other. Ilse projected an optimism based on nothing but her own determination. When confronted with new obstacles, the twins heard her say, "*Wenn schon, denn schon*," a German idiom that could mean, as she used it at different times, "What will be, will be," or, "If you are going to do something, do it with all your energy. Go all out!" or, "If something is worth doing, if it must be done, do it right." They had watched Ilse save part of her small bowl of what Stefan called "slop" for Karl, who desperately needed more nutrition. Karl regularly asked his family, "What can I do for you?" When the children could not eavesdrop, Karl and Ilse shared their worries and also their hope that the war would end soon and they would be free.

Marion would later speak of the "core of our existence":

We were there with our mother and father, and always felt their protection. One night, when the curfew had passed for everyone to be in their barrack, my mother was not there. Every second seemed like hours, minutes like days. I remember shrieking, a primal shriek that did not stop even as others tried to comfort me. I will never forget the relief I felt when my mother finally entered the barracks. I could breathe to live another day. No one could sleep because of the noise I made. I remember, too, even then, my father's eyes sparkled with energy.

His tremendous vitality imbued all of us with a sense of optimism and will to survive. At times, he would hold my hand, and I would feel safe.

Encouraging their children to stay strong, Karl warned them about people who were known in camp jargon as *Muselmänner*, German for Muslim men—a term of uncertain origin, but slang used by prisoners to describe those prisoners who had given up their fight for life. Muselmänner had a blank, distant look and seemed to have lost all hope and the will to live. Karl and Ilse told the twins not to go near them, as if their condition were contagious.

At times it may have seemed to the Hesses, too, that all their dreams had been dashed, irrepairable, forever out of reach. Their property and their lives were in German hands. They had no freedom and no safety. And they worried about Ilse's large family suffering the same fate. Germans had stolen their homes and livelihoods in Germany and Amsterdam. Yet, with escape impossible, they chose hope as a weapon and found some level of peace and a path out of fear in beautiful dreams. They talked about attending the theater together one day, listening to fine concerts, and taking fabulous journeys far, far distant from Bergen-Belsen.

■   ■   ■

At his young age, Stefan correctly understood camp life; trouble was everywhere. A considerably graver danger than the family may have initially recognized had already begun to threaten them. In May, 150 tubercular prisoners from the hellish Dora work camp (later named Mittelbau) had arrived in Bergen-Belsen, where no medical facilities existed. Yet a hospital existed there on paper, the need was huge, and the Germans had no intention of building any real clinic for Jews or other prisoners. Far more crucial to the Germans than the danger of disease was the fact that Soviet forces were advancing into Poland. The Germans' dark secret was in danger of being revealed to the world.

During the winter of 1944, belatedly the German Foreign Office cabled the change in the Sternlager's status to SS Major General Karl Schöngarth in the Netherlands: "Due to considerable changes in the character of the camp, Bergen-Belsen is no longer in a position to receive Jews and members of enemy states…who have been made available for exchange operations." Elusive and formal to the point of obscurity, the telegram avoided mention of the disaster unfolding in the Sternlager, the Soviet liberation of camps in "the East," or the Germans' new plan for Bergen-Belsen as a repository for Jews in any state of health from camps threatened by Allied liberation.

That first transport of Dora's diseased prisoners portended the Nazis' drastically altered vision of the Sternlager from a protected internment camp to a place of starvation and harsh labor, and then to a convenient dumping ground for ill and exhausted prisoners. As early as March 1944, concentration camps began sending their diseased prisoners to the Erholungslager, the "Recovery camp" Bergen-Belsen. In May, another 150 prisoners arrived from Dora. In June and again in August, sick and weak Jews and other prisoners were transferred from Dachau. In July, more came from Sachsenhausen and in August from Neuengamme.

In August, the Sternlager's work details erected large tents for a women's camp behind the shoe squad building, outside the main gate. Three days later, the first women's transport from Auschwitz arrived at Bergen-Belsen. Thousands more women would arrive over the next weeks.

On November 1, Anne and Margot Frank, probably already stricken with typhus, were transported, along with some three thousand other female prisoners from Auschwitz-Birkenau. They arrived in frigid, open freight cars to the Celle station, then walked the three miles to Bergen-Belsen. They crowded into tents without lighting and rested on a thin layer of straw, unable to go outside to the latrines without stepping on another prisoner.

These wretched conditions gave way to even worse a week later, on November 7, when a heavy gale ripped several tents to shreds, leaving the women and girls standing in the cold wind and hail. Some spent the rest of that night jammed in the kitchen tent, the next day in the shoe squad shed. The following day, with an hour's notice, several barracks, including some from the Sternlager, were evacuated, dismantled, and moved to the new women's subcamp. The exchange Jews who had slept in those barracks were forced to find shared bunks in other Sternlager barracks.

On November 25, Himmler ordered crematoriums and gas chambers at Auschwitz-Birkenau dismantled and blown up. By December 1, as train after train brought prisoners like so much freight, Bergen-Belsen's population swelled to over 15,000, more than double its capacity of 6,000. Instead of about 160 prisoners, during those frigid winter months each barracks held about 600. The death rate spiked. When the camp's death rate was lower than the numbers arriving and the barracks could not hold more prisoners, another tent city was constructed, offering no protection from the freezing temperatures.

Ilse's mother, Fanny Hirschberg, as a young woman. She died in Stutthof concentration camp. *Courtesy of the Hess family*

Karl's mother, Rosalie Hess, with Ilse around the time of her marriage to Karl. *Courtesy of the Hess family*

Nazi students burning books in 1933. *United States Holocaust Memorial Museum, courtesy of the National Archives and Records Administration*

Karl and Ilse on their honeymoon in Switzerland in 1934, the year after Hitler was appointed chancellor and used the Reichstag fire to make himself dictator. *Courtesy of the Hess family*

Ilse at the beach in 1935. *Courtesy of the Hess family*

Teddy, the Hesses' cuddly Scottish terrier, in Karl's Mercedes convertible, in 1935, before Karl obtained a transfer from his employer and the Hesses were able to leave Germany for the Netherlands. *Courtesy of the Hess family*

Ilse in 1938 with the twins. *Courtesy of the Hess family*

Ilse's parents, Fanny and Willi Hirschberg, on their one, specially permitted trip from Germany to the Netherlands to meet the twins. They never saw their grandchildren again. *Courtesy of the Hess family*

Jewish businesses and synagogues across Germany and Austria were vandalized, robbed and burned down on November 9–10, 1938, Kristallnacht. *Courtesy of the National Archives and Records Administration*

Map of Germany's May 10, 1940, invasion of the Netherlands, Belgium, and Luxembourg, published in *Time* magazine's May 20 edition. *Courtesy of* Time *and PARS International*

Ise and the twins at the beach in
Zandvoort, Holland, August 1939.
Courtesy of the Hess family

Stefan and Marion in 1941. *Courtesy
of the Hess family*

Karl with the twins in Amsterdam,
1941. *Courtesy of the Hess family*

Tickets to America in 1941 meant that Karl's parents, Josef and Rosalie Hess, could flee Nazi Germany and survive. *Courtesy of the Hess family*

Napkin rings and an ashtray hidden for the Hesses by the twins' nanny Marretje Pasterkamp, along with other treasures including irreplaceable family photographs, in a suitcase under her bed and returned after the war. *Courtesy of the Hess family*

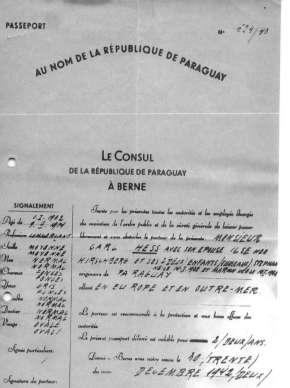

A falsified Paraguayan passport helped save the Hesses' lives by allowing them to be deported to Bergen-Belsen rather than Sobibor or Auschwitz. *Courtesy of the Hess family*

Prisoners at the Westerbork transit camp in the Netherlands observe Hanukkah. The Hesses were imprisoned here, then deported to Bergen-Belsen in Germany. *Courtesy of the Kamp Westerbork Memorial*

Mass grave at Bergen-Belsen concentration camp. An estimated fifty thousand people, most of them Jews, perished there. *Sergeant Morris of the British Army No. 5 Army Film & Photographic Unit*

Captured SS guards at Bergen-Belsen are forced to load the corpses of the victims. *Sergeant Midgley of the British Army No. 5 Army Film & Photographic Unit*

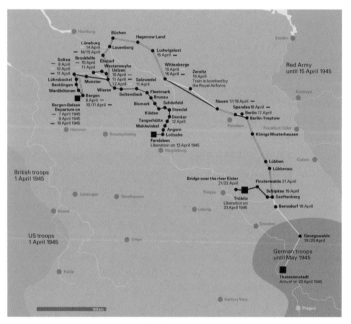

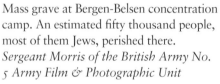

A re-creation of the routes of the three trains that transport Bergen-Belsen prisoners from the camp. The route of the "Lost Train" that carried the Hesses to Tröbitz and liberation is shown in red. *Courtesy of Bertold Weidner, Weidner Händle Atelier*

The death warrant for Kazimierz Cegielski, one of the most feared Kapos at Bergen-Belsen. Karl testified at his trial. *Courtesy of the Hess family*

The ashtray Ilse gave Karl for his birthday on January 3, 1946, inscribed, "Tonight we will not be taken." *Courtesy of the Hess family*

Advertisements that Karl and Ilse placed in newspapers after the war seeking information about Ilse's mother, Fanny Hirschberg, who had died in Stutthof concentration camp. *Courtesy of the Hess family*

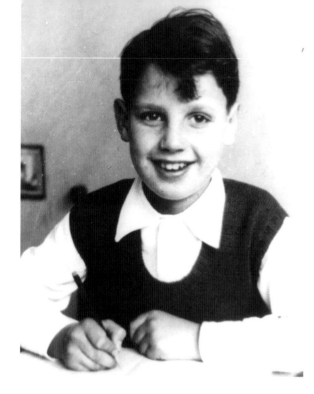

Stefan in school in Amsterdam after the war. *Courtesy of the Hess family*

Marion in school in Amsterdam after the war. *Courtesy of the Hess family*

The Hesses in front of their apartment building in Amsterdam after the war.
Courtesy of the Hess family

The Hesses traveled to America on the RMS *Queen Elizabeth*. *Reprinted under
the Creative Commons Attribution 3.0 Unported License, available at https://
creativecommons.org/licenses/by/3.0/legalcode*

Ilse in America. *Courtesy of the Hess family*

Marion (to our far left) meeting Eleanor Roosevelt in 1947. *Courtesy of the Hess family*

...even (as he spelled his name in America) and Marion learning how to use ...opsticks from the mayor of Chinatown. *Courtesy of the Hess family*

...se and the twins with the Hesses' new Pontiac. *Courtesy of the Hess family*

Steven and Marion in the front yard of the Hesses' first house in America, in Queens. *Courtesy of the Hess family*

Steven as a Boy Scout. *Courtesy of the Hess family*

The new U.S. citizens celebrating at the iconic Horn & Hardart automat in New York City, July 1, 1952. *Courtesy of the Hess family*

May 3rd, 1956.

REGISTERED.

Schade - Enquete Commissie
Keizersgracht
Amsterdam / Holland.

Gentlemen:

We, the undersigned, CHARLES and ILSE J. HESS were arrested
June 1943 and taken from our residence, Zuider Amstellaan 235,
Amsterdam - Zuid to Camp Westerbork.

During our stay there, we saw thousands of people being deported
to the concentration-camp Auschwitz. Already at that time we
were informed, that this camp meant death for most of the inmates.

The German commander of Westerbork postponed the transportation
of some people by a procedure which was known as the
" PUTTKAMER - STEMPEL ". The meaning of it was to pay a high
ransom to the German authoroties, in order to be kept in Camp
Westerbork or ultimately to be shipped to another camp but
Auschwitz.
Since it was a matter of life or death for our family, we informed
our Dutch friends in Amsterdam to hand over our diamond-broche,
worth fl. 60.000 to Mr. Puttkammer, who was in charge of the
whole transaction.

Enclosed you will find a photostat, confirming the facts.

Our claim of restitution is in accordance with the treaty of the
United States and their Allies and the German Bundesrepublik.

We are American citizens and declare under oath, that above
statements are true.

Sincerely yours,

CHARLES HESS

ILSE J. HESS

enc./

The Hesses' restitution claim for the broach that Ilse surrendered in exchange for the "Puttkammer Stamp." *Courtesy of the Hess family*

Ilse and Carl (as he spelled his name after immigrating to America) on their one and only return to Europe, in 1961. *Courtesy of the Hess family*

Carl at home in America. *Courtesy of the Hess family*

That fall and winter, daily food rations decreased to a soup consisting of water with a few bits of kohlrabi and a ten-inch loaf of bread shared by six people. In the barracks, prisoners slept three to a bed, furiously fighting each other in the night for every inch of space. Karl described the "satanic pleasure" that the SS took in forcing prisoners "to move into different barracks every few weeks."

Steven remembers, "I shared a bed with an old woman—well, everyone looked old. There were three slats to keep the pallet on top of it. Those slats were your prized possession. One night, I woke up all wet. I was terribly embarrassed. I thought I'd wet my bed, but it was that woman. People's humanity had been taken from them."

During Anne Frank's first days in the makeshift tent shelters, she was well enough to move about to some extent. Hannah Goslar, a school friend of Anne's imprisoned in the Sonderlager, the Special camp, heard of Anne's arrival and called to her through the barbed wire. Defying camp rules, Hannah tossed a small package containing socks and bread over the fence to Anne. Another desperate prisoner grabbed the package as Anne shrieked in dismay. A few days later, Hannah returned with a second packet, gathered at some cost to herself, and that time Anne caught it. With small moments of friendship and caring, the prisoners maintained a form of resistance, fighting the Germans as they could.

The Hesses' health was deteriorating. Karl's body was ravaged by starvation, his face and legs twice their normal size from "hunger edema," a condition caused by low blood protein. Ilse and the children shared one portion of soup at lunchtime, claiming that the "slop" was too revolting to eat, so that Karl sometimes had three portions. Like all Belsen prisoners, he obsessed over one thought—how to obtain more food. Some days, prisoners too weak to eat gave Karl their portions. Even on days when he was the lucky recipient of seven liters of kohlrabi, he, Ilse, Marion, and Stefan remained as painfully hungry as before, their meals no more than "an appetizer."

Winter 1944 blew in hard and cold, that December bringing heavy snow and, with it, increasing death in Bergen-Belsen. More than two thousand inmates died, including more than three hundred in the Sternlager, the so-called "privileged" camp. Prisoners were compelled to drag the dead to pits they had dug near the Prisoners' camp at the far end of Bergen-Belsen, then sprinkle the corpses with quick lime. Even so, the camp reeked with the stench of death and decay.

■　　■　　■

Jews across Europe dreamed of Germany's defeat, but the war was far from over. In November and December 1944, the Soviet military achieved major successes in the east, driving the retreating Wehrmacht back towards Germany. Hitler retreated from his Wolf's Lair command bunker in eastern Prussia and re-established his headquarters in the Reichstag in Berlin. Axis forces had withdrawn from the Greek mainland, and the war in Italy reached a stalemate. The British had become skilled at intercepting V-1 rockets with anti-missile defenses mounted on rail cars, but the Germans had developed V-2 supersonic rockets. Silent and faster, with larger destructive power than V-1 rockets, the V-2s were the world's first guided ballistic missiles. V-2 attacks rained death and destruction on Britain, Belgium, France, and the southern Netherlands and proved difficult to defend against. Launched from ground sites or dropped from above, with minimal loss of German personnel, V-2 rockets killed and wounded thousands.

Throughout fall and into winter, the Allies fought furiously in Western Europe, as American troops, aircraft, and other matériel arrived almost daily. Beginning in September, Allied forces made slow progress in freeing the Netherlands, fighting town by town to retake the country. French troops took back Strasbourg in eastern France, and by November 2 the Allies had liberated most of Belgium. There, Allied progress halted.

Probably the most significant fighting in Western Europe that winter of 1944–45 raged in the heavily wooded Ardennes region of Belgium, Luxembourg, and Germany where, four years earlier in the same corridor, Germany had stunned the Allies by invading France and the Low Countries. In another surprise move, instead of continuing to pull back its forces, on December 16 the Wehrmacht attacked. In a bold, last-chance move to retake Belgium, German forces surprised Allied troops by advancing south and west through bitter cold and deep snow. Into early January, the Germans continued their advance. Battle lines formed the shape of a bulge near the small town of Bastogne, Belgium, where American troops seemed on the verge of annihilation. Hitler appeared to be on the cusp of a masterful military victory, leading to jubilation in Berlin.

On December 22, German commanders sent a message demanding surrender to American general Anthony McAuliffe, who was holding on in that bulge in Bastogne. Without a moment of hesitation, McAuliffe replied with one word, "Nuts!" and the battle raged on. By the end of December, the Wehrmacht formed a plan of attack on Bastogne based on a gamble that low, heavy cloud cover would continue to protect German advances.

Instead, luck fell to the Allies. A bright sun shone over formations of American aircraft dropping supplies to beleaguered Allied troops. Three days later, General George Patton's Third Army broke the Bastogne siege, but the Battle of the Bulge raged on as Germany fought to turn back Allied advances. In New Year's speeches to the German people and the Wehrmacht, Hitler lambasted the "Jewish international enemy of the world" and declared that "like a phoenix from the ashes…Germans will rise from the ruins of our cities."

■   ■   ■

December 1944 heralded frigid winter temperatures, hovering at or near freezing. In Bergen-Belsen that bitter cold December, it may have seemed to the imprisoned Jews that conditions could sink no lower, but they did, falling to another level of hellish cruelty. Karl explained in his memoir: "The first command for those poor people [the thousands of new arrivals] was that they were forbidden 'to die in the barrack.'…In front of this barrack, there were hundreds of corpses lying each morning. They had to be undressed by their fellow-sufferers who had possibly another few hours to live. They then were dragged, thick ropes tied around their arms and legs, to a collection area and thrown with pitchforks onto a wagon. For the children, the view of the corpses was as normal as it should have been of dolls and rocking horses."

CHAPTER 12

Walking Dead
JANUARY 1945–MARCH 1945

B y late 1944 and early 1945, conditions on the Eastern Front were deteriorating so rapidly that Himmler decided to evacuate camps near the front, hoping to hide the Germans' crimes from the world. He ordered surviving prisoners transferred to camps in Germany. Frustrated that the ill, exhausted prisoners previously sent to Erholungslager, Bergen-Belsen Recovery camp, had not returned to work, he assigned SS Captain Josef Kramer, Auschwitz II-Birkenau's tough *Lagerführer* (camp commander in charge of operations at the camp's main killing site), to replace SS Major Adolf Haas in Bergen-Belsen and impose harsher discipline.

Kramer's first directives at Bergen-Belsen canceled bread rations for twenty-four hours and abolished the few remaining privileges—not that the already starving prisoners had many privileges to lose. Next, Kramer ordered four barracks emptied to make room for diseased inmates arriving from Poland. His actions created even more hardship and chaos; no barracks existed for the evicted prisoners, who were forced to sleep on the floor of other barracks. His third order: Kramer disbanded the vestiges of the Elders' Council, which had negotiated with the SS on camp issues including job assignments. Kramer replaced the Council and also some SS guards with Auschwitz *Kapos*, prisoners who assisted in enforcing camp discipline—typically convicted criminals, some of them Jewish. The Germans granted Kapos release from prison plus a few camp privileges—a small room to themselves, less physical abuse, extra food rations—in return for enforcing SS orders. The Kapos' reputation for brutality preceded them, sending new waves of fear and misery through the camp. Kramer also brought a number of female SS guards from Auschwitz and assigned them and their Doberman pinscher attack dogs to manage the women's camp.

In January and February 1945, the frigid temperatures conspired with the camp's brutal conditions to make survival in Bergen-Belsen even more difficult. Snow shrouded the camp, increasing the spread of disease and tormenting prisoners standing for hours during Appell. Many dropped from weakness, some developed frostbite, others fell down dead. Sleet, snow, and freezing rain blew through the barracks' broken windows and leaking roofs and turned the camp's barren dirt into deep mud bogs.

During that record-cold winter, the camp's meager rations again plummeted. Assessing the situation, Commandant Kramer reported that at times no bread reached the camp for two weeks. This despite the reality—ignored by the commandant—of a Wehrmacht bakery turning out bread for German troops only a mile from Bergen-Belsen. Furthermore, the camp held only an eight-day supply of potatoes and a six-day store of kohlrabi. Kramer noted that when he began his tenure as camp commandant, the average daily mortality was between 250 and 300. "The incidence of disease is very high.... The sick gradually pine away until they die of weakness of the heart and general debility." Kramer explained that he ordered the sick to attend Appell because "the people were too lazy to go even for a short time out of their barracks, and then they all said: 'We are sick.'"

The twins' friend Marion Stokvis recalled that the children played a game to ease the constant pain in their stomachs: "When you are going to spit, you wait a minute, and then you can swallow your spittle. It's just like you have something to eat or drink. It was a game."

But starvation was no game. Deaths in Bergen-Belsen eventually reached between five and six hundred per day, out of a population of some forty-one thousand prisoners. The harsh Häftlingslager and the more recently established women's camps suffered the largest numbers of deaths.

The Hesses wore all of their clothing in layers, partly to fight the piercing cold, partly to keep their clothes from being stolen by other desperate inmates. In Bergen-Belsen, everyone's clothes had become thin, ragged, and dirty. No matter how many layers they wore, the family suffered in the bitter cold. The clothes that Ilse had packed in Amsterdam and Karl retrieved still fit the twins, who had not grown taller during their year in the Sternlager. Stefan's boots still had plenty of growing room. By the end of winter 1945, the twins, then seven years old, weighed thirty to forty pounds. Karl weighed about ninety pounds. Ilse's weight was somewhere between those numbers.

"I do have some quite vivid memories of Belsen," Marion said in a United States Holocaust Memorial Museum interview. "First of all I do remember the general bleak cold lay of the land, how very cold and barren and wet and uncomfortable I felt all the time. I remember certainly what we ate—or the only things that were there to eat, which was basically kohlrabi, which in the beginning of the war was still—I think it was called turnips, a kind of turnip. In the beginning of the war, they were cooked, and near the end of the war they—we ate them raw."

Steven, too, said, "I remember the hunger and the misery. We used to sit outside and pick lice out of each other's hair because they were itchy. Remember, we never had a bath. We were filthy. So, we picked lice. If a mosquito bothers you, you flick it away. We didn't realize we were in a place of death. We didn't realize…this was our everyday existence."

Marion's most enduring memories of Bergen-Belsen, like Steven's, are a kaleidoscope of fear, cold, hunger, and the sense that color had drained from their existence: "What do I remember? Mostly, cold, fear, total misery, and grayness all around. Of course, the seasons came but for some reason, I don't remember sunshine. I don't remember flowers, although they must have bloomed somewhere. I don't remember birds, although they could not have been totally missing."

Steven said to me, "I know we 'played' with other children, but we were so malnourished, itchy, often very cold, I question how much enthusiasm was possible. Our mother remembered us as 'gray.' We would not complain, talked little, did not cry, did not move unless told to. We, like all others, were decaying. You have to understand that we had no childhood. We were not children."

As Karl remembered this time in his memoir, "There was no more bread, only raw kohlrabi. Like starving little birds, our children sat on their three-tiered beds. No more did they speak. No more did they laugh. They did not complain, they did not cry. They were just apathetic."

■   ■   ■

In early 1945, as the Hesses struggled to survive, German troops held on in uneven retreat across Europe, winning some battles, but more often pulling back as the Allies advanced from the east and west. In February, after a five-month campaign, Canadian, British, Polish, and U.S. forces liberated Belgium. In the southern Netherlands, as winter set in, the Allies pushed the Wehrmacht east to the strategically critical Maas River along the Dutch-German border. Fighting subsided as soldiers and Dutch citizens alike endured intense cold and hunger. The 3.5 million Dutch living in occupied northern Netherlands, including Amsterdam, were increasingly reduced to scouring the countryside for fuel and food during what would be known as the Hunger Winter. On edge, patrolling SS troops, Wehrmacht soldiers, and Green Police executed Dutch civilians for even minor infractions, including breaking curfew. Fighting resumed in February as more than three hundred thousand British, Canadian, and Polish soldiers pressed Axis soldiers back toward the Rhine and into Germany.

In a sign of Germany's growing desperation, a new conscription law changed the draft age for young men from seventeen to sixteen and raised the age for older draftees to sixty-five; increasing numbers of eligible conscripts went into hiding. Women between seventeen and fifty, whom Hitler had once exhorted to stay at home to raise large families, stood ready for mobilization; as many as one hundred thousand women served with the Luftwaffe in searchlight and antiaircraft units during the war.

In early 1945, German troops still held territory in western Poland, two hundred miles east of the Polish land they had occupied at the start of the war. The Red Army had liberated its own homeland but stalled in eastern Poland waiting to resupply and shift some forces south to Hungary and Yugoslavia.

With that shrewd tactical twist—like a move in a deadly game of chess, holding its troops in readiness, awaiting Germany's next foray—the Soviets exposed Germany's underlying weakness: the Wehrmacht was dramatically overextended. The Reich's expanse of conquered nations had become its greatest liability.

Now under extreme pressure, Germany could not defend its beleaguered allies or maintain control of its occupied territories. Some of its partners, including Romania, Bulgaria, Slovakia, and Hungary, instead of aiding Germany, either surrendered to the Allies or threatened to desert the Axis, requiring Germany to send troops to Central Europe. Across Europe, German troops were spread too thin, unable to keep pace with the Allies' combined militaries and the seemingly limitless supply of American trucks and other resources. In Northern Italy, German forces and pro-Fascist Italian fighters remained locked in battle with the Allies and Italian anti-Fascists.

When Hitler's acting chief of staff, Heinz Guderian, communicated the ominous news of massive Soviet offensive preparations, Hitler flew into a fury, shouting, "It's the biggest deception since Genghis Khan! Who is responsible for producing all this rubbish?" Perhaps he was recalling his own devious ploys that preceded Germany's invasions of both Poland and the Soviet Union.

On January 12, the Soviet Union launched its broad offensive into Poland, forcing Hitler to shift troops east, away from the raging Battle of the Bulge. Against his generals' advice, he chose to send most of those units to the Southern Front, to Hungary and Yugoslavia, not east to Poland, where the Soviets were poised like a dagger at the heart of the Reich. Later that month, a marauding Soviet submarine torpedoed and sank the MV *Wilhelm Gustloff*, once a luxurious German ocean liner launched in Hitler's presence. As part of his "Strength Through Joy" campaign to win the support of German labor, some sixty-five thousand German vacationers had enjoyed its low-cost cruises. In what would become the worst maritime disaster in history, an estimated nine thousand passengers fleeing the advancing Soviets died when it sank, an ominous portent of the dangers Germany faced.

In the heavily wooded terrain of the Ardennes and southwestern Germany, Allied and German forces remained locked in ferocious combat in early January, the Allies gaining ground at a slow and costly pace. After a brief clearing in the weather, freezing rain, thick fog, and deep snow enveloped the region, hitting the under-provisioned Germans the hardest. Running short of matériel and with their troop strength depleted, German forces were pushed back, fighting fiercely for every foot of lost ground in the Fatherland. Hitler Youth and other conscripted boys as young as sixteen fought alongside seasoned Wehrmacht troops. Over a million troops engaged in the four-week Battle of the Bulge, including some six hundred thousand Americans, fifty-five thousand British, and five hundred thousand Germans.

When the guns quieted on January 13, Germany had lost close to one hundred thousand men. Britain lost fourteen hundred. The battle was a turning point in the Allies' advance into southern Germany, but it was also one the costliest campaigns the United States ever fought, with more than one hundred thousand dead, wounded, or missing in action. A few weeks later, American soldiers on grave-registration duty reported that "bodies were stacked twelve to a pile, with Germans in separate groups." The civilian death toll numbered three thousand; fifty thousand soldiers on all sides remained unaccounted for.

■   ■   ■

Bodies were piling up in Bergen-Belsen that winter too. Ilse left the barracks in the wee hours every morning for her work cleaning the sick bay, which started at 3:30. And every morning she met the same guard who eagerly asked her, just as he had asked Karl, how many people had died in the night. Her response never satisfied him, but every day a prisoner assigned to pull a cart from one barracks enclosure to the next picked up bodies to throw into the pit.

As Marion would tell me, "You never knew where you stood: one more day of survival or the day of your death. The corpses piled in front of your barracks gave testimony to this reality."

Steven remembers, "So you basically had just emaciated skeletons. So these people were just grabbed by the legs and arms and tossed onto the pile. And I remember vividly learning to count on bodies. . . . they were in rows and just rotting. . . ."

Marion explains, "You lived in an alternate reality, a continuing horror show where there were fleeting moments of believing you could survive IF you obeyed orders and had the strength and spirit to endure. BUT even on a daily basis you were shocked out of that notion because yet another special act of cruelty and inhumanity would occur over which you had no control: it could be YOU the next time."

■   ■   ■

From the end of 1944 into 1945, a seemingly endless flow of evacuation transports arrived at the already overcrowded camp. In December 1944, when Kramer took command, 15,257 prisoners clung to life in the camp. On January 1, 1945, there were 18,465; two weeks later, 22,286. No reliable figures exist for February. At the beginning of March, 41,520 filled the camp far beyond its capacity.

As Karl wrote in his memoir, "More and more transports kept arriving. One day, two thousand prisoners came, arms linked, always five in a row. When this transport halted and the prisoners had to let go of each other, they dropped. Half of them were dead."

Between December 1944 and the spring of 1945, as the Allies pushed into Poland and Germany, thousands of freight cars moved hundreds of thousands of prisoners from camp to camp. The SS evacuated concentration camps ahead of the fighting, murdering many prisoners, leaving thousands behind, and moving thousands to Erholungslager Bergen-Belsen. In early 1944, when the Hesses arrived at the Sternlager, Dutch Jews made up the majority of prisoners. As more and more transports arrived, Jews, Sinti, Roma, and other captives from across Europe and North Africa crowded into the barracks.

Trainloads of Poles and Hungarians, mostly women from eastern camps, reached Bergen-Belsen and then were directed south for labor in munition factories at Buchenwald and Flossenbürg. Several groups from the Neutrals and Hungarian camps were transferred to Switzerland or other neutral locations for ransom or release. Controlling the complex movements of prisoner transports and troops ordered to shifting battle fronts demanded sophisticated coordination from Berlin.

■   ■   ■

Barracks and inmates moved continually around Bergen-Belsen that winter, as male and female inmates in teams of four to six were forced, despite painfully swollen legs and bellies and matchstick arms, to unload materials, assemble the new barracks, and carry heavy three-tiered beds from one barracks to the next.

The young French-Jewish Sternlager prisoner, Francine Christophe, recalls in her memoir, *From a World Apart: A Little Girl in the Concentration Camps*, how the SS continually screamed at them:

> *Los, Los, Schweine Juden!*
> *Schnell, jüdische Kuh!*
> *Raus, Schweinerei!*
> *Zu fünf, Scheisse, Schmutztück!*
> Move, Move Jewish pigs!
> Quickly, Jewish cow!
> Get out, swine!
> In fives [rows of five], you shits, you garbage!

One prisoner arriving from Sachsenhausen was stunned to find that in this so-called Recovery camp's barracks, no beds, no mattresses, no straw, and no benches awaited them—only bare muddy floors where they would lie "packed like herrings." Even prisoners arriving from Auschwitz in late 1944 and January 1945 declared conditions in Bergen-Belsen shocking.

To prevent starving prisoners from attacking the food distribution, five guards accompanied the vats of thin soup that prisoner laborers carried to the barracks. In the two prisoners' camps, where Polish Jews were held, some inmates turned to cannibalism. Thousands of Bergen-Belsen prisoners suffered from abdominal typhus (a bacterial infection spread through food), dysentery, stomach diseases, tuberculosis and, from early 1945, spotted fever and typhus (both spread by lice). Margot Frank, and then her sister Anne, nineteen and fifteen years old, were among those who succumbed to typhus in that sordid time and place, probably in late February, their bodies thrown into pits or left among the uncounted dead.

Ilse had been raised in a family whose members were leaders in their Jewish community; Karl had an Orthodox upbringing. They both knew Jewish history. Seeing Jewish corpses in growing piles, they may have felt reverberations from millennia of deadly persecution—from Egyptian pharaohs; Persian, Greek, and Roman leaders; Europe's crusaders; and Spanish kings and queens enslaving and murdering Jews. They themselves had run for their lives from their oppressors and were close to death in hellish Bergen-Belsen. They were living the ancient story of oppressors trying to kill them simply because they were Jews. Karl and Ilse may have thought about that history and felt haunted by it. Or their thoughts may have revolved only around how to survive each day.

■   ■   ▪

Although Karl frequently warned his family to stay quiet, remain in the background, and avoid attracting attention, resistance to the Nazi order ran deep inside him. He could not refrain from bending strict German orders.

In a letter included in Karl's memoir, a fellow prisoner on one of Karl's work details, Sally Vorst, recalled that Karl "did his best to sabotage the work," save the prisoners' energy, and protect them from punishment. He remembered that Karl sometimes divided their work group into two parts so that when they returned through the gate "it seemed that we had performed twice the work while we had only done half of it." Another worker on that crew, N. Coster, wrote that while the group was digging trenches, Karl "took care that we could goof off and we worked only when our tormentors were in sight. He faked and started shouting orders at the moment when the guards were coming.... The Germans hated him."

In his memoir, Karl wrote, "I was perfectly aware of the fact that we, too, would have to pay the final price. I had resigned myself to the fact the four of us would never survive this hell. I prepared for my own death. On the outside, as well as within, I was completely calm. Towards Ilse, I always emphasized that we would have to start on our last road courageously. The fifth of February 1945 would be the day of my death." That was almost literally true.

The winter cold kept its grip on Bergen-Belsen that February, but work in the camp continued with no break. The temperatures hovered in the thirties, clouds hung low and somber, and a biting wind was blowing on February 5 when Karl was assigned to the "sand crew," digging trenches. Because he could speak perfect

German with guards and Dutch, French, and English with prisoners, he was made the group leader.

As he had helped Jews in Amsterdam's Schouwburg escape from the Germans' clutches, and protected his family with all of his strength, Karl took a chance that wintery Monday and allowed the prisoners under his supervision to rest from their labors. Just as the twins had taunted the guards, coming close but not too close to the guard station, Karl unwittingly pushed the limits of his ability to help his fellow prisoners. It was a bold move, not his first in Bergen-Belsen. But this time the risk turned disastrous.

On that fateful day, Karl did not see the guards returning to the work site from their break. Furious at his deception, they beat Karl, then dragged him to a pit of sewage that flowed through a pipe from the camp. Filled with human waste, the basin measured about eleven feet by six feet and was somewhat deeper than Karl was tall. Obersturmführer Rau and two other German camp leaders arriving to participate in Karl's punishment ordered him to clean out a stoppage.

As Karl recounted in his memoir, "First I tried to alleviate the stoppage with a pole. When this did not proceed fast enough for the SS, they ordered me to undress. Thus I stood on a bitter cold day, on the rim of the basin, clad in nothing but my pants. The SS threw me into the excrement and ordered me to dig up the filth with my hands. Since the waste pipe was at the bottom of the basin, I had to dive into the filth while they beat me with their rubber truncheons. Twice I tried to crawl out of the basin. Each time, they threw me back into the nauseating filth."

Karl begged for a reprieve. Maliciously, the guards agreed and dragged him to the Appell grounds. "At that moment, while I was lying on the ground," he recalled, "I was beaten and kicked so badly by the two SS men that I knew my end had come. Calmly I asked section leader Hertzog to shoot me and end this satanic torture. High in the sky a flock of crows was screeching. Diagonally opposite, I saw, through the partly open door of the crematorium, a heap of corpses. Those were my last impressions of this world. This mistreatment lasted four hours."

Sadism pervaded the camp after Commandant Kramer's appointment. Karl's persecution was extreme, but cruelty was a growing part of devolving camp routines. The SS guards and officers seemed to be monsters, but there may have been many factors at work in their cruelty. Karl's beating would be a lesson to others considering any form of resistance. But also the guards and low-ranking Nazi officers, unlike the prisoners, would have read newspapers and heard the ubiquitous reports of disastrous war reversals and their nation in ruins—an end to the Nazi dream and a blur of humiliation. It's likely that they were angry at the Jews, whom they believed had caused the Allies to turn against the Reich. They may have been angry, knowing that fate had cheated them and blaming the Jews: in the best of their imagined futures, they would not return home to heroes' welcomes.

Before them on the ground lay a Jew who looked more Aryan than their Austrian-born Führer and whose whole being, it seemed, was the embodiment of disobedience. He had mocked them behind their backs. And so they beat him; they intended to beat Karl as they had beaten others on that Appell ground—until he died. And yet, though they came close to killing him, they did not.

It may not have been crows that Karl heard screeching over his head. Marion had looked for birds around Bergen-Belsen and not seen any. The twins seem to have witnessed the horrible punishment inflicted on Karl.

Their friend Marion Stokvis remembered seeing the Germans dragging two horribly beaten men to the latrines and pushing their heads under over and over again. When she and the other children suddenly realized that one of the bloodied men was the twins' father, they stood rooted to the spot, terrified that the Germans would kill him. She remembered Ilse being there, and the twins running to their mother.

Karl wrote in his memoir,

> From the kicking, my head was swollen so badly that it looked like a clown's head, the kind one puts over one's face at a circus. My battered ribs hurt. In the camp, my fellow-sufferers stared at me with shock and horror. Even those who had themselves shared in the most brutal mistreatments had never seen a man so badly beaten about, almost beyond recognition. My eyes were closed, my mouth hung somewhere in my face and not even Ilse recognized her own husband. Ilse decided that I was not going to return to work under any circumstances, come what may. She took care that I got a plank-bed in the hospital, which was a tremendous achievement because a mattress became vacant only after someone died.
>
> That same evening I had a high fever, pneumonia and pleurisy. As Ilse told me later, the doctors had given up on me. She also told me that I kept asking for a mirror and that she had forbidden everybody to let me have one.

For nine weeks, I was lying in the hospital barrack, never thinking that I would describe my own death. To my right and left, people died like flies.

Ilse said that after Karl's beating, she recognized him only by his coat. It was fortunate that she worked in the recovery barracks, the sick bay, where she could help him with her watchful and loving presence and keep him as comfortable and clean as possible. Prisoner doctors could monitor his condition, but nothing more. They had no medicines or equipment to work with, and they were pessimistic about his recovery. Ill and injured prisoners in the sick bay simply rested from labor and either recovered or died.

After Karl regained enough strength to be able to talk with his children, Marion and Stefan visited him in the sick bay, probably accompanied through the gates by Ilse. "Those times with my father were special," Marion told me. "I could hear the death rattle from cots to the right and left of him. Not all moments were grim—we laughed, he told funny stories. He asked whether I had dreams and aspirations. I told him that one day I hoped to see a whole loaf of bread and have a sandwich all for myself."

Before Marion left, Karl asked her to hold a small piece of a broken mirror and his tin drinking cup filled with weak coffee-water for him so that he could shave. Marion explains, "Almost too weak to perform the task, he wanted to look as well as possible. He wanted to show the Nazis that he could not be demeaned."

Marion also recalls that they reminisced in the sick bay about one of the family's few happy moments in Bergen-Belsen, just a few weeks earlier: "For our birthday [January 14] in the camp, my parents gave us each two slices of bread with butter and chocolate sprinkles [*Hagelslag*] on the inside, a favorite breakfast food from Holland. It was the best birthday present ever, and we extended the sandwiches over a three-months period! Years later, I learned that my father sold his wedding ring to make this wonderful treat possible."

Steven wonders about the timing and existence of this sandwich gift. Perhaps this delight was given after they were liberated, he has speculated. How could that treat have been possible, when the camp was running out of even the most basic food stores? (Possibly, the camp's active black market, which included the SS, made such a trade feasible. Sometimes when they were too sick to eat, prisoners saved bits of bread in their pockets.) And how could scraps of food have lasted for months in the conditions of the camp? The details are perplexing, but the family's devotion to each other at that low time is the core of the memory. Talking and dreaming with Marion, Karl lifted them all out of their imprisonment in Bergen-Belsen and into a better future—his commitment to saving his family providing strength they all needed in his long fight back from the edge of death.

CHAPTER 13

To Survive
MARCH 1945–APRIL 1945

T here were always airplanes overhead late in the war, and you always heard cannon fire," Steven told me. "People did know that the war was coming our way."

As the Allies pressed Germany from both the east and the west, prisoners in Bergen-Belsen were bewildered and angry. British and American planes alternated flying during the day and night, rumbling low over Bergen-Belsen, bombing the nearby Wehrmacht base and supply lines that made the area an active war zone. Why had no Allied bombs dropped on the railroad tracks serving the camp or the surrounding fields where SS were stationed? For some three years, the Allies had known about the German programs to annihilate Jews, but the Allies' objectives remained tightly focused on ending the war, not on saving the millions of Jews and others imprisoned by the Germans.

Trapped in an emotional and physical nightmare, the prisoners' only options were to give in to their misery and let life slip away or to hang on to their remaining strength and hope for rescue even as conditions in the camp grew more desperate. Transports continued to rumble into Bergen-Belsen's nearby rail station from the Eastern Front and from camps in southern Germany. As late as April 1945, two large transports brought fifteen thousand arrivals, some of whom were housed in a temporary camp at the Wehrmacht base nearby. The endless flow of transports may have been the handiwork of Eichmann, who later proclaimed he would "leap into my grave laughing" because he had five million deaths on his conscience.

Inmates battled each other for space and over meager possessions, which in the overcrowded camp could mean the difference between life and death. At 3:00 every morning, on her way to work cleaning the Erholungslager, Ilse felt her way through the cold, dark, dirty barracks where there was no heat or electricity, stepping around inmates whose arms and legs hung over the sides of the overcrowded bunks or who slept side by side on the floor. One day in her barracks, two deportees claiming a small saucepan found in the mud fought each other for it until they negotiated a trade—a few precious lumps of saved sugar for the pan, to be used as a chamber pot that would save its new owner and her daughter, both ill, from having to walk to the latrines in the cold nights.

Marion remembers, "Your life was the clicking of marching boots, leather straps and cudgels ready to strike, hunger, cold, shouting and screaming and always feeling like a penned animal. You could see but you could not say [what was happening] or comprehend or understand. You endured and became dead to feelings."

She explains, "Everyone wanted to sleep next to us, because we were little and skinny and the bunks were very narrow. People just told us where to sleep."

Steven told me, "I was bunked with a very large woman and one morning she was dead. I just remember it was one of my better days because I actually had the space to myself."

Wedding rings changed hands for watery soup, bread, threadbare, filthy clothing, or more space to sleep. The twins then reached into the pockets of the dead for crumbs that might remain there. Marion remembers, "Just seeing thousands of bodies was something that I thought was an everyday happening. And I remember there was always a tremendous conversation about who would get the jacket or the shoes or whatever the dead body had on. And people really watched other people die and to some degree like vultures would—would try to grab whatever was on that body that may be of some use." Steven would recall, in a Holocaust Museum interview of the Hess family, "Basically what happened was that if somebody was near the end they became a veritable commodity because they had a certain amount of clothing on them. And so anyone who died would be stripped right away so basically you had a lot of naked bodies."

As conditions continued to deteriorate, food and water were impossible to obtain. The death rate soared.

The twins remember sand, dust, and especially the mud and terrible cold, night and day that spring. One young girl, left for dead on a pile of bodies ready to be thrown into the pit, called out in a weak voice. Rescued, she died a short while later, and her body was thrown back onto the pile. Ilse told a reporter for the *Washington Post* that "it was so crowded, people were not allowed to die in the barracks. And every morning, there were piles of corpses in front. And the children were looking for bread between the corpses."

According to Steven, "After a while, you can only get so hungry. We reached a peak when you don't get any worse."

That spring, a bomb destroyed the electric grid that ran the camp's pumping station; after that, fresh water no longer reached the camp. Throughout Bergen-Belsen, even water was severely rationed, each prisoner allotted two cups a day. In the Prisoners' camps, which housed Polish Jews, at least one corpse floated in the only water tank. By April, the camp's water supply ran even lower; buckets of fetid, unpurified water sat outside each barracks. A clear running stream nearby could have been fitted in a matter of a few hours with a simple purification system and a pipe running down to the camp, but this was not done—supposedly no purification equipment was obtainable because of the war. Just a few miles away, a water truck supplied the Wehrmacht camp; the soldiers there suffered neither grinding hunger nor thirst. But no such truck drove through Bergen-Belsen's gates.

By spring, Commandant Kramer understood that the war was lost and, after the inevitable surrender, Nazi leaders would be tried for war crimes. The Allies had threatened postwar punishment of those responsible for mass murder. Yet Kramer remained committed to Nazi ideals and to his role operating the deadly camp. When he wrote Richard Glücks, the head of Section D (concentration camp administration), that spring to report on the camp's situation, he must have known that he was writing for two audiences—his superiors, but also the Allies, who had already liberated a number of camps and would eventually be judging him. And yet his words betray appalling crimes and shocking callousness: "The number of sick," he wrote, "has greatly increased, particularly on account of the transport of detainees, which have arrived from the East in recent times—these transports have sometimes spent eight to fourteen days in open trucks [rail cars]. An improvement in their condition, and particularly a return of these detainees to work, is under present conditions quite out of the question.... [O]n one occasion, out of a transport of 1900 detainees over 500 arrived dead."

Kramer reported that about 7,500 exchange Jews remained in the Sternlager. SS Hauptsturmführer Ernst Moes had notified Kramer that "these Jews would be removed in the near future. It would be much appreciated if this could be done as soon as possible," Kramer wrote, "for in this way accommodation could be found for at least 10,000 concentration camp prisoners." Kramer's purposely careless math makes it clear that his true concern was pleasing his superiors, not improving the camp's overcrowding, abominable conditions, and inhumane treatment of the prisoners.

Kramer also noted that Moes, who had inspected a number of camps including Bergen-Belsen, had objected to transporting the exchange Jews, sick with spotted fever and other highly contagious diseases, away from Bergen-Belsen. Kramer pushed back, reluctant to delay the evacuations from the east, where he had served as commandant. Arguing for the transport of Jews without regard for the spread of disease or the prisoners' health, he continued: "The removal of these internees is particularly urgent for the reason that several concentration camp Jews [the Prisoners' camps arrivals from Polish camps] have discovered among the camp internees their nearest relations—some their parents, some their brothers and sisters. Also, for purely political reasons—I mention in this connection the high death figure in this camp at present—it is essential that these Jews disappear from here as soon as possible." Kramer was not eager for prisoners to talk to their relatives, to share stories, to draw a fuller picture of the Germans' crimes.

Kramer's extraordinary statements reveal his detailed knowledge of the camp's daily life. His letter demonstrates how fully he understood the situation of unchecked disease and cruelty in Bergen-Belsen. He knew exactly which transports from Natzweiler concentration camp in Alsace had carried spotted fever to the camp and when prisoners from camps in Germany and further east had brought typhus. He also knew that people were desperate to connect with members of their torn-apart, fractured families. He displayed no shred of compassion. His descriptions of the inmates' suffering and health ring hollow and technical, as if the camp's victims were vermin and their tortured existence simply a logistical problem. And yet in the same letter he requests more beds, blankets, and eating utensils for twenty thousand prisoners—perhaps for the eyes of the Allies, who would soon seize Nazi records and punish those convicted of war crimes. Perhaps Kramer believed that this letter would allow him to portray himself as a victim of circumstances.

His cold calculations had served him well as Lagerführer at Auschwitz II-Birkenau. He had applied those same skills to the starving, diseased Bergen-Belsen prisoners. Yet, his power and influence in the deadly camps had become a potential noose around his neck. Kramer made a special effort to point out problematic "political" aspects of Bergen-Belsen's dire conditions. Perhaps the Soviets' condemnation of the Germans when they liberated Auschwitz in late January had made clear to him the potential consequences of the Allies' evolving knowledge. Discovering Auschwitz's horrors, Colonel Vasily Petrenko, commander with the Red Army infantry, had exclaimed, "I who saw people dying every day was shocked by the Nazis' indescribable hatred toward the inmates who had turned into living skeletons."

Attempting to cover his tracks, Kramer sought simultaneously to please the *Gruppenführer*—"I assure you that from this end everything will be done to overcome the present crisis"—and to whitewash his own role. He portrayed his work simply as a job in which he took orders and tried to overcome difficulties he had not created. In both regards, his misreading of the gravity of his own responsibility renders his letter absurd. While inmates died of starvation in Bergen-Belsen, Kramer knew that there was eight hundred tons of food stored on the Wehrmacht base two miles away.

■　　■　　■

Appell had ended some time before April. Few Jews could stand for the roll call. Who would count and report on those Jews who lingered between life and death? As Kramer had complained, many simply lay on their bunks or on the floor, too sick to move, days away from dying. Many ill prisoners had given up thoughts of rescue. Deadly conditions prevailed in every corner of Bergen-Belsen. No barbed-wire fence, no gate, no section of the camp could hold in the rampant scourges of disease, hunger, and thirst.

Even the Kapos who beat and insulted and murdered the prisoners night and day succumbed. The SS were increasingly terrified of contracting any of the numerous painful, disfiguring, and potentially lethal camp illnesses. Among the diseases spreading untold misery throughout the camp that March and April, spotted fever, tick-borne and highly infectious, caused profuse sweating, pain, diarrhea, and deep sores that reached to the bone. Typhoid fever afflicted prisoners with temperatures over 104 degrees, delirium, exhaustion, and bloody stools. Varieties of epidemic typhus were spread by lice, rats, fleas, ticks, and chiggers—all in abundance in Bergen-Belsen. Many prisoners shaved their heads to keep deadly insects at bay, with no success. With no resources for hygiene and sanitation, they suffered from countless infections. The "privileged camp" had become a scene of horror.

As Ilse would remember, "I . . . and my husband, we very often talked about [death], because we just could not imagine that a family of four would ever survive this—I cannot even call it living hell—this dying hell. . . . we almost were jealous of people who were dying. . . . The moment someone closed their eyes forever, there was absolute peace on their faces. There was no horror, no fear, no tears. It was just a picture of rest." The picture of peace that Ilse seemed to envy did not last. The look of release on the faces of the dead often quickly turned to hideous grimaces and expressionless staring eyes.

Among Bergen-Belsen's dead were once successful lawyers, actors, merchants, politicians, scientists, and teachers, the intelligent and the ordinary, funny and thoughtful, outgoing and withdrawn, families and single people—an array of the range of humanity. For some years, the camp's crematorium, designed to hold just three bodies at a time, incinerated the mortal remains of thousands upon thousands of deceased prisoners, the unsanctified ashes rising in threads of smoke next to the Appel grounds. In February 1945, some seven thousand people had died in Bergen-Belsen, in March, eighteen thousand died, and some nine thousand in the first half of April. By some time in the spring, the crematorium was no longer in use, unable to keep pace with the massive number of corpses.

Attempts to burn bodies in a pyre fed by wood from the local forests also proved unworkable: protests came in from the German forestry department, which opposed the deforestation, and from the Wehrmacht in the nearby base, who could not bear the stench.

■   ■   ■

While Bergen-Belsen continued to operate as a harsh and deadly camp, the Allies drew closer to the German homeland. The Wehrmacht had launched an offensive against the Red Army in Hungary, but it was soundly repulsed. Seizing the moment, Soviet forces burst forward from the east, taking their revenge for the beating they had suffered at the hands of the Germans. The Red Army advanced across Poland but then paused at the Oder River on the Polish-German border, some thirty miles from Berlin, waiting to coordinate with Allies invading from the west.

As Soviet forces in Poland halted their drive, U.S. forces preparing to cross into Germany—Patton's Third Army, Hodges's First Army, and Simpson's Ninth Army—were also holding fast along the Rhine River on Germany's western border, coordinating with British field marshal Bernard Montgomery's meticulously planned invasion from the west. When Red Army units entered Austria, in contrast to their experience further east, the Soviets found no ghettos or camps awaiting liberation there. Adolf Eichmann had declared the country Judenfrei three years earlier, in August 1942, as the last transport left Vienna for the killing fields of Belarus.

On March 27, the last V-2 rockets to strike Britain killed 135 people. During the war, over a thousand rockets had killed close to 3,000 British people and nearly 2,000 Belgians. On March 31, General

Dwight D. Eisenhower, Supreme Commander of Allied Expeditionary Forces in Europe, broadcast a demand for a German surrender.

By that time, German generals and many civilians had accepted the reality of their defeat. They now hoped that the British and Americans would sweep swiftly across the country to occupy as much of the country as possible, before the Soviets roared into Germany and imposed Communist rule.

■   ■   ■

Even as most Germans, civilians and military, understood that defeat was imminent, in Bergen-Belsen the SS still shouted at the prisoners, beating, hounding, and starving them. The inmates' struggle to survive, their constant fear, and the brutality they suffered all took their toll; some turned against each other. In his account of Bergen-Belsen, *After Daybreak: The Liberation of Bergen-Belsen, 1945*, Ben Shephard reported the recollection of one survivor: "Our hut [barracks] was like a madhouse," where the smallest provocation, theft, or suspicion of theft led to vicious arguments. Prisoners thrown together sometimes carried deep grievances; some French Jews, remembering Germany in World War I, harbored bitterness toward German Jews.

It was probably early in April 1945 that Ilse's once satin-black hair turned white and she lost partial sight in one eye. As Karl was recovering in the Erholungslager, she had spiked a fever, vomited, shaken from chills, and hurt all over. She had contracted one of the many diseases rampant in Bergen-Belsen. A prisoner doctor diagnosed Malta fever.

Ilse remembered, "No one ever had heard of it except one Greek doctor . . . Dr. Allalloof. He was the only doctor who ever had heard of [Malta] Fever. And it's a kind of malaria which develops in the tropics and I must have caught the bug. And due to this doctor—he didn't have any instruments—he didn't—there was no antibiotics at that time—he didn't have anything—I survived. I myself always had the feeling when I got up in the morning...I will survive the whole German army...."

Prisoner doctors provided great service to their fellow prisoners but were hampered by the absence of equipment and medicine; perhaps, in her feverish state, Ilse had not heard Dr. Allalloof's diagnosis correctly. Malta fever had been distinguished from malaria in the late nineteenth century, but it is unlikely that Ilse had either disease. As Steven explained to me, "My parents said that a Greek doctor diagnosed a very rare 'Malta fever.' I think that was not possible. Chances are my mother got typhus, the major killer in Belsen, from lice." Ilse, like all of the prisoners, knew that the Allies were approaching—and that she and her family were racing against time for their survival.

■   ■   ■

The section of the SS that operated Germany's concentration camps had an intimidating name—SS-*Totenkopfverbände*, the "Death's Head Units"—wore impressive, shiny black jackboots and held life-and-death power over the prisoners. But by April 1945, they knew that Germany's defeat was imminent, and they did not walk so proudly. At that time, some German people still did not understand that Germany had lost the war—they still believed in Hitler's "rise from the ashes" vision. But most of the SS in Bergen-Belsen *did* understand. Some who were locals deserted their posts in early April, disappearing into the countryside ahead of the advancing Allies. As Karl wrote in his memoir, "The allied troops kept coming closer—thirty miles, twenty-five, ten miles. The SS got nervous. The kitchens did not function any more. The corpses were not picked up any more and piled up like mountains, thousands per day. A sudden order: 'The camp will be transported.'"

While thousands upon thousands more prisoners continued to arrive at the camp, Himmler in Berlin realized that the British army was nearby and would soon take over Bergen-Belsen. Hoping to hide evidence of German atrocities and possibly negotiate a dignified handover of the camp, he ordered three trains to arrive at Celle between April 6 and April 11 to transport approximately seven thousand Sternlager prisoners, along with Hungarians, citizens of neutral countries, and special cases, to Theresienstadt.

Ilse explained,

> Well, one day—it was exactly on April the 9th, 1945—a group of our coprisoners were told that they had to leave the camp and that they could just carry what they were wearing—we didn't have much more—and they were leaving the camp by train. And so it was on April the 9th they were leaving not knowing where to go—where they were going. On April the 10th a group of about five or six hundred people, among them my husband and my two children, also were told that we would leave the camp. My husband at that time weighed maybe ninety-six

pounds, but his spirit was still there. He couldn't walk, but he could talk. So he still was convinced that we would not survive, especially not after the Germans told us we would go by train direction [sic] east to be gassed. So, we were loaded into trains . . . cattle cars.

As Karl wrote in his memoir, "The first part of the camp left. A few trucks were supposed to transport the severely sick. When they arrived, the healthy ones stormed them. Without any consideration, women and children were thrown to the ground. Those who found no space on the wagons had to walk the five kilometers. From previous reports, we knew that whoever could not keep up on the way was shot. We let the first transport leave in the vague hope that the English, by then only fourteen kilometers away from the camp, would be able to liberate us. But a bridge was blown up and that delayed their advance."

The Hesses' evacuation was not a source of much joy to the family. Too much had been suffered, too much irretrievably lost—and far too much uncertainty lay ahead. On Tuesday, April 10, they prepared to leave the camp. Ilse carefully packed a few essential pieces of clothing. Karl came across a "suit," worn only a few times, that probably Ilse had originally packed during her brief return to Amsterdam and stored in their packs. In the camp then it proved invaluable. Karl was able to barter with another prisoner, trading it for something he valued more—three-fourths of a liter of kohlrabi. "It was the first day that once more I was standing on my legs," Karl remembered, "i.e. that I practiced walking like a child.... We stumbled out of the barracks into the throng of thousands of people who were lying, sitting or standing on the camp road, each ready to jump and grab a seat on the three trucks which were to take us to the railroad station. There ensued a wild melee. The section leader pulled his gun to keep us in check."

Because that section leader remembered Karl from a work detail and respected him, he made room for the Hesses on the life-saving truck, a rare instance of human compassion amidst the horror. Karl was still so weak that he might not have been able to make the three-mile walk.

■   ■   ■

The train awaiting the desperate throng of twenty-five hundred Jews had a few passenger coaches and a long line of about forty-five cattle cars. Next to the train, a mountain of raw kohlrabi that prisoners themselves could load into the cars constituted the only provisions for their journey.

The Hesses who stood on the Celle station platform that spring day were vastly different from the family that had arrived there in winter 1944, fourteen months earlier, bewildered and frightened but healthy and strong, unaware of the hell that awaited them. On April 10, the family limped and walked along the lengthy train and saw that every seat in the few battered, dirty passenger coaches had already been taken. Up to eighty people had crammed into some of the cars. Finally, they found a cattle car of female Hungarian prisoners—almost full, but with just enough room for their family. They helped each other clamber aboard the rubbishy, smelly train. It had no water and no provisions for sanitation for the fifty-seven people—fifty-four women and three men—who claimed spots in that car. This was not a glorious moment. The family was injured, ill, barely alive, herded like cattle into a train car akin to a dark, windowless cage. But they were alive, and they were together. Amid the terrifying sounds of SS men and women shouting and berating them, Dobermans lunging and snapping at their legs, and train cars bumping and clanking, they left Bergen-Belsen.

CHAPTER 14

Chaos

APRIL 10, 1945–APRIL 15, 1945

Long-dormant optimism heartened the weary Hess family as their train rumbled away from the Celle spur track, leaving the nightmare of Bergen-Belsen farther and farther behind. They left Bergen-Belsen around midnight on April 10. Yet the worries and the harsh conditions of their life in the camp followed them. As Karl wrote in his memoir, "None of us knew how to manage at all with these few square meters, since there were neither seats nor any other provision for human beings. We arranged ourselves along the walls [about thirty-two feet long] so as to leave the middle free for the few pieces of luggage. Despite the fact that we traveled towards an unknown fate, our inner excitement was mixed with a scant joy. For the first time in years, we were outside a barbed wire."

But Karl and Ilse's spirits fell again as they considered where they might be headed. According to Karl, they had heard in the camp "that we were to take an extended trip, which was to last fourteen days, in cattle cars.... The trip was supposed to lead to the gas chambers." Karl found that rumor convincing. Ten years earlier, he had predicted that only 5 percent of Europe's Jews would survive the Nazis. He had never wavered from his belief that the Germans would pursue their murderous obsession until the moment of their defeat. Karl's belief that the Jews aboard the train were headed for the gas chambers would be reinforced a few days into their journey, when he was taunted by a sneering German. As he explained in his memoir, "A few days after our departure from Bergen-Belsen, the engineer informed us that we were supposed to be taken to Theresienstadt to be gassed. This terrible piece of news did not shake us too much after what we had already gone through."

Ilse had heard a different malicious rumor: their train would cross a mined bridge over the Elbe River. The bridge would explode and send them crashing to their deaths. After all that the Hesses had endured, nothing seemed too barbaric for the Germans.

Those horrifying predictions were lies. The SS spread misinformation to inflict more pain, twisting the knife in the wound. Months before the Hesses' train left Bergen-Belsen, all German gas chambers had been shut down or blown up and those camps liberated. And there were no mined bridges ahead. Their train and the two others that left Bergen-Belsen that week, overloaded with Sternlager Jews, were heading to Theresienstadt, a so-called model concentration camp in German-occupied Czechoslovakia. Each train took a different route, as the engineers sought undamaged tracks and safe passage. The three trains would cross paths at several points along the way, then set out again in uncertain directions. Barbed wire no longer surrounded the Hesses, but the Germans still controlled their fate.

Having starved and killed thousands of "exchange Jews," as Germany's defenses were crumbling that April, the German Foreign Office revived its scheme of using Sternlager Jews as hostages in negotiations with the Allies. But instead of trading carefully selected Jewish prisoners for German prisoners of war, as originally planned, the Germans plotted to use them as if they were weapons of war, to extract more lenient surrender terms from the Allies as the future grew increasingly bleak. Theresienstadt seemed the ideal location to hold the Jews for that purpose. The Germans never comprehended that the Allies had no interest in compromising war gains for hostages.

Germany's elaborately constructed fiction of Theresienstadt as a model camp still held sway over even the International Committee of the Red Cross. Theresienstadt, in contrast to Bergen-Belsen, had originally been established as a civilian internment camp, nominally subject to inspections and the Geneva Conventions. And following the deportation of Danish Jews to Theresienstadt, the Danish Red Cross and International Red Cross had in fact jointly inspected that camp in June 1944. In yet another of the Germans' smoke-and-mirrors deceptions, the camp had prepared in advance for that visit: Sports teams competed on grassy camp fields where, on other days, prisoners sometimes lined up without coats, food, drink, or rest for an entire day as group punishment for a minor infraction or to acknowledge a Nazi holiday. The captive Theresienstadt Jews' orchestra and chorus performed Verdi's *Defiant Requiem* for the dignitaries just days before many of the musicians were deported to Auschwitz. Yet the camp easily passed the outside world's inspection.

In reality, during Theresienstadt's five years of operation, more than 150,000 Jews, including 15,000 children, had been held there for months or years before being transported to their deaths, mostly at Treblinka or Auschwitz. By the week of April 10, 1945, when the three trains left Bergen-Belsen, death marches had brought some 15,000 prisoners to Theresienstadt, almost doubling the camp's population and spreading typhus. Back in February, Himmler and other SS leaders had negotiated with Jewish groups in Switzerland for the release of more than 1,200 mostly Dutch and German Jews from Theresienstadt to Switzerland in exchange for an offer, never received, of a million dollars. Himmler's scheme to transport the exchange Jews between fast-moving battle zones risked the prisoners' lives for frantic and imagined end-of-war gains.

The first of the three trains to depart Bergen-Belsen, on April 8, became known as the "Farsleben Train." Almost by chance, it was liberated on April 13 outside the small village of Farsleben, near Magdeburg, some eighty miles from Celle, by American army troops. The soldiers billeted the rescued Jews in German homes nearby. Later those prisoners were taken west toward American screening centers. Some soldiers later reported having cried at seeing their condition. The second train, which held Hungarian prisoners, left Celle on April 9 and would be the only transport from Bergen-Belsen to reach Theresienstadt, on April 20. In retrospect, the Hesses felt fortunate not to have boarded that transport. In addition to deaths from disease during that journey, around forty-five prisoners died when Allies mistakenly bombed the train, believing it to be a German troop transport. In the maelstrom of the trains' traveling through a war zone, estimates of the numbers of dead from that attack would vary from forty-five—the number in Karl's memoir—to fifty-six, plus many more wounded.

The Hesses' train, later known as the "Lost Train" which was the third to leave the camp, rolled north from Celle late in the evening of April 10 or in the early hours of April 11 and traveled through the night, attempting to find a clear path to Czechoslovakia. But the Allies were closing in on that region from both east and west, leaving the train with an unpredictable, narrowing corridor of safety. Travel conditions were harrowing. Although the Germans did not plan to murder the Jewish prisoners on the Theresienstadt-bound transports, the miseries of Bergen-Belsen traveled with the twenty-five hundred Jews packed into the Hesses' train. The diseases, exhaustion, and lack of food that ravaged the Sternlager continued to kill them even as their train left the camp behind.

The SS had made no effort to separate the sick from the healthy in the windowless cattle cars. Among other illnesses, almost all of the prisoners had dysentery. Francine Christophe, who was on the train, would describe clothes "stiff with diarrhea" and hair "matted with lice eggs." Some prisoners had shaved their heads, but lice still attacked them. As Christophe would write, "And we scratch ourselves until we bleed." From day one, excrement, dirt, and blood from beatings and untreated gunshot wounds covered the floors, which were choked with the comatose and the dead, making them slick and revolting. The cars reeked. In a meager effort to create a small measure of order, the SS guards who slammed shut the large sliding doors of each carriage had chosen car leaders. They named Karl leader of his car, which allowed him, Ilse, and the twins to sit near the door. They could press their faces toward what little fresh air wafted through the cracks—a breath of freedom.

As the Hesses' train rumbled away from Celle, it slowed to allow prisoners to throw dead bodies from the train cars, an average of over fifteen per day left by the tracks. I suspect that Karl, at the door, weak, starving, and unable by himself to observe the ordinary respect due to the dead, managed that unhappy task for his car of mostly women. As he wrote in his memoir, "The train hardly stopped when one of the corpses would simply be thrown out of the car to find his last resting place, unburied, next to the tracks.... The short supply of food was soon used up. Since the travel from Bergen-Belsen had not been prepared for in any way at all, there had been no arrangements made for feeding the prisoners. After a few days, hunger drove us out of the train. Even with the SS shooting off pistols as soon as somebody left the car, one took the risk to get out of the train."

Ilse explained:

> I think that this was one of the last trains ever to roll through Germany. No one knew where we were going.... We stopped all the time. It was cattle cars.... About six hundred people died on this train—on both trains.... And their bodies were just thrown out of the train.... at the next stop. And ten men got up and prayed. And then it went on and on for the next stop to throw out the bodies.... We—eighty percent of us had typhoid fever. I had it too. And this is a very contagious sickness even in a private room in a hospital. So imagine to have this in a cattle car.

Initially the SS did not permit anyone to leave the train, but they soon realized that the absence of toilets made stops unavoidable. Steven explained to me, "Whenever we stopped the doors were slid open to get rid of bodies and, I would guess, human waste. People who still had the will and the strength would lower themselves from the high car opening. Our mother had two bricks to hold a metal pot for cooking—grass, or anything that might be edible alongside the roadbed. Our father would sneak off to find food."

Traveling through that first night, April 10–11, the train turned due north, away from the large rail junction at Hanover. Twenty-five miles south of Celle, it was the obvious route to Theresienstadt. But Hanover lay in shambles after eighty-eight British and American bombing raids had destroyed nearly its entire city center. The final raid had occurred just two weeks before the three trains left Bergen-Belsen.

The Hesses' train made its way along the flat, alluvial Lüneburg Heath and stopped at the town of Soltau, some fifteen miles from Bergen-Belsen. Meanwhile another of the Bergen-Belsen trains was following the Elbe River south towards Magdeburg, intensifying fear among those prisoners who had heard the rumors about a mined bridge.

■　　■　　■

On April 10, the same day that the Hesses boarded the train, the Red Army under Soviet commander in chief of the Western Front, Georgy Zhukov (from the Soviet perspective, Germany was the Western Front), burst out of its bridgeheads in northern and southern Germany. The Soviets captured Königsberg on Germany's

Baltic coast and fought inch by inch to within thirty-seven miles of Berlin, almost forming a noose around the city—and then they halted, awaiting a coordinated assault on the capital with the Western Allies.

Moving swiftly from the west, British and American forces continued to push north and east across Germany from their gains in the Ardennes. They took Cologne, wrested control of a key bridge across the Rhine not far from Karl's birthplace of Fulda, then moved deeper into the interior. They closed in on Buchenwald and Bergen-Belsen and battled eastward where the Hesses' train wandered in search of a clear path. Allied bombs and fighter planes battered the country in seemingly nonstop raids.

In the threatened capital, Hitler remained sequestered in his bunker under the Reichstag, counting on a miracle to save Germany. Roosevelt's death on April 12 at first seemed to be that stroke of luck, but America's smooth democratic transition of power placed Harry Truman in charge and dispelled Hitler's hopes. However, his Kampf—his struggle to destroy European Jewry—remained at least partially intact, and no doubt gave him satisfaction.

■   ■   ■

The Hesses' train turned east from Soltau. From there they traveled past Munster and Uelzen, and pushed north again, in the opposite direction from Theresienstadt. In that mostly flat landscape, native Moorland sheep, unique to that area, grazed placidly in the nature reserve of grassland, marshes, and small lakes as the Bergen-Belsen train rolled passed. Perhaps spring lambs gamboled in the heath. During stops, the prisoners would have seen the bombing damage all around them, even in small villages. Travel was slow, cautious, frightening, their route unclear.

I thought about the Hesses' frightful journey. Some years before, Karl had traveled Germany in his Mercedes convertible for his job with United Silk. And Ilse had very likely accompanied her mother on buying trips to Berlin for the department store, probably by train. It seems likely that, during the brief moments when the Bergen-Belsen train's door slid open, familiar sights and scents helped Karl and Ilse to find their bearings and—perhaps—to recall better times.

But the once picturesque small towns they passed held still active remnants of the German war machine, prime targets for Allied bombers. On their fourth day of travel, the train stopped in Lüneburg. Before the war, the rushing Ilmaneu River and a small water mill had made the city a center for tourists. Excursion boats toured nearby lakes. But the town had also become home to a Luftwaffe bombing range, a production plant that churned out large quantities of mustard gas, and a concentration camp. And yet the city remained largely unscathed by Allied bombs. Ironically, military barracks there saved it from Allied fury; the Allies planned to use those barracks for billeting their own soldiers and to hold military tribunals in the city at the war's end.

Just days before the Hesses' train reached Lüneburg, though, Allied bombers had mistakenly attacked a train loaded with about 400 Jewish prisoners awaiting transit in the city's rail station; more than 250 died in that attack. The SS had then force-marched 140 survivors of the attack the sixty miles toward Bergen-Belsen. Three days before the Hesses' train reached Lüneburg, Wehrmacht soldiers shot and killed 70 of them who were too weak to join the march.

Shortly after the Hesses' train passed through Lüneburg, SS guards on the train taunted the prisoners, telling them that soon after they left the British had liberated the city and its camps. They had almost been rescued.

■   ■   ■

The Hesses understood that the Germans had once considered Sternlager Jews useful, but since the country's collapse, the Germans had expended almost no effort to keep them alive.

Steven described the conditions on train to me: "Once again, only kohlrabi, a pail for a toilet, about fifty-eight dying companions in the filthy car."

Karl would remember, "Sometimes the train stopped for one minute and sometimes it remained standing in some lonely place for a whole day. This, of course, we never knew in advance. On the fourth day, I left the car and went, as if guided by a divining rod, to a nearby forest, and there I found…a potato field, which I dug up with my bare hands. It was a gold mine. Sixty-four potatoes I stashed in my pockets. I returned to the train like a king. Ilse always had to pull me into the car, since I was too weak to get up there by myself."

Trains not on war-related trips were frequently forced to wait on sidings for military transports to pass. One fortuitous stop had put the Hesses' train near a farmer's field. Karl's determination to provide for his family brought them life-saving food they desperately needed. In a whisper, Karl told Ilse and the twins about his treasure.

Discovering the potatoes was a critical first step in staving off starvation, but the potatoes were far from an edible meal. Cooking the potatoes to make them digestible—and protecting their prize from some forty other starving people in the same cramped space—proved equally daunting.

Karl was not alone in his quest for food. All Bergen-Belsen prisoners on the train were teetering on the knife-edge of starvation, and others, too, scavenged during stops. Some had found the potato field. Some gathered nettles and made dirty soup they later realized did little to assuage their hunger, but instead increased their stomach pain and diarrhea. Some had saved bread or other bits of food from the camp in their pockets. One had a secret metal container from which he pulled scraps of food, even a piece of chocolate.

Francine Christophe would describe her fellow prisoners as if they had become wild animals. She admitted, "We have become wolves." Prisoners fought for every drop of gritty gruel.

To celebrate their good fortune, the Hess family decided that each of them should eat six potatoes as soon as they could prepare them. Because eating raw potatoes could cause stomach cramps, their next challenge was to make a fire and collect water. A few people on their transport had means of starting fires and had begun cooking their own precious bits of food. The Hesses gathered twigs and dry leaves, lit those flammable bundles from others' fires, and carefully carried their tiny torches back toward their own car, helping others to start fires as they went. Placing small stones around smoldering bits of wood, they turned to the next arduous chore—water. Steven told me, "Marion and I would walk up to the huffing engine and carefully hold out cups to catch hot water from the steam engine pistons."

Marion added, "We actually ate leaves from trees. By that time, we weren't particular."

Karl remembered how they kept the cooking fires going:

> Ilse would lie flat on the ground and fan the fire by puffing for hours, while I had to keep searching [as far as eighty yards from the train] for more and more new pieces of wood, and breaking them. Later on, we were the fortunate owners of two bricks on which the bowl stood more firmly. How often, during cooking, a shrill whistle would sound—a sound that the train was going on! Then, we first threw the glowing hot, irreplaceable bricks into the car. Afterwards, we jumped, with the children and the boiling water, onto the train that, in most cases, was already moving. [At times] the train had hardly stopped when we "installed" our "kitchen" in front of the car. This way our potato cooking some-times took one hour, sometimes [due to the unpredict-able length of the stops] more than one or two days.

They ate the potatoes and made soup from whatever they could find—and lost more weight. The train moved ahead fifteen miles, then stopped at Lauenburg, a Hamburg suburb on the Elbe River. Another formerly scenic small town, once dotted with red-roofed buildings, narrow cobbled streets, and a castle—now ravaged by Allied bombing. Far beyond the horizon, over three hundred miles to the east, lay Stutthof concentration camp, its subcamps sprawled out around it.

Stutthof's main camp had held Ilse's mother, though Ilse did not then know where her mother had been or how she had fared during the six years since the war began. The separation had tormented Ilse. By the time the Hesses' train stopped in Lauenburg, Ilse's mother, Fanny Wallheimer Hirschberg, had been dead for perhaps two years. She died of typhus in Stutthof, at age fifty-one; she had carried a picture of the twins in her pocket until the end. Stutthof prisoners still alive in April 1945 would suffer a brutal final month before liberation; the SS forced many of the prisoners to wade into the cold Baltic Sea and machine-gunned them to death.

Ilse had contracted the same disease that killed her mother, and her own health was deteriorating. Both Karl and Ilse hung on to remnants of their former strength, sustained by love for their family. As Karl described their dire circumstances in his memoir, "Ilse had a very high fever. Most of the time, she, herself, was not aware of it, but her eyes were so glazed that there was no need for a thermometer." She was suffering this life-threatening illness in impossible conditions: "The nights were horrible. The doors were locked and the people simply could not contain their natural needs. A severely ill man in our car evacuated into his eating bowl, and in the darkness he wandered around with his full bowl, trying to reach the hatch [a ceiling-high air vent] of the car. The women screamed because he kept stepping on sombebody all the time. Nobody dared remove his shoes, since one never knew what kind of unpleasant surprise the night might bring.... Stefan and Marion could have been an example for the whole car. They were little heroes. Never a word of complaint. No tears. They suffered quietly through their sleepless nights."

■   ■   ■

Across Germany in spring 1945, the American, Soviet, and British troops liberating the camps were appalled that the German people—that any people—were capable of perpetrating such horrors. On April 8, two days before the Hesses boarded the train, American military radio operators sent a secret radio message to the resistance at Buchenwald concentration camp, some 160 miles south of Bergen-Belsen: "KZ BU [concentration camp Buchenwald]. Hold out. Rushing to your aid. Staff of the Third Army." Three days later American troops entered Buchenwald.

In Bergen-Belsen, prisoners observed with rising concern that the SS were disappearing. New fears seized the barracks. Perhaps their entire camp was slated for liquidation. German cruelty had taken many forms over the two years of its existence, and the inmates suspected the worst possible final days.

As American troops fought their way toward the camp that the Hesses had left behind, Commandant Kramer's last order created an episode so bizarre and disturbing that even now, with the benefit of hindsight, it seems a break with reality. He forced prisoners still able to walk to drag the naked corpses from the heaps throughout the entire camp over the bumpy, unpaved central road to mass graves dug in the Prisoners' camp section of Bergen-Belsen. Over four days, two thousand prisoners tied braided cellophane rope or leather straps from cut-up shoes to the limbs of the corpses, or simply clutched the lifeless arms and legs, and in a long procession, dragged bodies to the pit they had dug—and still left thousands of the dead unburied. As the gruesome task continued, at Kramer's command, other prisoners pulled out musical instruments they had brought in their luggage and played dance music—a "distraction," Kramer explained, from the sights, foul smell, and terrible misery of their task.

■ ■ ■

On April 12, the Hesses' second day on the train, survivors in the camp, ill and exhausted, would have seen an astonishing sight. The British army had, by chance, discovered Bergen-Belsen, a sight horrifying even to seasoned soldiers as the emaciated, diseased, ghoulish-looking prisoners stared at the soldiers through the wire fences.

As British and Wehrmacht forces battled nearby, through a long night of meetings on April 12 and into the early hours of April 13, British lieutenant colonel Richard Taylor-Balfour and the Wehrmacht commander negotiated a local cease-fire. They agreed also, with Himmler's approval, that the handover of Bergen-Belsen would take place formally on April 15. Under the agreement, both sides agreed to delay the immediate release of some sixty thousand desperate or dying Bergen-Belsen prisoners in order to prevent the spread of their diseases into the world outside the camp. British soldiers posted warning signs around Belsen's perimeter: "Danger! Typhus."

The agreement—hastily wrought in the midst of an active war zone by soldiers, not skilled negotiators or political leaders—also permitted the majority of SS camp personnel to withdraw without punishment. British military authorities, urgently engaged in the nearby battles, did not pursue those who fled before liberation. Before departing, the SS burned all of their files, making the specific crimes of those who had served there—some 425 men and 45 women—impossible to track.

The truce agreement also mandated that 75 SS personnel remain behind with Kramer to ensure a smooth handover of authority in the camp. A number of Hungarian soldiers who had fought alongside the Wehrmacht joined the 75 SS guards—50 men and 25 women—who volunteered to assist Kramer.

As part of agreement, the British required Kramer to accompany British intelligence officer Captain Derrick Sington and several noncommissioned officers (NCOs) on a camp tour. In his book *The End of the Holocaust: The Liberation of the Camps*, Jon Bridgman relates Sington's account: Kramer balked: "They are calm at present," he said. "It would be unwise to risk a tumult." No one who had not seen a German concentration camp could have understood what the commandant meant by "calm" and "tumult." The British could not imagine the human powder keg inside the gates. They commanded Kramer to accompany the tour.

On April 15, looking determined and formal in a fresh uniform, his revolver at his side, Kramer waited at the camp gate for the British. Sington arrived in an open jeep at the head of a column of Sherman tanks. Kramer stood on the truck's running board as a guide while the British drove through Bergen-Belsen's gates. Sington's report reveals his stunned astonishment at the conditions and at Kramer's impermeable emotional and moral defenses: "I had tried to visualize the interior of the concentration camp, but I had not imagined it like this. Nor had I imagined the strange simian throng, who crowded to the barbed wire fences.... We had experienced gratitude and welcome in France, Belgium and Holland.... But the half-credulous cheers of these almost lost men, of these clowns...who had once been Polish officers, land-workers in the Ukraine, Budapest doctors, and students in France, impelled a stronger emotion, and I had to fight back my tears."

Sington's first chilling perceptions reflected stereotypes Nazis had promoted about Jews: "Strange." "Simian." "Clowns." The Germans had successfully reduced their Jewish victims to the appearance of subhuman beings—like nothing Sington had seen in war or peace. But unlike the Nazis, Sington recognized the prisoners as very real brutalized human beings. He dismounted from his vehicle and shook hands with one, a former Dutch journalist, who had smiled a greeting. He climbed back into the truck again, barely able to maintain military demeanor and hold back his tears. The British soldiers rolled along the camp's central street in procession, agog at the horrific state of the prisoners. As Joseph Bellinger would describe in "The Lethal Liberation of Bergen-Belsen," a "bluish mist had formed and was hovering above the ground and between the buildings." There was also an overpowering stench of sewage and rot. Kramer responded easily and promptly to Sington's questions about numbers, informing him that some forty thousand prisoners were currently held in the camp, and another fifteen thousand prisoners, "habitual criminals, felons, and homosexuals," were currently imprisoned in the overflow camp at the nearby Wehrmacht base. In reality, those more recently arrived overflow prisoners also included Jews and others transferred from the horrific Dora labor camp.

Sington spoke through a loudspeaker system mounted on his jeep that roared out the news—Bergen-Belsen is liberated. The British had taken charge, but prisoners were not yet permitted to leave the camp because of the danger of spreading typhus.

"Now the tumult is beginning," Kramer warned Sington.

Shouting, cheering crowds of the diseased and emaciated prisoners ran towards them, surrounding the British vehicles, yelling at them, "You must deliver us. It is FRIGHTFUL, this camp." "God Save the King." Sington had expected a reception resembling Britain's liberation of Belgium. There joyous citizens had thrown flowers and fresh fruit into the soldiers' trucks. In Bergen-Belsen, the prisoners, possessing no such delights, showered Sington with twigs and leaves. Kramer flicked the debris off his immaculate uniform, as Bellinger notes.

Sington would remember, "Suddenly a German soldier began firing his rifle into the air" to calm the chaos, then lowered it, "firing only just over the heads of the prisoners." Sington leapt from the truck, pulled his revolver, and commanded the soldier to stop shooting. Suddenly a dozen Kapos darted into the fray, attempting to keep order, as was their mandate. They beat prisoners with heavy truncheons, striking with such force that the Kapos bent double with the effort. Sington watched in mounting horror: "Half-way across the road I saw a thin creature on his back trying to ward off blow after blow from a thick stick."

Even to the sympathetic British officer, an ill, starving Jew had become something horrible, a "creature," a Nazi stereotype of a lower race of beings. Sington would later understand that most of the prisoners were racing not toward him, but to the unguarded kitchen. Their most urgent need was food.

During a tour with Kramer of the Wehrmacht camp's enclosure for overflow prisoners, Sington witnessed a guard shoot a prisoner attempting to dig potatoes in that camp's field. Furious, Sington ordered Kramer to pick up the victim and carry him to the hospital. When Kramer stared, dumbfounded, Sington pulled his revolver and pointed it at the camp commandant. Until that moment, Kramer had comported himself as if he were a general, pompously and with an expectation of mutual respect handing his sword to his equal on the opposing side—not comprehending the revulsion that he and the German nation had engendered.

As Bellinger recounts, later Kramer led his British captors back to his office. He leaned back in his chair and slung a leg onto his desk, ready for conversation—oblivious that he was about to be shackled hand and foot and imprisoned in a slimy basement room that stank of fish. He, too, would soon be deported from Bergen-Belsen, his destination an Allied military prison in Lüneburg.

During the first two nights of Bergen-Belsen's liberation, riots tore through the camp. Prisoners who still retained some strength stormed the camp's kitchen and food storage shed. They may have been horrified as well as overjoyed to discover a food storage shed full of Red Cross packages that had been sent to the prisoners; some of the packets had been looted by the SS. The rampaging, defiant prisoners killed and roasted fifty pigs at an SS compound, but they did not discover the eight hundred tons of food stored nearby in the Wehrmacht camp. That same night, prisoners also bludgeoned seven Kapos to a bloody pulp.

The next day the camp quieted, and the British took stock of its eighty barracks and the some sixty thousand prisoners held in the main and Wehrmacht camps. They estimated that thirteen thousand corpses littered the camp's grounds—but prisoners continued to die at an appalling rate. The total number of victims in Bergen-Belsen can only be estimated. Authoritative sources put the numbers near fifty thousand. The authorities compelled both female SS guards who had remained at the camp and local civilians to help put the shrunken, rotting, dead bodies into a mass grave. The British located a water pump and pumped water from the nearby stream to the camp, which had been without water for six days. Health experts would later question whether that untreated water contributed to the post-liberation death rate, though it may have also saved some lives. Occupation authorities established a medical center and a displaced persons camp near Bergen-Belsen. A month later, on May 21, to prevent the spread of disease, British soldiers burned Bergen-Belsen to the ground.

■   ■   ■

For prisoners in the dark cars on the Hesses' train, day and night merged into a dim fog. The clacking wheels, coughing and moaning of their fellow prisoners, and the booming, shrieking sounds of war around them merged into what seemed an endless journey as the train changed directions, stopped, and moved onward again toward an unknown destination. Then, as Karl would write in his memoir, "Other horrors were lying in wait for us. Suddenly airplane formations appeared on the horizon—Americans!"

The prisoners had heard about mistaken Allied attacks on prisoner transports, as British and American planes crisscrossed Central and Northern Germany. With total disdain for the Jews' survival, Germans had made no effort to paint Red Cross symbols on trains carrying prisoners. And so, Karl explained, American planes "attacked our train, assuming it to be a troop transport. At roof level, they strafed all cars. I yelled to our people to lie flat on the floor, face down, hands folded in the nape of the neck. Despite the short duration of the attack, it seemed endless. The planes left and I told everybody to rise. Stefan remained lying down. My heart stopped; I thought he had been hit, but one second later, he, too, got up. That one second seemed to me like hours, even today."

As Steven would tell me, "I vividly remember machine gun bullets coming through the arched train car roof and letting in sunbeams in which the dust swirled. My father was on top of me. Our mother on Marion. I was crying because we were both bones and ribs. It hurt. Of course, we had no idea what was happening. One day the dust-filled dark car suddenly had shafts of sunlight coming through the roof. What did I know about machine guns and airplanes? But I well remember sunlight streaking through the holes and dust swirling in beams of light. I remember the sunbeams. I remember my father's ninety pounds against my ribs."

The planes returned and attacked again. Twenty-five hundred terrified prisoners leapt from the train in a desperate bid for safety. Six hundred others were too ill to get out of the cars. Karl described how terrified the twins were: "Marion was crying and shaking with terror. Stefan was pale as wax but very calm. With both children, we ran cross-country, further and further, no matter where to. Through a backyard we reached a small farmhouse. The children could not even eat the bread the owners gave them and hid this wealth under their filthy coats. As if by a miracle, this attack had not caused any casualties. The following train, however, also from Bergen-Belsen lost forty-five persons."

The realities of their precarious situation extinguished any thought of escape, even as the family stood in a friendly farmhouse

CHAPTER 15

In the Fog of War
APRIL 15, 1945–APRIL 23, 1945

As the Allies made hard-won advances throughout Europe and Americans clung to encouraging war reports, Karl's parents and sister, who had fled to the United States in 1937 and settled in Manhattan, received terrible news. HIAS (Hebrew Immigrant Aid Society), a Jewish refugee organization, informed them that Karl had been killed. After his beating in Bergen-Belsen, the SS probably believed they had finished him off and listed him as dead. But Karl, Ilse, and the twins were still alive and still fighting desperately to survive as their train lurched away from Bergen-Belsen, the engineer seeking a route to Theresienstadt that remained safe from the constantly changing active battle zones.

Karl and Ilse were also operating in ignorance of the facts: traveling on that train, they did not know that Bergen-Belsen had been liberated on April 15. Sealed off from the world in the dank rail cars, the Sternlager Jews from Bergen-Belsen continued to travel north—some ten miles through low rolling hills and verdant valleys from Lauenburg to Büchen. In their only possible act of rebellion on that SS-guarded transport, the prisoners ripped off their despised yellow stars.

After nearly a week into the journey, the train had progressed only about 160 miles, mostly north, in the opposite direction from their intended destination. At Büchen, their train finally turned south on the Berlin rail line and then passed through Hagenow Land rail junction. That nearby small town had once been home to a century-old synagogue, but the numbers of Jews had dwindled over time, and when the Hesses' train rumbled past, the few Hagenow Jews who still had lived there before the Nazis came to power had already been deported and murdered.

From Hagenow, the train continued south and made a brief stop, perhaps for fuel, at Ludwigslust, named for a magnificent palace in the town. In stark contrast to that elegant showplace, the town was also the site of Wöbbelin concentration camp, created in February that year to hold prisoners evacuated from other camps. The Allies had designated Ludwigslust as one point along a two-hundred-mile north-south line where Allied militaries advancing from east and west would make contact. On the day that the Hesses' train passed, the shrinking corridor between the armies was about seventy miles.

On the sixth day of their journey, April 16, the train finally stopped at Wittenberge, a factory town and shipping hub at the confluence of two rivers. Its railway workshop, Singer Sewing Machine factory, and chemical factories had labored in service to the Nazis' ten years of war. Wittenberge, too, held a concentration camp. The train remained standing at that station, its progress impeded by heavy aerial fighting. Then it finally pulled out of Wittenberge, the Jews anxiously watching fires burning and the ruins of small towns they passed. Continuing air attacks in the skies above them kept the train moving south, rumbling past the small town of Glöwen and then stopping at Nauen, which held Germany's high-power radio transmitters, whose frequencies could penetrate seawater and connect with submarines without their needing to surface. Also from these towers, Berlin radio beamed its version of war news, in English, to most of the world, circumventing the censorship of Britain's cable network. The Allies placed high value on these reports and had not targeted the facility during the massive Berlin bombing campaign.

Karl described the prisoners' desperate search for food: "The journey continued in the direction of Berlin. On the way, we stopped at a small station [likely in Nauen]. On the opposite tracks stood a German armored train of the anti-aircraft defense. Driven by unbearable hunger, our people dashed for the field kitchen attached to the train, begging for some food. No success!"

Watching the melee unfold, Karl and Ilse saw the guards beat back the throngs of starving Jews. Karl exited the train to speak with a railroad worker, who told him that the Americans were only seven miles behind. "I crawled underneath the train to the opposite side where nobody was standing," Karl recalled. "The cook, diverted by the begging masses, did not see me. I stole a can of 'K' rations, about two pounds in weight, contents unknown. Back to our train. Secretly we opened the can—meat. Ilse, happy and proud of her thief, and the enthusiastic children kept staring at the loot. This was a find that today could not be compared to even a shipload of foodstuff. We felt like eating everything right away. Reason, however, and many years of experience warned us, and we rationed it carefully."

The passengers reboarded. Doors slammed shut and the train moved on, stopping next at Spandau, on the northern edge of Berlin. If the streets of this small town could have told stories, perhaps the Jews would not have wanted the train doors opened at all. Center of the German armaments industry, the town also held fearsome Spandau Prison, site of Gestapo torture. The Jewish community of Spandau, present since the fourteenth century, had been deported and murdered, the synagogue destroyed. At this stop, the prisoners witnessed a nearby Allied bombing. Their own numbers had continued to dwindle day by day, mile by mile, as more of the "privileged" Jews died and the survivors coped with the distressing reality of the grisly, upsetting corpses all around them. There was no open ground, and no peaceful setting to dispose of the dead.

The train departed Spandau and headed deeper into Berlin. Surely, I thought, the Jews onboard must have held their breath as they went around the German capital. According to Karl's memoir, when they stopped at Lichterfelde, a freight station toward the southern edge of Berlin, he once again left the train in search of food:

> As was my habit, I went looking for loot, an old filthy pillow cover under my jacket and an eating bowl in my pocket. After having crossed many tracks, I got to a German food commissary. We had torn off our Jewish stars a few days before and the SS, feeling slowly but surely that their days were numbered, ignored us.

"Do you have anything to eat?!" I asked the Red Cross nurse on night duty.

"Who are you?"

"I am a refugee."

"The kitchen is not working yet, we only start at seven o'clock."

"Don't you have anything at all to eat?"

"Well, some cold macaroni with ham, but you can't eat it like this; it has to be heated up first."

You can imagine how enthusiastically I accepted even the cold food. After filling my belly so that the macaroni almost came out of my nose, I filled my bowl, too, in order to bring it to Ilse and the children....

Radiant with happiness about the wonderful meal, I ran back to the train—which had left.

Karl stood motionless at the train station in Lichterfelde for an hour, for once having no idea what he should do.

■   ■   ■

Unknown to the Hesses and the other Bergen-Belsen prisoners in the train—and to the people of Berlin enduring constant bombing—news about the Germans' concentration camps was spreading like a wildfire across Western nations. As the Allied military liberated camps, they saw the reality of what a handful of Western political leaders, including Churchill and Roosevelt, and to some extent Senator Harry S. Truman, had known for at least three years. Speaking at the April 1943 "United Rally to Demand

Rescue of Doomed Jews," Truman had called Hitler "mad" and Mussolini "degenerate." He had gone on to tell the crowd what the world was just beginning to grasp: "The Jews...are being herded like animals into the Ghettos, concentration camps, and the wastelands of Europe. The men, the women, and the children of this honored people are being starved, yes! actually murdered...."

On April 12, 1945, three days before Bergen-Belsen was liberated, U.S. generals Dwight Eisenhower, Omar Bradley, and George Patton toured the liberated Ohrdruf concentration camp in Germany. Eisenhower immediately cabled the Admiral William Leahy, head of the Joint Chiefs of Staff in Washington. Following that experience, stunned by the brutality, Eisenhower immediately ordered all American nearby units not engaged in active fronts to be sent to Ohrdruf. He urged members of Congress and journalists to view liberated camps and document the horror. Later, Eisenhower would describe his experience in his war memoir *Crusade in Europe*:

> I have never at any other time experienced an equal sense of shock.
>
> I visited every nook and cranny of the camp because I felt it my duty to be in a position from then on to testify at first hand about these things.... [A]s soon as I returned to Patton's headquarters that evening I sent communications to both Washington and London, urging the two governments to send instantly to Germany a random group of newspaper editors and representative groups from national legislatures. I felt that the evidence should be immediately

placed before the American and British publics in a fashion that would leave no room for cynical doubt.

The news media was busy that day. April 12 was also the day that President Roosevelt died. Even so, the media leapt at the chance to view the sites. Congress proposed an official American agency to investigate and record war crimes. In the United States, editorials, political cartoons, and news stories decried the German nation. On April 23, a day that would be of great significance to the Jews on the Lost Train, the *New York Times* reported,

> Every German will view the pictures of inhumanities practiced on the prisoners at the Buchenwald, Belsen, and other Nazi torture camps. Editorials from newspapers throughout the world showing the revulsion with which the Germans are viewed because of the treatment of prisoners will be "required reading" for all citizens of conquered Germany.
>
> Such a plan was being perfected tonight by information services of Britain and the United States in cooperation with Allied Supreme Headquarters.
>
> These services are assembling a pictorial layout of scenes at both Buchenwald and Belsen together with pictures of men and women wardens captured at the camps. The photographs will be reproduced on large boards for display in every community in conquered Germany....
>
> ...German people must be made to assume responsibility for acts of their Government....

One of the most notorious German criminals, Josef Kramer, commandant of the Belsen camp, has been removed....

"We are told," Eisenhower said in an interview, "that the American soldier does not know what he is fighting for. Now, at least, he will know what he is fighting against." Liberation photos were so disturbing that editors of *Illustrated London News* placed photographs of atrocities at Bergen-Belsen, Buchenwald, Nordhausen, and Langenstein in a detachable four-page supplement "intended for our adult readers only."

■   ■   ■

Karl, alone by the tracks, was near despair: "As if I had been hit over the head, I stared at the lonely tracks, blaming myself. For years, I had never been separated from my family, and now I should lose them like this!...But the train was gone."

Finally, Karl left the freight station. Fueled by his driving hunger, he hailed a bus heading into Berlin, the crosshairs of Soviet shelling and bombing attacks. The driver allowed him to ride without paying. He described the scene: "Imagine this—a Jew, a bum, in rags, filthy, without a single cent, without identification papers, in Berlin—a few days before the city was stormed by the Russians. A gigantic heap of rubble. Excited masses of people. Like a beggar I stood in front of an inn."

A passerby spoke to Karl. Switching from Dutch to perfect German, Karl told the man that he was hungry. The man then took him inside and ordered food and beer for him. "Slowly the terrible shock that I had endured with the leaving of the train lessened," Karl remembered.

Karl was amazed by his German benefactor, the second stranger who had offered him urgently needed help. Kindness. Generosity. Long missing from his life except from his family. The food and drink gave Karl some relief from the constant pain of starvation. But the human warmth may have been as much balm as the bus ride and the macaroni. "I returned to the freight station, Lichterfelde, like a criminal who is driven again and again to return to the scene of his crime," Karl recalled. "I did not trust my eyes; there was a long freight train filled with Jews that was en route from Bergen-Belsen also to the east. Onto the train I went, fervently hoping to once more reach my wife and children. The train kept rolling for hours."

This was the second of the three trains that had left Bergen-Belsen carrying Jews toward Theresienstadt. The first had gone through Magdeburg, near the village of Farsleben, where, on April 13, it was liberated by American troops. The "Lost Train," the third Bergen-Belsen train, was the Hesses' train, which had roared away from Berlin's Lichterfelde station carrying Ilse and the twins far from Karl. But with incredible luck and his typical determination, Karl had anticipated that train's direction and found the second train, carrying Hungarian Jews from the camp. He still believed the fiendish SS rumor that the three trains were headed to "the East"—to the gas chambers. Yet Karl, who had fought for five years to keep his family safe and together, would keep fighting to share whatever fate held for them. Without hesitation, he boarded the "Hungarian Train."

■   ■   ■

The German war effort was imploding, but in many parts of the country the Wehrmacht continued to fight fiercely. Massed German artillery wiped out a U.S. Ninth Army bridgehead across the Elbe River near Magdeburg. Stiffening German resistance slowed the Western Allies' advance towards Berlin, but their progress was relentless, impossible to stop. They whittled down the area near Berlin still in German hands. Berlin radio reported that Western Allied armies were on the point of making contact with the Soviets. The U.S. Third Army and the Red Army threatened Cottbus, a German city of about seventy thousand a few miles east of the Hesses' two trains. Allied bombs had leveled a factory there, where forced labor assembled German aircraft. To the west, the U.S. First Army seized Leipzig with a wild tank charge through the city center.

On the Western Front, during the first two weeks of April, Allies took more than a half-million Germans prisoners, including the Nazis' head of U.S. propaganda. In France, heavy naval and air bombardment struck a German pocket in Bordeaux; Polish troops of the British Eighth Army battled their way into the town. In the Netherlands, the Allies fought from the north and south, but made slow progress.

■   ■   ■

Traveling at high speed at night, the Lost Train halted some fifty miles later in a forest near Lübben as engineers considered their options for avoiding the Soviet front coming from the east and Americans moving in from the west. From the forest, the train continued its journey south about ten more miles and arrived at Lübbenau. An air raid greeted their arrival, and yet a Lübbenau pickle factory managed to supply the Lost Train with pickles and pickled cabbage.

Karl mentions in his memoir passing through a "small town," very likely Lübbenau. Standing watch at the train's door, which was somehow still open, Karl spied Ilse! "Finally at four thirty in the afternoon, [my train] passed, at high speed, through a small town—and I just caught a glimpse of Ilse, waving to me from her train that was standing still. But my train rolled on without pity. Twenty, thirty, forty, fifty kilometers."

As Steven explained to me, "Our father missed our train in Berlin while looking for food. Through the luckiest of luck, he managed to get on the Hungarian train and then back to us. The two trains did pass each other a few times, so they were not completely separate."

In its unpredictable progress through war's chaos, the trains had encountered one life-threatening obstacle after another. Downed bridges. Bombs that sometimes missed the train by less than a mile. Strafing attacks that did not miss. Disease-bearing lice that the twins had learned to fear. As the train rolled on, mile after mile through the pounding war zone, nothing felt real except the deadly, painful hunger and thirst, the shrieking train whistle, grumbling wheels bearing them forward, and the trail of bodies left behind.

Karl was exhausted; he had been awake the entire previous night. His train had raced about ninety miles south from Berlin. He and Ilse would later speak of that day as a "miracle," as if events had been guided by providence. It was also a testimony to their love and unflagging efforts—worrying and hoping, hiding under a station, standing watch at the door—to find each other.

"Finally, at ten thirty in the evening," Karl would write, "we stopped in Senftenberg. I jumped out of the train, and glory of all glories, some time later Ilse's train also came in and we were once more reunited. To this day, Ilse claims, half-jokingly, she had known in those frightful hours that I would find my way back. I, however, cannot but feel this great happiness for just what it was, the very greatest miracle that ever happened to me." The Hungarian Train, which Karl had left, continued south and would reach Theresienstadt on April 20, via a route that was blocked to the Lost Train just a short time later.

"Since he was German," Steven explained to me, "he blended in with other Germans. He wasn't wearing a prison uniform, and by 1945, the Germans themselves were mostly bedraggled. He sneaked onto another train, then hid under the station, miraculously spotting the train that held our family."

Ilse remembered, "No one knew where we were going. This train kept rolling for ten days, day and night." The train pressed on from Senftenberg through a lovely countryside of lakes and forests they could not see, and arrived in the small town of Schipkau. At that moment in their journey, they thought about the rumor they had been told, that the family was headed for Theresienstadt's gas chambers. Karl and Ilse, talking through everything that they had been through and seen, no longer expected that fate—understanding that it was illogical at this point. While they didn't realize that Theresienstadt held no gas chambers, they knew that the Allies were winning the war. Their train would never reach the Czech border. Even so, they were weakening, and the Germans still held them prisoners.

Karl's frightening experience in Lichterfelde gave him pause, but it did not deter him from leaving the train again to find food for the family. "I had firmly decided never again to leave the train—but hunger kept driving me. I walked four kilometers until I reached a small village. The peasants were already putting all their belongings onto carriages to flee the ever-closer approaching Russians. I went to see the commander of the local Nazi office, realizing that he was the one who would have most of the provisions. 'Just take whatever you want.' I did not have to be told twice."

Karl stuffed his pockets, and then the commander also gave him a sack of potatoes weighing one hundred pounds. Gratefully, he turned back toward the train, dragging the treasured sack, which weighed more than he did. In his memoir, Karl described his dilemma:

> With a bleeding heart, I had to throw away one potato after another so there would be no more in the sack than I was able to carry with great effort, weak as I was. There were four kilometers ahead of me. Sparks were dancing in front of my eyes. Under the heavy load, my back was bent almost to the ground. Again and again, I had to part with a few potatoes, until a long "potato trail" showed in back of me. Stumbling over my own feet, I dragged myself meter by meter. The more potatoes I threw out of my sack, the heavier my load seemed to get. Exhausted, my knees buckled under me. I did not walk any more. I did not drag myself any more. I crawled. I crawled on all fours until a terrible thing happened to me.

It pained Karl to relinquish precious potatoes, one at a time. To him, each one represented the possibility that his family would survive. But the macaroni he'd eaten in Lichterfelde was about to take a toll. He had eaten so much that, suddenly, he suffered an attack of diarrhea: "I soiled myself, soiled myself like a newborn baby. At that moment, I stopped being human. I was disgusted with myself. Cold sweat covered my face and body, but I had to plunge ahead. The evening in Lichterfelde floated before my eyes like a ghost, and gave me strength to overcome those last hundred meters still ahead of me. The happiness of my loved ones when they saw the wealth of potatoes rewarded me a thousand times for all I had gone through."

Ilse surprised Karl by pulling a clean pair of underwear out of their pack. Karl made his way to a nearby forest and washed in a small brook. He bathed, standing in "mud up to his knees," then returned to the car, refreshed inside and out, though his legs were still coated in mud.

On his return, Karl learned from Ilse that the SS had ordered all prisoners who could still walk to get off the train and prepare to march—where, they didn't know. By that time, Karl, Ilse, and the twins had been through too much to experience real fear. Karl explained, "So we remained in the car calmly, a good example for those who had already taken their places in front of the train with their luggage. After a few minutes, nobody was 'in any condition to walk' any more, and it seemed that the SS was not in any condition to battle the Jews any longer. After a short sit down strike in the cars, we again started cooking on the tracks until the train started moving."

Where the SS intended to march the prisoners is unknown. They may have planned to shoot and murder them all. Or the prisoners might have been forced to join the thousands of others on death marches moving away from the front lines. Instead, fortune smiled on the Jews of the Lost Train that night. The bold decision not to obey this order—likely made from deep exhaustion rather than a surging spirit of rebellion—probably saved their lives. At least a third of prisoners on those marches died along the way.

Relentlessly, the train set off again, but turned north, the engineers flailing for direction. Large British air strikes had hit railway targets near the German-Czech border, making a border crossing to Theresienstadt treacherous and uncertain. There seemed no clear route either forward or back.

■　　■　　■

April 20 was Hitler's fifty-sixth birthday. Nuremberg fell that day. Fierce tank battles threatened Berlin's suburbs. Unrest and rioting were reported in many German cities. The Red Army and Western Allies had fought to within about thirty-five miles of making contact. Yet Hitler emerged briefly from his command bunker under the Reich Chancellery that day and awarded Iron Cross medals to a detachment of Hitler Youth who had seen battle, some as young as twelve.

After traveling just sixteen miles through flat, pastoral terrain, the train stopped at the small red-brick rail station at Finsterwalde. Then it made another turn, this time heading west, making eight miles to Doberlug-Kirchhain, two towns side by side, population about fifteen thousand. Luckily, the station's maintenance supervisor resided in its two-story brick building, ready to assist any train experiencing breakdowns. The train continued another twelve miles to Langennaundorf, a farming town that sometimes held more cattle than people. In better times the countryside might have felt like a bucolic paradise, but these times were far from peaceful. Which direction to turn? Allied planes roared overhead. The thunder of Soviet tanks and trucks pierced the countryside's former tranquility. Finally, the engineer was compelled to stop at a bombed bridge over the Black Elster River. Forced to admit defeat in the wandering quest, the engineer attempted to back out of his difficulties. Steven told me what he remembers about the situation: "The train encountered blown-up tracks and had to reverse or possibly repair, I'm not sure. My father was on top of me trying once again to protect me. Once, the train passed Tröbitz, a village in northeast Germany, and suddenly stopped at the Black Elster River with the discovery that the railroad crossing bridge had been destroyed. The train could proceed no further. There the train had to back up to Tröbitz, but for unknown reasons this could not be done. So a small 'shunter' locomotive was obtained from a nearby factory. However, shunters are used to pull a few cars around a factory rail connection, not to drag nearly fifty full-size cattle cars. For that reason, our train had to be uncoupled in two parts. The separate halves were shunted back to Tröbitz, which had just been occupied by the Russians."

The train became lost and then stuck in place in the middle of a forest. On April 23, in the early hours of the morning, rifle shots rang out near the train. Karl, still the car leader, took charge: "I asked my people to remain calm and not to leave the car under any circumstances. Very quietly I sneaked out of the car, crawled along underneath the car and ran along an embankment to see what was going on."

Ilse remembered,

Finally, after thirteen days, on the 23rd of April 1945, at five o'clock in the morning, the train stopped. It stopped for a little longer than it used to do the last ten days. My husband opened the [door]. . . . and looked out and it was daylight. He jumped out of the train and he saw a man standing in a kind of a, it looked to him, a small forest. He—normally he wouldn't have dared because the moment someone was leaving a train the SS guards would jump out and threaten to shoot. But no SS men jumped out. So, my husband walked toward this man, and he looked at him and he saw a Russian uniform. My husband put up his arms and said, 'Do you speak English?'"

Karl saw soldiers—Soviets, soldiers of the Sixth Cossack Division of Marshal Georgy Zhukov's army! He ran toward them, speaking English, French, and then, as a last resort, German. In fact, he might better have drawn on his early studies and tried Hebrew. As Karl wrote in his memoir, "A Russian lieutenant answered, 'I am a Yid, too.' I jumped up and down like [a wild man], fell around the Russian's neck, and he spontaneously reciprocated my burst of joy. Obviously, as a sign of his own great excitement, he pressed a filthy handkerchief into my hand that was filled with sugar. Like a madman, I ran to the train. I felt like an angel of peace, bringing this wonderful message of good luck to my fellow prisoners. All of the Jews tumbled out of the train like crazy."

"WE WERE FREE!"

CHAPTER 16

The Road Home
APRIL 23, 1945–JUNE 15, 1945

Karl wrote in his memoir, "Like a swarm of grasshoppers, the Jews flooded [off of the train] onto the road and fell upon the village of Tröbitz, a few hundred yards away.... Everything was stormed—bakeries, food stores, shoe stores, private houses. No cellar, no stable, no barn was spared. Like madmen, they all lay on the street and stuffed themselves with immense amounts of food, hoping to make up for all they had missed for years in just one hour. The cows were dragged out of the stables, goats and rabbits killed, chickens had their necks wrung right then and there."

In April 1945, most of Tröbitz's men and teenage boys were away fighting for Nazi Germany, some likely killed or taken prisoner in Germany's war for an Aryan empire. With a pre-war population of about seven hundred, the small rural village was now inhabited mostly by women, children, and the elderly, some of whom had taken refuge there after fleeing from the advancing Soviets. The Red Army had taken control of Tröbitz just hours before the train from Bergen-Belsen was blocked by the bombed bridge; Soviet vehicles, including tanks, occupied the streets. Nearby towns had hung white sheets in their windows and on their rooftops, announcing their surrender. Because the residents of Tröbitz had not surrendered, the Soviets occupied the almost deserted town.

The maybe six hundred remaining residents were vastly out-numbered by the Bergen-Belsen survivors, who deserted the train and rampaged through the town. The storm of skeletal Jews rav-aging their village that early dawn as fighting went on nearby must have been terrifying. And, when they learned more, the situation was probably even more confusing. Jews had never lived in Tröbitz. To the villagers, "Jew" was only a word—something they had heard the Nazis railing against for over a decade, a dangerous people, a threat to the German *Volk*. They probably knew nothing about the horrors of the camps.

Prepared for possible village resistance, Soviet soldiers helped the Jews to break open the doors of homes, barns, rabbit hutches, and chicken coops. One soldier took an egg from his pocket and handed it to a survivor, the mother of memoirist Francine Christophe.

Ilse explained, "I cannot even say that they were laughing or smiling or hurrays . . . from all the people who jumped out of the train. I think we just were all too weak, too worn out to enjoy the first few moments. And everyone only had one thought. Food! . . . Since I could not leave my children alone, my husband took a partner, a young Hungarian woman, and they went together to hunt for food for us. . . . It was very difficult . . . my husband still was extremely weak, my children hardly could walk, and I was wracked with about 102 temperature."

Karl was concerned about Ilse's fever, but she had brushed off his worries, as if typhus were a minor annoyance. She may have repeated the words she had spoken, whispered, or thought so often in the camp, "*Wenn schon, denn schon.*" The family knew that she was suffering, understood that she would never give up. She chose to remain on the train, keeping the twins safely out of harm's way and avoiding the mad race to town.

Gradually, the prisoners returned, laden with all the food they could carry. Karl dragged a dog cart, typically used for chores, or for children's entertainment: "I, too, arrived…with all the splendors we had dreamed of in our hunger fantasies, back at our car. Ilse…was again, by force of habit, lying on her stomach in front of the car, puffing into a fire to bring potatoes to a boil."

The reality of freedom had not fully registered with the Bergen-Belsen survivors. The train that had brought them to this place was no longer their jail or home base. The SS guards were themselves prisoners of the Soviets. Stefan quietly reported to Karl, "Pappi, we don't have to be afraid that they would catch us. I watched the Russians take away our SS guards."

As Karl explained in his memoir, "Despite the fact that we were free, nobody believed that it really was so. The imprisonment of many years had completely crippled the people's minds. Thus, all of us, loaded down with our loot went back to the empty train, never realizing that we had no more business there at all."

While Karl was in Tröbitz, two Soviet soldiers had been watching Ilse lie on her stomach and blow into the small fire. They used hand signals to make her realize she did not need to do that anymore. The soldiers had been through every building in the town, scouring for possible resistance. They explained that this farming village held enough food for everyone.

Marion and Stefan greeted their new situation with the innocence and spontaneity of childhood. These "model" children, who for two weeks on the train had remained silent and unobtrusive, whooped with joy upon spying Karl's wagon, then "hopped, danced, and jumped" with delight, ready to eat. Karl's eyes filled with tears at their burst of childish energy. They announced to him that their mother "had promised by way of celebration that they would be allowed to eat the potatoes without the peel" that day, but their eyes were on the treasures their father had brought.

Having traveled this far in the story along with the Hesses, I, as chronicler of their wretched odyssey, couldn't help but exult in their life-saving discovery of food in that small farming community. And I thought, too, about the blessing I've had in my own life, never to have felt the stab of true hunger, much less starvation.

Together the four Hesses unloaded the wagon into a corner of the car, already piled so densely with others' scavenged food there was hardly room for more. Out from the wagon came "a beautifully assorted load, things to put on bread in all variations from marmalade and cheese to pickled liverwurst, jars of vegetables, meat, poultry and fruit, and enormous quantities of each, bags of sugar, flour, oatmeal and barley, a few pounds of butter and fat and the most wonderful spices." Some of the Jews in the car had already eaten too much, too quickly, and were "doubled up with painful cramps." As Steven told me, Karl and Ilse were more prudent: "Our parents were very careful about limiting food intake at first, for them and for us. Some starved survivors ate voraciously, got sick, and died."

During those times of severe rationing, homes in large German cities would not have held such a wealth of food. The train's starving passengers could not have been luckier than to have been liberated in a farming region whose residents—men, women, and children—produced food, planted their own gardens, butchered their cattle and pigs, made their own cheese, and knew how to live off the land. Yet, in the absence of the men at war, it is likely that the region's farmers were helped in those years by forced labor from one of Germany's hundreds of concentration camps.

■ ■ ■

For the first time in five years, the Hesses now had some control over their lives, and for the first time in five years, they felt able to share with others. They offered some of their loot to a woman in their car whose mental state had become unstable; she had returned from the town with nothing but thermometers, toothbrushes, clothes hangers, and scrub brushes.

The prisoner mentality that had at first held them all in the hated car brought them back to the train to eat. But, as they began what Karl gratefully termed a "royal repast," Ilse suddenly grabbed Karl's shoulder and whispered, "What on earth are we still doing here! Come on, let us carry the stuff back to the car and go to the village."

Mortal danger had threatened the family for so long that they continued to speak in mute gestures and soft tones, as if any overheard word could cost a life. Whispering was another ingrained habit that would take time to unlearn.

The family finished their meal, reloaded the cart, and turned toward the village. When Karl first returned with the loaded wagon, it had seemed huge, barely manageable even with help from his Hungarian partner. After eating a real meal and feeling the crushing weight of imprisonment begin to lift, they loaded the rest of the food into the cart that then seemed "little," though it was still difficult for the weak family to manage. Karl remembered, "Like two little horses, Marion and Stefan pulled on the shaft of the wagon and Ilse and I had to make quite an effort to lift our heavy load across the tracks."

Many of the former prisoners on the train had already come to the same realization about leaving the train and occupied a number of Tröbitz's houses. Karl recalled, "After a short search, we found a tiny little house at the end of the village. It was a so-called 'retirement house' where the old peasants live while the younger generation moves into the 'main building.' 'Our house' seemed to be unoccupied and locked."

Karl did not know what he might encounter when he pounded on the door of the front house. Though overrun, Tröbitz was enemy territory. When a woman answered, he demanded that she give them the keys to the small back apartment. Intimidated, she handed over the keys "with lightning speed." Relieved, the Hesses explored the cottage's "large kitchen and two small rooms," "very plain and simply furnished. Two big beds, covered with white linen." A sofa. The little house looked like heaven.

Some of the evicted Germans moved to nearby villages to stay with friends. Others lived in barns or in cellars below the occupying Bergen-Belsen survivors. Steven told me, *"The weather was beautiful and we discovered food, real beds, toilet paper, soap, warm water—after a year and a half without these things. And, we were ALIVE!"*

■   ■   ■

At first, the Hesses were so filthy they hardly dared to touch anything. Behind the house, Karl discovered a large pile of wood and coal briquettes. The woman who owned the house helped them to light the stove, and the family's washing operation began. They filled every container they could find with water and heated it on the stove. As Steven would remember, "The very first thing that my mother did, though she was the sickest of us all, was to scrub us as we stood in a large laundry tub. She would have been grateful for sandpaper."

Karl wrote, "Ilse and I, too, could not do enough to get rid of all the dirt, inside and out, in this manner." "Years of longing for warm water make me smell and savor the warm water to this day."

A knock on the door interrupted their cleansing. A Soviet entered and told Karl he was suspected of being a "hidden" German. He was under arrest. Ilse explained, "I couldn't imagine what the reason was. They had watched my husband, and since—because of his blond hair and his perfect German, they thought he would be a German Gentile hiding among the Jews who were liberated from a concentration camp and they wanted to arrest him. It took some time to convince them that he was Jewish."

With frantic hand signs and garbled language, the Hesses persuaded the soldier that they were Belsen survivors, but Karl and Ilse were shaken. The incident reminded them how precarious this new refuge actually was. They were no longer prisoners, but neither were they free. Soviet soldiers now controlled their lives.

After that scare, the family turned to the next step in recovering from their ordeals and prepared their second feast of that day. Again, out from the cart came prepared meats, canned fruit, bread, and jam. They compared it to dining in the finest restaurant. Their bellies full, the long day came to an end. They were more than ready to sleep in a bed for the first time in years. Ilse had slept with the twins in Bergen-Belsen and Westerbork, and she could not bear for them to sleep at any distance. Because of her illness, the children took turns sleeping at the foot of her bed, with the other twin on the sofa and Karl on the second large, soft bed.

Steven told me, "I do remember what a weird feeling it was to sleep in a bed."

And Marion remembers that "it was white, and I said, 'I don't want to sleep in anything that looks like that.' It was so unusual."

■   ■   ■

Not all of the prisoners were as fortunate as those who had leapt from the train and rushed to Tröbitz. Around eight hundred of them lacked the strength even to seek food and shelter. Many of those invalids would die in the coming days, and some infected survivors who had moved into the town grew sicker and died. The Hesses lost close friends who had settled in the house next to theirs.

Death in Tröbitz was not the same numbing mass experience the Jews had endured in the Sternlager. Many of the survivors had forged close friendships during their transport, in Bergen-Belsen, and in some instance, in Amsterdam. Not able to share food before or during their journey, they had shared what they could, even if it was only the means of starting cooking fires or words of comfort.

Karl had felt personally responsible for those in his car, advising them how to protect themselves during attacks, taking on himself the hazards of patrolling outside.

Soviet soldiers ordered the remaining Tröbitz residents to help the survivors prepare a Jewish cemetery near the town's graveyard. Every day, a funeral procession moved through Tröbitz's main street with the most recent victims. Without access to motorized vehicles, the survivors pulled their dead in sad caravans of ten to twelve dog carts to a mass grave; hundreds of those who had lived through the worst of the camp had come achingly close to escape—only to die in Tröbitz. Written on the marker for the mass grave are the words "Here lie six hundred and seventy-five Jews from the concentration camp, Bergen-Belsen. The light of freedom came too late for them. They died on the threshold of their homeland."

Neither had the survivors forgotten the many corpses they had thrown or lifted from the train car. The train had held Jews of widely varying ages, from infants to men and women over seventy. Not knowing the names or ages of the dead, they remembered the locations and said prayers for them also. According to Karl, "We mourned one hundred and ninety-five dead on this trip of thirteen days."

Some of the townsfolk watched the funerals and some, too, held funerals for their own friends and family members. Out of fear of the Red Army, nineteen Tröbitz residents had died by suicide. A few villagers had volunteered to help nurse the Jews in the makeshift Soviet sickbay, and some of those volunteers had died. The Jews' invasion of their village was a disaster to the residents. About nineteen Tröbitz residents, including the mayor, died of infectious diseases, mainly typhus.

Karl continued to worry about Ilse, her fever stubbornly and dangerously hovering at 102–103 degrees. He urged her to stay quarantined from the other families and reminded her and the twins, "One single louse was enough to tear our family apart."

■   ■   ■

As the family's urgent necessity for washing diminished, their days revolved around food and recovery. Their first meals, eaten with restraint, soon gave way to feasts that satisfied their overwhelming hunger. As Karl would write, "At half past seven o'clock we sat at the breakfast table heaped with the most marvelous things. It meant nothing to Stefan to eat ten to twelve crafty sandwiches plus two eggs. As for me, I can say—and this is to be taken literally, that during the time in Tröbitz I ate as much in one day as I would normally eat in one week. Every day we baked huge cakes and torten; we made roast goose, reveled from morning to night and still could not get enough of all the glorious stuff. This is how starved we were and how we enjoyed all the beautiful things." He remembered, "Now glorious days began for us. Wonderful weather. There was a big garden with young vegetables behind the house. We were the masters. I stole two bicycles. It was very important to have two bicycles. One always had to be prepared that the Russians would take one away."

Karl awakened early every morning, at 5:30, to bike the half hour to a neighboring village, where he picked up eight liters of milk. Shelves in Tröbitz food stores had been stripped bare. None of the survivors felt that they could yet share milk from the cows they had claimed or meat from the livestock they had butchered. That camp mentality would take time to unlearn. Karl was not alone in commandeering bikes and making trips to neighboring towns.

Marion told me, "A forever memory was getting up early with father and riding from our little village to forage for food. It was spring, and I remember an allée of trees, a warm sun, blue skies, and spring flowers growing everywhere. It looked magical and new and fresh. And then, the bounty in my father's bicycle rack, a chicken, lovely fruit, and vegetables. A whole loaf of bread!"

There is no record of how Karl managed to acquire that food. Had he or Ilse found a way to hide money in their packs? Was he permitted to cable his family in America? Were townspeople generous with the emaciated survivors? What did Marion mean by "forage"? Karl did not write in his memoir about the means by which he acquired this food for his family—or about the shocking dissonance of the abundance in these rural communities while in camps nearby, Jews had been deliberately starved.

To recover his strength, Karl took long bike rides, some as long as twenty-five miles. Ilse and the children swam in a lake at the edge of town that had formed over time in a former coal pit. The family thrived. They called their days in Tröbitz "glorious."

■　　■　　■

Yet not all was glorious for the Bergen-Belsen survivors or the Tröbitz residents. Soviet soldiers still ruled the town, and some of their actions crossed from sympathetic and caring to criminal. Karl would remember, "The Russians marched through the village in gigantic formations and some of them stayed on in Tröbitz. Even if we owe our lives to the Russians, we have to say that there are some unpleasant memories for us."

Vigilant about the spread of disease, the Soviets set up a hospital and brought in physicians and nurses, aided by the Jewish doctors among the Bergen-Belsen survivors and by a few Tröbitz volunteers. The Soviets checked every house, every day, for typhus. If they discovered someone with fever over ninety-nine degrees, they took that person to the hospital, a place simply for quarantine with no medicine to offer, a sick bay. Anyone taken there who didn't have typhus already was likely to contract it.

As Ilse remembered, "Now the Russians were deathly afraid that they would catch the typhoid fever. They would make house calls every day. They would go from house to house and room to room and see whether anyone would be in bed sick. As soon as they would see someone with fever they would take them to quarantine, shave their hair. They were afraid they would catch it. And keep them there until they were either better or dead." Ilse was still unsure which diseases were rampant. She did not realize that she and many others had typhus, not typhoid fever, a very different disease.

In danger of being taken from their home, Ilse hid in the garden or behind the coal shed when Soviets knocked at their door. If she didn't have time to run, Karl tried to stall their entry while she grabbed a brush and pail and scrubbed under the furniture. The deception worked. Once again, the family's joint efforts saved them from disaster. The Soviets never suspected that anyone working so vigorously could have the disease.

Sometimes, Soviets did not knock at the village doors. Instead they burst into homes, bent on rape. If other family members were home, the soldier drew his revolver. One evening, standing on the village road, Karl observed a Soviet walk down the street, then break into the nearest house. Karl heard a scream. After twenty minutes, the soldier came out and pushed into the next house, and then the next.

Ilse was careful not to appear on the streets. She and Karl concocted a scheme for her to escape from a Soviet intrusion. They placed a chair outside under the high bedroom window. Ilse practiced jumping on the bed, then up "through the window and onto the chair, all in one leap" before she could be seen. They had come up with this plan when one day Stefan, beaming with excitement, came inside holding hands with two Soviet soldiers. They had asked the seven-year-old child to introduce them to his mother.

Karl remembered an evening when "we sat there in the evening after dinner, with bated breath and terribl[y] excited. Suddenly the door opened and a Russian entered the room. Ilse jumped up to run away. With a gesture, he calmed Ilse down and made it clear to her that she should sit down. He was from the G.P.U. (secret police) and was looking for Russian soldiers. He explained to me in sign language that I should give a kick in the behind to any Russian soldier who would dare enter a private house. So, this cloud, too, passed us."

■　　■　　■

While Tröbitz remained a calm center in the final stormy weeks of war, the conflict still raged around them. As the Hesses' two trains—one carrying Ilse and the children, Karl following in the other—pulled out of southern Berlin, the Red Army under Marshal

Zhukov's 1st Belorussian Front battled ferociously toward the city center from the east and south. A few days after the Hesses were liberated, the Red Army completed its encirclement of Berlin. The Soviets began intense bombing and shelling of the city center, the reverberations shaking even the *Führerbunker* four levels below the street. The next day Zhukov, supported by Ukrainian troops, launched the final assault. Hitler blasted "treacherous" and "incompetent" military commanders who, understanding their precarious situation, had deserted Berlin and moved their units further west to engage the Western Allies. There, they believed, they would receive better surrender treatment than from the Soviets.

Germany had murdered more than half of the Soviet soldiers it had captured since 1941. Some three million Soviet POWs died by shooting, gassing, or starving, or were worked to death in forced labor or concentration camps, including Bergen-Belsen before the Sternlager was built there. At least twenty thousand Soviet POWs were buried near the camp. German soldiers feared retribution—similar treatment in Soviet hands. Their fears would prove valid. The Soviets took some three million German POWs, and as many as a million—one in three—died in Soviet hands. By contrast, fewer than one in twenty-five German POWs would die in Western captivity.

During the fury of the Berlin assault, on April 24, Himmler made a startling proposal while negotiating with the Swedish Red Cross (SRC) about Theresienstadt transfers. He asked the SRC to relay a conditional surrender offer, unauthorized by Hitler, to the Allies. His belated efforts to save Germany and himself were in vain. Both Churchill and Truman stood fast. The Allies would accept nothing short of total, unconditional surrender.

When Hitler heard the news of Himmler's offer, he became furious, condemned Himmler as a traitor, and sentenced him to death. But the Nazi government and Axis alliance were in shambles. Powerful Nazi officials had begun to disappear from sight. By late April, Himmler, the powerful SS Reichsführer whose name had struck fear into the hearts of Jews and other victims of the Germans, was on the run, sought for treason. He shaved his mustache, dressed in the stolen uniform of a common soldier, and attempted to elude Allies searching for him and other powerful Nazis. Soviet soldiers captured the disguised Himmler and turned him over to the British. Denied clemency, he committed suicide. Eichmann, who had been a traveling salesman before rising to become SS-Obersturmbannführer, escaped from an American prison camp and for five years lived in disguise in Lüneburg Heath, a few miles from the ashes of Bergen-Belsen. In 1950, with help from the Vatican, he traveled south to Italy with his family and lived anonymously in South America, along with thousands of other Nazis. Years later, he would be captured, tried in Israel, and hanged.

Hitler's closest ally, Mussolini, also tried to escape but failed. On April 27, 1945, Italian partisans captured Mussolini, heavily disguised and attempting to reach Switzerland. The following day they executed Mussolini and his mistress, then hung their bodies upside down in a plaza in Milan.

As the Nazi regime crumbled, Hitler informed a few top officials that he planned to die by suicide. In his will he named former U-boat commander Admiral Karl Dönitz his successor as *Staatsoberhaupt*, head of state. On April 30, in an underground bunker behind the Reich Chancellery in Berlin, Hitler and his newlywed wife, Eva Braun, committed suicide. Braun killed herself by taking cyanide provided by the SS. Controversy had surrounded the method of Hitler's suicide, shortly after Braun's, but that debate has ended. He swallowed a cyanide capsule, then held a Walther pistol to his head and fired. Following instructions Hitler had left in his will, the SS took his and Braun's corpses out of the bunker, poured gasoline on them, burned them, and buried the ashes.

Ignoring the suicide of Germany's leader, Goebbels urged the people of Berlin to defend the city to the death, though months earlier he had noted in his diary that millions of citizens had already fled west ahead of the advancing Soviets. On May 1, 1945, a day after Hitler's death, Goebbels, too, tried and failed to negotiate a ceasefire; later that day, he and his wife killed not only themselves but also their six children. Reichsmarschall Hermann Göring, who had overseen the Luftwaffe, was arrested by the Nazis for possible treason; freed by a Luftwaffe unit, he raced to U.S. lines in order to surrender to the Americans, not the Soviets. He died by suicide during the Nuremberg trials.

The narrow corridor that had allowed the Hesses' train to slip between Soviet and American armies closed on April 25 when Eastern and Western Allies met in the small town of Torgau, less than thirty miles from Tröbitz. On May 2, the Red Army raised the Soviet flag over the ruins of the Reichstag. Berlin's Lustgarten Park, site of numerous mass rallies supporting the Nazis, was a bomb-pitted wasteland.

■　　■　　■

In Amsterdam, the winter of 1944, continuing into early spring 1945, had been devastating for the Dutch people. The Allies had liberated southern Netherlands before the Battle of the Bulge, but their attempts to advance farther north into the Netherlands had been stymied. Throughout the bitter winter, a German blockade against the Allies cut off fuel and food shipments to the city, and the Germans shut off its electricity. Sweden managed to send flour, which the Dutch baked into "Swedish bread," but that humanitarian effort made little impact on the city's hunger. In an arrangement negotiated through the International Red Cross, Germany permitted some American and British humanitarian food drops. In one of many displays of gratitude, some Dutch farmers spelled out "Thanks, Boys" in their tulip fields. Nonetheless, some twenty thousand Dutch died of starvation in what would be called the Hunger Winter.

Many Dutch people lived in cellars that winter to avoid bomb attacks and street violence, emerging only to pursue their search for sustenance. By spring, official daily food rations had fallen to 320 calories per person, about an eighth of daily adult needs. Meat coupons were worthless; butcher shops had no meat to sell at any price. As they had done during the early years of German occupation, Dutch people from the cities trekked miles to the countryside, wearing packs, riding bicycles, or pulling carts, bartering for food to carry home. The Dutch dismantled their furniture and walls of their houses and the desolate empty houses of deported Jews, and they burned the scavenged tinder for heat. They consumed tulip bulbs and sugar beets. In 1945, the Netherlands' birthrate plummeted. Its death rate soared.

Canadian and British infantry, a Polish armored division, American, Belgian, Dutch, and Czechoslovak troops, and American and French air forces joined the fight to liberate the Netherlands. Yet even as the Germans lost ground, Nazi leadership tightened its grip on the country. Dutch Resistance, emboldened by German defeats, mounted increasing attacks that triggered murderous mass reprisals from the Germans.

Increasingly fearful about the war and Dutch Resistance, the SS and the German Green Police executed citizens on the streets for offenses as minor as curfew infringements. Informed about a priest who was hiding twelve Jewish families, the SS stormed the church, herded them all into the street, and shot them. In the last months of the war, Reichskommissar Seyss-Inquart ordered between eight hundred and fifteen hundred executions, many of them carried out by members of the SD, who were so committed to the Nazi obsessive hatred that they were glad to act on their own initiative.

After the Allies liberated southern Netherlands, they halted, wary that the Germans might breach all the dikes and flood the country. Fighting resumed in the country's eastern and northern provinces in April when Canadian, British, and Polish forces entered the Netherlands from the east, fighting along "Hell's Highway" and advancing west canal by canal. On April 19, the First Canadian Army fought to the North Sea, breaking Germany's vise-like grip on the Netherlands. Amsterdam and regions in the west, where German forces were stronger and civilian populations denser, remained trapped under occupation, awaiting liberation by German surrender.

Between September 1944 and May 1945, as the Soviets fought in the east, the British suffered some sixty-seven hundred losses in the Netherlands; Canadians, four thousand; the Americans, eleven hundred; and the Poles more than six hundred. Nearly twenty-five thousand Dutch civilians died in the fighting.

On Dönitz's fourth day as German president, May 4, at Lüneburg Heath, he surrendered all German forces in the Netherlands, Denmark, and northwestern Germany to the British, signaling the end of World War II in northwestern Europe. On May 5, General Johannes Blaskowitz, German Supreme Commander of the Netherlands, agreed to surrender terms in the small Dutch town of Wageningen, where, in an almost ludicrous irony of history, no type-writer could be found to create the formal document. After a harried search, the document was created, and on May 6 General Blaskowitz signed the surrender in the presence of Canadian lieutenant-general Charles Foulkes and Dutch Prince Bernhard. Two days later, in Amsterdam, German soldiers confronted victory celebrations by firing into the crowd, killing thirty-two and wounding more than two hundred people.

On May 7, 1945, at 2:41 a.m., Dönitz's representative in Eisenhower's headquarters in France signed surrender documents mandating all German forces to cease operations on May 8. Because of the time difference, Soviet forces announced their Victory Day on May 9.

Across Europe and North America, wild celebrations marked victory in Europe—V-E Day. Yet on the Dutch island of Texel some sixty miles north of Amsterdam, the fighting had not ended. There, a group of captured Georgian soldiers forced to fight for the Germans refused orders to return to the mainland to support the embattled Wehrmacht. They turned on their German comrades also stationed in Texel and killed hundreds while they slept. On May 20, two weeks after V-E Day, Canadian troops quelled the ensuing combat, the final battle of the Second World War in Europe. German soldiers operating a weather station on the small

Norwegian island of Svalbard surrendered to a local seal-hunting vessel on September 4, the last day of the European war.

Eisenhower later commented on the war's longevity and destruction: "Germany was defeated after the Battle of the Bulge....By January 16, 1945, it was all over, and anyone with sense knew it was over. But then there was that statement that President Roosevelt made about unconditional surrender in 1943.... The whole spring campaign should have been abandoned." Eisenhower was referring to Roosevelt's firm demand for nothing short of unconditional surrender—and Truman's endorsement of that position. The Allies had summarily rejected Himmler's proposal of conditional surrender. Historians would later suggest that the Allies' intense bombing campaign extending into May 1945 could have been shortened and the Soviets' costly push into eastern Germany halted earlier; in its final months, World War II had become inseparable from Soviet territorial ambitions and the looming Cold War.

■   ■   ■

In his memoir, Karl would describe the surreal situation: "The war had ended. Under Russians' sponsorship, we had a big victory celebration in the village. Every speaker expressed his feelings in the language of his own group, including Hebrew. For eight weeks, the world was not aware of the fact that our transport had been stranded because the Russians had already employed a policy of secrecy....For [eight weeks] we lived in this weird world, as alien to us on the last day as it had been on the first."

The trapped Tröbitz Jews gained their freedom through a coincidence of time and place. Neither the Western Allies' nor the Soviets' maps showed the hundreds of German concentration camps throughout the Reich and conquered lands. Most were discovered by troops battling nearby. Bergen-Belsen had been liberated on April 15, but the Hesses, then far from the camp, were an anomaly—free from the camp, but still captives. On what would later be called Elbe Day, April 25, Soviets battling from the east and Americans advancing from the west after fierce fighting in Leipzig met up for the first time. They met at the winding Elbe River in two locations, both about twenty-five miles from Tröbitz, greeting each other warmly as if long-time comrades in arms. Amidst exchanged handshakes and information, the Soviets eventually mentioned the stranded Tröbitz Jews, most of whom were from the Netherlands, and proposed that the Americans arrange their return home.

On June 15, 1945, a warm, sunny day, forty-five American trucks drove into the village to pick up the stranded Jews. The excited children watched from their doorsteps or ran as if toward a circus parade, following the roaring trucks emblazoned with large, five-pointed white stars on the doors. As Karl would say in his memoir, "It was wonderful seeing these fresh American boys jump out of their cars."

Steven told me, "We quickly learned to beg for sweets from the Americans, of which they seemed to have an endless supply. My first so-called English lesson—'Hershey Bar' and 'chewing gum.'"

More good fortune: Ilse's condition had improved. Whether she had contracted Malta fever, as she and Karl then believed, or typhus, as was likely, they guessed that the blessing of her survival derived from her miserable days cleaning the sickbay; she may have acquired some immunity through those smaller repetitive exposures. The eight-week interlude after Bergen-Belsen held much

CHAPTER 17

Love, Hope, and Reality
JUNE 16, 1945–JANUARY 1, 1947

I n mid-June 1945, hundreds of thousands of people were on the move across Europe. Civilians from eastern countries desperately fled toward the West to avoid trading Nazi dictatorship for Communist domination. People liberated from forced labor camps from France to the Soviet Union traveled in all directions, some searching for family that no longer existed. Soldiers. Shopkeepers. Thieves. Families. The healthy and the strong. The ill, lame, weak, and wounded. Nazi officials, sympathizers, and members of the SS stationed in occupied countries looking for places to disappear or making their way home shared trains and walked roads with Jews liberated from concentration camps seeking home, family, and a way out of hell.

Allied soldiers, too, moved across Europe, pacifying the countryside, establishing control, and setting up camps for displaced people (DPs) with nowhere else to go. To manage the turmoil, U.S. forces established huge screening centers. The Tröbitz Jews' first stop on their journey to the Netherlands was an American center in Leipzig, sixty miles from Tröbitz, where officials had set up operations in the former base of the Luftwaffe's 14th Flak Division.

As Ilse remembered,

> After about ten weeks we were notified that we would be picked up by the Americans. Hurray! Hurray! And one beautiful day, they came with big trucks, the American army, to get us out of Tröbitz. . . . I would like to say this was the end of our horrible story, but the story still had a . . . pretty bitter in-between. First, we were taken by the Americans to Leipzig to an old army camp because they really didn't know what to do with all these hundreds of thousands of people, Jews and Gentiles alike, who all of a sudden marched back and forth through Germany. So, we stayed in this camp, and slept again on cots and straw until . . . they got us trains to go back to Holland.

By chance, the Hesses were assigned to a barracks room shared by five acquaintances. The large echoing space held lockers but nowhere to sleep. Accustomed to much worse, they simply turned over the wooden lockers and slept, again on hard wooden beds. Fearing lice, the Hesses refused straw mattresses offered to them. Instead of eating the miserable food from the center, they unpacked provisions they had brought from Tröbitz.

During their eight days at the center, far more distressing to the Hesses than the spartan barracks or throngs of detainees, which may have included Nazis and Nazi sympathizers returning home, was the resurgence of ill will on the part of Dutch Jews toward German-Jewish Dutch refugees. The "old, underground battle," as Karl called the hostility, erupted anew.

That animosity had begun in the mid-1930s when thousands of German Jews fleeing the Nazis began entering the Netherlands and the Dutch economy was still struggling under the impact of a worldwide Depression. Furthermore, a large number of Dutch Jews leaned toward Orthodoxy in their observances; German Jews tended to be more liberal or, like the Hesses, only loosely observant. Thus the influx was not only an economic burden, but a religious and cultural clash. The Dutch government's antipathy towards the German Jews mirrored that of some Dutch-Jewish citizens. Although the Netherlands had taken in thousands of fleeing German Jews, so hostile were the Netherlands secretaries general to the incoming Jewish refugees that when asked by the Nazis whether they would protest their deportation, the officials responded, "No, they are German citizens. They are not our responsibility."

Those officials had not yet grasped the extent of Nazi antisemitism—or that Jews who were Dutch citizens would be the Germans' next target. No Dutch official resigned in protest at the deportation of either group, and persecution by some Dutch Jews of the German-Jewish refugees erupted again after the war. When the Dutch-Jewish liaison in the Leipzig camp tried to sabotage the German Jews' return to the Netherlands, Karl and others immediately recognized the threat. They united in an iron-willed protest, demanding reinstatement of their transportation.

On happier days that held no conflict, the Hesses rode a bus into the city of Leipzig. They were buoyed by the sight of an elegant restaurant, taken over by the Belgian military, that featured a large window sign: "Forbidden for Germans." Karl and Ilse well remembered signs in Amsterdam's restaurants, theaters, shops, and parks: "Forbidden for Jews."

"I remember Leipzig," Steven told me. "We found some small arms ammunition—it was a German former army camp—and threw some in a bonfire. A potentially deadly 'fireworks.' We survived that, too."

On the Hesses' eighth day at the center, June 23, 1945, Ilse and several friends, delighted with even their limited freedom, again ventured into the city to acquire ration tickets for food and clothing. Karl's thoughts had not turned to the state of his wardrobe; he was content with his "white German navy pants and a Belgian military shirt." But Ilse was thinking ahead, eager to discard the "smock-like apron" she wore as a dress, taken from a corpse in Tröbitz. Without the ration tickets, what would they wear in the days ahead, and how could they acquire food in their lives after detention?

While Ilse and her friends were in town, the order came through for the Netherlands Jews to prepare for immediate departure. Karl and the other nervous husbands paced, waiting for their wives' return. They brought their children and luggage to the bus yard and watched the stream of buses leave. Aware that this was their final chance to make the train, the men implored the driver of the last bus to return for one more group. No response.

As Karl explained in his memoir,

> We sat there in the barracks yard. The children cried
> with excitement and kept running outside the gate to
> conjure up their Mammis. Finally, after three hours,

the women came back, holding their ration tickets like trophies. When we told them the reason for our excitement, they did not know whether to cry or laugh. Before their departure for Holland, they would have liked to "outfit" themselves. Fortunately the driver did come back, but he held out very little hope that the train would still be there. But, if a person is lucky, he is lucky even in Leipzig. The train had not left yet. At the station, everybody received a package from the American Red Cross.

The family hustled into their train compartment, stored their luggage, and marveled at having real seats, a stark reminder of the distance they had traveled since being shoved into a disease-ridden cattle car at Bergen-Belsen. Karl commented that he felt like royalty "in a grandiose local train," though there was no glass in the windows.

The airy train crossed Germany from east to west, some four hundred miles over four days and nights. The ravages of war outside the open window gripped Karl and Ilse. Their train rumbled northwest past Halle in the scenic Harz Mountains, and farther west past Kassel, both cities bombed to near total destruction, shocking the family. The days were cool; they were thankful it was summer. The nights were miserable for them, crammed into the crowded seats.

Karl remembered, "We curled up as tightly as possible to leave the most possible space for the children. The sight of the cities, however, made up for our sleepless nights. One could not imagine that all the rubble we saw could be cleared away in the next few years. Gigantic Rhine bridges lay in the water, and, with them, the freight trains loaded with coal and war material. For kilometers, there was not a house, only here and there an undamaged smoke-stack of a factory."

In western Germany, they stopped briefly in Krefeld, the location of United Silk, where Karl had worked before the war. Karl strolled on the platform, hoping to glimpse familiar sights. He chatted with a stranger, who turned out to be a United Silk employee. Karl learned that the factory had escaped major damage, though much of the town had been heavily bombed. The British had appointed his former boss as Krefeld's "supervisor." The news relieved his concerns—it seemed that his former company and colleagues had survived. Karl would not have known at that time about the company's forced cooperation with the German war machine.

On June 27, the train carrying Jews and others hoping to repatriate hissed to a halt in Valkenburg, a Dutch town near the Belgian border. Karl remembered, "The closer we got to the Dutch border, the greater our excitement grew. Soon we saw the first advertising signs in the Dutch language. We felt at home once more."

■   ■   ■

Their reception was sobering. The screening process at the Dutch border was intense and aggressive as the Dutch strove to filter out former Nazis, Nazi sympathizers—and German-Jewish refugees. Over the five years since the German invasion, more than 650,000 Dutch had been deported—or gone enthusiastically—to Nazi Germany. More than 100,000 of those were Jews transported to concentration camps. Additionally, some 500,000 Dutch citizens forced to labor in German fields and factories were making their way home. More than 20,000 Dutch men had volunteered for the German military and served in special volunteer units. About 65,000 Dutch Nazis (NSB) and collaborators had fled the Netherlands as Allied forces closed in on Dutch cities. Many of those Dutch Nazis, having witnessed Germany's collapse, had already begun filtering back into their own homeland.

The Dutch government wanted to know who was attempting to enter the country, but their nationalistic wrath especially targeted their enemy, the Germans—even those who had fled the Nazis. The Dutch minister of justice proposed to forcibly deport all holders of German passports, a plan that would be implemented in 1946, resulting in several thousand expulsions.

According to Karl, "In Valkenburg, the train stopped. There were strict controls directed towards collaborators and people who had voluntarily worked in Germany because there were a great many Gentile Dutch on our train who were being repatriated."

Camp guards collected the refugees in a large room. Officials called each person individually, then placed them into groups that they dismissed or led elsewhere. Karl remembered, "After the room had slowly emptied out so that one could survey the scene, we realized that almost without exception, only German Jews were left."

The Hesses waited long hours before the guards directed their group to another room. After midnight, border police handed Karl a lengthy, menacing, garbled questionnaire:

Printed at the top: "Stefan Hess."

The official filled in more information as Karl stood and watched, appalled.

"Punishable Act: German"

"Politically Reliable-Unreliable-Suspicious: SUSPICIOUS."

Karl attempted to reason with the official. This was not even his name; this form named his son. In exasperation, he let it burst out that he had assumed that the Dutch and the Allies had won the war—but according to this form, apparently they had lost. The officer apologized, but he explained that new laws made Karl German and that he would be treated as such. In September 1944, while the Hesses suffered in Bergen-Belsen, the Dutch government-in-exile denounced anti-Jewish laws but classified German Jews as stateless people of Jewish origin and therefore "enemy nationals." Deprived of citizenship for ten years by Nazi Germany; surviving the Germans' cruelty in Amsterdam, Westerbork, and Bergen-Belsen; suffering disease and a deadly train journey through a raging war zone, the Hesses and other German Jewish refugees were aghast as the Dutch labeled them as "suspicious" and imprisoned them in a school with members of the SS and the NSB.

Karl explained, "The building was already overcrowded with German Nazis, Dutch traitors and similar rabble. Our wives refused to sleep under the same roof with this mob and preferred lying down on the stone floor in the entrance of the school. There were strictest orders against this, but the guards could have done nothing except shoot. Commands and orders did not work any more with our women. After two days of protest, finally one of the Nazis' rooms was cleared for our women."

Karl and Ilse were trapped again. Twice they had told themselves they were free, first when reaching Tröbitz and again when they left Tröbitz. Yet once more they were captive, and they felt betrayed again by the Dutch. Karl and Ilse had fought and kept their family together against all odds, but in that center, the Dutch separated them, herding Karl away like a criminal.

The next morning, with ten minutes' notice, guards loaded the imprisoned men onto trucks and drove them to the nearby Vilt internment camp, a site surrounded by barbed wire that Karl described as a "concentration camp." At the entry gate, they were met by a sign with the dreadful words: "*Voor Galg en Rad*"—which Karl translated, "For Those Who Are Destined for the Gallows or to Be Broken at the Wheel"—an ancient prison sign, never removed. A Dutch Nazi worker there assigned Karl a number to wear across his chest at all times—all too reminiscent of the burning anger he had felt for four years while forced to wear the Nazis' Jewish star, like a brand or target.

Designated as leader of a work detail, Karl was required to report—"in snappy posture"—three times a day in front of a Dutch Nazi whom the camp's commander had designated as "sub-commander." Karl and his group of eighteen pushed wheelbarrows loaded with stone from a gravel quarry behind the camp through public streets. They performed deep knee bends while being struck on the head as local Dutch citizens, believing them to be German Nazis, mocked them. Punishment drills. Work commandos. A tidal wave of memories. Karl had escaped the Nazis, yet now the Dutch had confined his family for the crime of being born Jews in Germany.

The guards threatened the refugees with four days imprisonment in a cellar and confiscated their belongings and their Red Cross packages. They did not find Karl's meager luggage. Experienced with camp life, he had hidden his few possessions under his bed.

Once a week, Dutch guards took the male prisoners, their camp numbers still attached to their clothes, to visit their families. Karl found his children filthy and tired. The family hardly spoke. Karl needed the brief time to eat. Ilse called the food in the camp "fodder" and set out the last of their provisions from Tröbitz. The Hesses' Dutch friends on the train had been billeted in a nearby hotel; they were not permitted to visit or bring anything to the Hesses. Karl saw the food as starvation rations, "like in the 'best days' in Bergen-Belsen." Furious, feeling betrayed, he kept a diary of his treatment and collected testimony from other prisoners.

Marion told me, "My mother later told the story that I was very belligerent in this camp and bit a girl about my age so severely she needed medical care. I think she was taunting me [perhaps about the accusation that Karl was a Nazi collaborator]. My mother remembered it because it was so out of character."

Eight days passed. The shaken Hess family was loaded onto a train headed farther north on the Dutch-German border. To their horror, they were imprisoned again, this time in a former monastery. Ilse explained, "Because the Dutch government, all of a sudden faced with thousands of people coming back, not only Jews but Gentiles from all over Europe, said, 'Now you are not stateless any more. Now you are German again and we have to take you to camp.' So they took us to an old empty monastery near the German border where we were again locked up." Again they slept on floors, received poor food, and soon looked like camp inmates. Another eight days later, in early July, over two months after their liberation in Tröbitz, with no apology, the Dutch informed the Hesses that they were free. According to Ilse, they stayed there "until some of our Jewish Dutch coprisoners, lawyers from Bergen-Belsen, intervened and we could finally could trek back to Amsterdam."

As Steven told me, "My father made a huge fuss and got a lawyer. We were freed after ten days."

In his memoir, Karl wrote, "This is how we entered the land in which our children were born. By muted drums."

■   ■   ■

As Karl noted, drums did not roll and flags did not wave to welcome the returning Jews. The Hesses came back to a nation bearing the ravages of war—destroyed buildings, empty storefronts, poverty, and a haggard population, many grieving. White sheets hung in many home windows, signaling that the owners had lost family in the war. A number of Jewish parents reuniting with their hidden children found the reunion difficult: Some families who had sheltered the children did not want to give them up. Some children did not recognize their parents. The economy had stalled; unemployment soared. Beginning in summer 1945 and continuing over a decade, some five hundred thousand Dutch would emigrate, many of them to Canada.

Throughout that summer, instead of marauding Green Police, the SS, and formations of German troops on the streets, Canadian troops marched through the cities, their bands playing bagpipes. In Amsterdam, bikes plied the narrow streets. Trees in full leaf, fresh ocean breezes, and gentle waves lapping in canals throughout the city may have raised the Hesses' sagging spirits when they were taken in early July to a house in Amsterdam for displaced people.

During the occupation, under German pressure, Dutch solidarity with their Jewish fellow citizens had crumbled. Indifferent or collaborative Dutch behavior had permitted the Germans to deport, in less than a year, nearly three out of four of the country's 120,000 Jews, most of them to Auschwitz and Sobibor. In stark contrast, only 40 percent of Belgian Jews and 25 percent of French Jews had been deported. Of the 107,000 Dutch Jews deported, only about 5,300—about one in twenty—returned.

The surviving Jews might have expected a warm reception by the Dutch or, at a minimum, sympathy for what they had endured. Instead, they often experienced blatant antisemitism. One Jewish survivor, Jacob Presser, who would later write several well-regarded histories of the Holocaust in the Netherlands, described the generally negative attitude of the Dutch toward Jewish survivors. As just one example, a teacher who held a Ph.D. returned to Amsterdam after "horrible suffering" that included the murder of his wife. After taking up his teaching position again, he heard his boss complain to a full hall, "The good Jews are dead, the bad ones have returned." Some Dutch debated creating a fixed quota for Jews. Before the deportations, a number of Dutch Resistance groups had not allowed Jews to join them—and never apologized or welcomed back the liberated Jews.

Young Lolke Wilders, who had been snatched from Amsterdam's streets and deported to Auschwitz, survived Josef Mengele's brutal medical experiments. He returned to find that his family was alive, hidden by Dutch priests. As an adult in the United States, in several interviews with me at his home, he spoke about his observations of the non-Jewish Dutch. "There were a lot of good people. On the other hand, there were a lot of bad people, Dutch, who were members of the NSB. They believed the Nazis because Hitler promised everything—a thousand-year Reich. The people really supported that man."

■　　■　　■

Karl and Ilse began contacting their non-Jewish friends who had agreed to hide their belongings when they faced deportation. Once again, disappointment and anger marred their homecoming.

As Karl explained in his memoir, "We started the hunt for all the things we had hidden. The Dutch 'keepers' were terribly disappointed that part of the Jews had returned and now wanted their things back. For months, I chased after our things and, with the help of the police and partly with the help of a crowbar, I succeeded in retrieving 70% of the hidden things. The rest had been embezzled."

Friends explained that the Hunger Winter had forced them to sell the belongings. Confiscations, exorbitant taxes, no fuel for their stove...Even so Marretje, the Hesses' former nanny, had kept their possessions intact. Marretje's brother brought their things from her home on the island of Urk to the Hesses. Silver platters, clothes, linens, paintings, and most precious, family photos—all that they had left in her care had remained hidden, safe, and untouched, under her bed.

According to Karl, "Considering the forceful experiences and the great human tragedy we had been a part of, these material disappointments were, of course, of minor importance. For us, it was only the pain of a small child on seeing his day of joy spoiled.

On the other hand, these conditions have opened our eyes to the manner in which the post-war world treated the Jews."

Ilse, the practical mother who had stashed extra underwear for the family and a tiny stove in her luggage, had also thought to sew a number of small diamonds into the lining of Stefan's then ragged coat, ready for bargaining the family out of emergencies. She had made lifesaving use in 1943 of her broach, delaying the time of their deportation and probably influencing, along with the forged Paraguayan passports, their deportation to Bergen-Belsen instead of Auschwitz. But she had not used the small diamonds. On their return, she cut out the lining and retrieved the few diamonds. One fell into the carpet, causing the family to crawl around the room, scrunching bits of the rug between their fingers until they found it.

■   ■   ■

Karl and Ilse were determined to push forward and prosper again in that complicated environment. Once, before the Nazis, they had loved being in Amsterdam. The twins had been born there. Perhaps they could love it again. They found an apartment at Valeriusterras 7B, near the beautiful 120-acre Vondelpark. Several canal bridges away from their former home, it had a different outlook that did not raise terrible memories from their former Amsterdam apartment. From those windows they had watched Jews assemble at the train station and wait for the last tram of the night to deliver the trapped Jews to the Schouwburg.

Soon after the Hesses arrived in Amsterdam, Karl applied for a job with the large Dutch textile corporation Van Vlissingen, which offered him a well-paid position. The twins, seven years old, had never attended school; Karl and Ilse registered them in the First Montessori School of Wielewaal, a short walk from their apartment. Optimistic, Karl bought a bike and took the children for rides. The family enjoyed walks in the park, which held gardens, a playground, and an iconic "fallen tree." Perhaps the family identified with the tree. Decades earlier, it had fallen over; instead of dying, it grew horizontally, put down new roots, and thrived.

Otto Frank, too, was among the Dutch Jews returning to Amsterdam. Liberated from Auschwitz, he had been taken by the Allies to France, where he learned of his wife's death and the probable deaths of his daughters in Bergen-Belsen. A month before the Hesses arrived in Amsterdam, Frank came back to the city where his German-born family had hoped to find refuge. As Carol Ann Lee recounts in *The Hidden Life of Otto Frank*, he, too, walked the streets, trying to put his life back together. Frank stayed in the house where his family had hidden and possibly visited the Montessori school his daughters had attended. There he would have heard about the fifteen other students who had died, and possibly would have seen Marion and Stefan. Frank checked and rechecked Red Cross lists and, in July 1945, saw the dreaded crosses, symbols of deaths, next to the names of his daughters, who had died in Bergen-Belsen.

■　■　■

The Hesses' battles in Amsterdam were not over. As he had done since Hitler assumed control, Karl continued to fight injustice. Over the difficult next year, he became embroiled in three highly publicized legal trials, the first on his own behalf to save his reputation and new job, the other two to combat the long reach of the Holocaust.

The textile company withdrew its job offer before Karl's contract was signed. In an emotional conversation with the president, Karl discovered that a former competitor, a man who had survived the war comfortably, had defamed him, claiming Karl had been a disloyal Dutch citizen and had "misbehaved" at Bergen-Belsen. A Sternlager friend, a lawyer, successfully represented Karl in a widely publicized libel suit that drew dozens of supporting letters that described his character, the many Jews he had saved while working in the Schouwburg, his resistance to the Germans in Bergen-Belsen, and the suffering that resistance had caused him. He won the case and received compensation, but the job did not materialize. Karl soon found another, less desirable position; money was tight for the family.

A second trial took on the Dutch government and its handling of German Jews in Valkenburg. Soon after reaching Amsterdam, using the notes that he had made in the camp and the testimony he had gathered from other Valkenburg prisoners, Karl wrote the Dutch government a letter of complaint, charging cruelty and blatant antisemitism. As he explained in his memoir, "This made for a very lively correspondence in which the concerned officers claimed that they were all lies. A short time later, we were brought to a military court in Breda. The former eldest of the Jews from Bergen-Belsen was present, as well as a Dutch lawyer in our defense and myself. We were able to prove to these gentlemen in the minutest detail that my depositions were correct. The trial ended with Colonel Van Delden writing us a letter informing us that he disapproved very much of his officers' behavior and offering his apology. The things that had been stolen, however, were never returned."

Karl's final legal battle with injustice, in June 1946, involved the Kapos of Bergen-Belsen, the criminals that Commandant Kramer had brought with him from Auschwitz to maintain order during the four deadliest months at the camp. One of the most feared of the Kapos, a Polish national and former prisoner in Poland, Kazimierz Cegielski, had been discovered in hiding and was being held in a British military prison. The British planned to try him in Lüneburg and identified seventeen possible witnesses.

On July 11, the British came to Amsterdam with "two trucks, one jeep, two officers, and five soldiers" to pick up their witnesses, according to Karl's memoir. He was one of three witnesses who appeared at the meeting location from among the seventeen who had been called. With a smaller group to transport, the British changed arrangements, and they traveled by train and car. Karl remembered, "We got into the cars and drove through Hannover, ghostly at night. Here and there in the ruins, one saw a candle burning. Obviously, one or the other cave dweller had found a room with three walls. At the edge of the city, the cars stopped. A very high ranking officer took us to a well furnished house. That night, for the first time, I got to know the English. A disarming friendliness and an extraordinary hospitality made my antipathy against the English abate somewhat. An English sergeant and a German girl served a princely meal, many courses, wine, coffee, cognac."

The next morning in Lüneburg, with a day to rest before the trial, the British left Karl and the two other Jewish witnesses at the barracks of "The Life Guards," the British regiment that in peacetime forms the royal bodyguard. The city appeared to Karl undamaged, as it had seemed when he rode past in the transport to Tröbitz. His observations had been correct: Allies had planned ahead for this time, keeping the huge base unharmed for their own later use.

Karl wandered the town and chatted with people he encountered. He saw empty shelves in the stores and Germans with gray, expressionless faces. He asked several people how life was for them now. The answers: "Our life is no life any more, without a trace of hope. We don't know where our children are..." He asked them how they felt about Hitler. One responded, "We seem to be the dumbest people on earth." Residents there would not have known, or admitted knowing, that Adolf Eichmann, indispensable Holocaust operative, lived with his family and worked with scant disguise a few miles from the trials. As Karl explained, "I did not even start [on] the topic of the Jews, because that litany to which I had listened for three months in Germany, after our liberation, slowly made me sick—every single one was so innocent."

Karl testified the next day, describing how Cegielski had started the prisoners' day by "beating us out of our beds at five o'clock in the morning" and "chased the sick and the weak to work with indescribable mistreatment" and how his sadistic behavior resulted in many deaths.

That evening, the British treated Karl royally, providing dinner and a cabaret show. As the show finished, the German actors stood at attention as a band played "God Save the King." Karl commented to the officer next to him, "If Hitler could see me, a German Jew, witnessing this scene here as a guest of the British army, he would certainly turn over in his grave." The week after Karl returned home, he received notice that Cegielski had been found guilty and sentenced to death.

News stories about war crimes trials riveted the attention of the Hesses, who felt a pain-filled sense of justice. The Belsen trials, also held in Lüneburg shortly after the Hesses reached Amsterdam, attracted international press. Forty-four Nazis, including Commandant Kramer, tagged in the media as the "Beast of Belsen," and eleven other defendants, including the SS who had chosen to remain with Kramer during the camp's liberation, were sentenced to death; nineteen were imprisoned; fourteen, acquitted.

In June 1946, a second Belsen trial in Lüneburg of ten defendants resulted in four death sentences for the massacre of Jews unloading at the Celle station where the Hesses, too, had disembarked from their transport to Bergen-Belsen. Across Germany, soldiers in the Wehrmacht, Nazi government officials, and the SS disappeared into the fabric of the country, almost all later claiming no responsibility, no knowledge of the Holocaust.

The Nuremberg trials, argued before the first international war crimes tribunal in history, began in November 1945 and continued until October 1946, laying bare the extent of German atrocities and the involvement of prominent Nazis.

■   ■   ■

The Hess family's return to Amsterdam was fraught. The shadow of the Holocaust still hung over the city. In August 1946, Karl sat down to write his memoir while the events were fresh and raw. For his birthday, Ilse bought an ashtray engraved with the words, in Dutch, "We will not be rounded up tonight."

Steven remembers "one bicycle excursion with my father in 1946. The big thing in that economy was 'barter.' Our father wrote to his sister in New York City to send a large cardboard box of cigarette cartons and mark the package 'Matzos for Passover,' so the contents would not be stolen. He let me go with him to the post office. Unfortunately, a customs inspector insisted that the box be opened. When he saw the contents, he took one carton, and we left with the rest...worth several hundred dollars I would guess."

Despite their regained freedom, the pain of the past often overwhelmed the family.

According to Marion, "There was no life in Amsterdam after the war. We were truly the walking dead. We had to learn to go to school—and just how to live again."

As Steven told me, "We were very wounded children, at least I was. I did what I was told. We missed a big chunk of formative years that could not be recovered."

The fate of her mother and numerous beloved members of her extended family haunted Ilse. She contacted the Red Cross and placed newspaper ads seeking information: "After 4 years of valiantly persevering, on January 21, 1945, our dearest mother, mother-in-law, grandmother, Fann[y] Hirschberg fell victim to Nazi terror shortly before the liberation of Stutthof, near Danzig. Anyone who knew this kind and helpful person will share our deep sadness. On behalf of all relatives...." Karl missed the members of his family that he had helped to save, now scattered in Sweden, Palestine, and America.

Marion explained to me, "My parents eventually decided there was no future for us in Holland and started the lengthy, costly process of coming to the States. But no one wanted Jews, even after all of that."

The Hesses had looked forward to leaving Germany and returning to Amsterdam, but they decided that their future lay in the United States and quickly applied for immigration. Their family in America sponsored their immigration, and the Hesses' papers came through relatively promptly. As had happened in the Netherlands, emerging information about the Holocaust did not soften Americans' resistance to increased immigration; a December 1945 Gallup poll showed that only 5 percent of Americans were willing to increase the number of European immigrants. Yet, in this moment, the Hesses' luck held. On December 22, confronted with Congress' unwillingness to increase immigration, Truman issued a statement ordering that, without increasing existing quota numbers, dispossessed persons would be granted priority for U.S. visas.

Marion told me, "I remember our return to Amsterdam mostly as a time of transition. We were neither here nor there. Our parents' fervent wish was to go to America. I had an eye infection just before a required physical. We all felt dread that [the eye infection] would prevent us from getting the green light to go."

An easy ferry trip to Britain contrasted starkly with the Hesses' disastrous May 1940 attempt to flee the Nazis. Their freedom to travel the seas and emigrate abroad had cost the world millions of lives over five years of world war in Europe. Yet their family of four had survived, a testament to the unbreakable spirit of each, to the bonds that held them together, and, as they often acknowledged, to miracles of luck in dark times.

In late December, on the rugged southern British coast, the Hess family boarded the RMS *Queen Elizabeth*, then the world's largest passenger ship, bound for New York. Steven remembers, "The first thing I discovered was a movie. I had never seen one, but that grand ship had a movie theater. I found my way to it, got a seat in the darkness and watched a movie I could not understand. *Pennies from Heaven*, with Bing Crosby. I was delighted and walked back on deck singing, 'pennies from heaven, pennies from heaven.' Three more words of English added to my vocabulary."

They experienced unimaginable extremes of emotion. Pain at their profound losses. Joy at their freedom. Hope in facing, together, the challenges of a new life. They crossed the ocean in a third-class cabin and reached New York at dawn on January 1, 1947. As the ship entered the harbor, Karl and Ilse woke the twins in time to see the Statue of Liberty.

"Now I get very emotional about it," Steven told me. "At the time, it meant nothing to me. I was just cold."

The Hesses sat on the pier all day, on a snow-covered dock, with their luggage, waiting for their relatives to come and pick them up. Surely doubts welled up about their welcome and about life in this huge metropolis. The twins did not even understand English. As night approached, their family, whom Karl had helped to save, came from work to get them and take them home. No longer contemplating what horror might await them or how they could survive one more day, at long last they could envision a life filled with possibilities. They were free.

Epilogue

On January 1, 1947, New Year's Day, Karl, Ilse, Marion, and Stefan settled in the building on Manhattan's Upper West Side where Karl's parents and his sister Meta and her family lived. They found that the funds Karl had sent ahead, with foresight to the future, had grown in value enough to give them a solid start in their new country. On April 5, 1940, five weeks before the German occupation, Karl had wired $4,243 (about $6,800 in 1947; $88,700 in 2022) to a friend in Maryland for him to put in a U.S. bank.

Shortly after their arrival, media interest in the displaced refugees brought the Hesses invitations to meet Eleanor Roosevelt and talk to local groups and the media. After that flurry of activity, the family looked forward to the ordinary life in the United States that they had longed for. Karl Americanized his name to Charles, or Carl, and worked as a regional sales representative for a number of textile companies. He bought a new car—no Mercedes, but a maroon Pontiac—and earned respect for his hard work and integrity. His first job in America included sweeping floors. Marion spent hours with her father going through his fabric samples, admiring the colors, the textures; she was impressed that he could crumple fabric in his hands, watch how it responded, and know the content and quality. A few years later, they moved to Queens, where neighbors loved to spend summer evenings on their balconies chatting with each other.

Carl spoke freely with friends about their life in Europe and sent copies of his memoir to friends and family. But the Holocaust remained a demon that never gave him peace, according to Steven. He had returned from Germany to Amsterdam angry at the treatment his family had received from the Germans and also the Dutch; later, he felt that some small, impossible justice had been served by the war crimes trials that extended for years. The October 1946 execution of Arthur Seyss-Inquart, Reich commissioner of German-occupied Netherlands, and the imprisonments of Ferdinand aus der Fünten, who had directed deportations from the Netherlands, and Albert Gemmeker, Westerbork commander, gave him some assurance that the criminals would be named, apprehended, and punished.

Over his lifetime, Carl felt grateful for their freedom in their new homeland. Unfailingly, he was the first in their neighborhood to raise a flag on national holidays. He urged the twins to give back to their country. As he had done in Europe, every day he would ask each one, "What can I do for you?"

Later he became somewhat moody and aloof, perhaps from fatigue after the week's travel away from home for work, or maybe,

Marion thinks, from "the weight of what happened to us." She remembers that when he talked about his life before America, tears often came to his eyes. No matter his mood or the stresses of work, his children and especially Ilse were his pride and joy, still his reason for living. He died in 1981 at the age of seventy-nine.

In the United States, Ilse continued searching for information about her mother, then grieved for her and for the large number of extended Hirschberg family members killed in the Holocaust. When the twins were in high school, she held a modest position in the diamond industry; she was respected as a skilled diamond weigher at the Diamond Dealers Club. Like Carl, she was passionately devoted to their family as it grew through marriage and grandchildren. Marion called her "the glue of the family," with the phone bill to prove it.

Marion says that before cameras stopped flashing and media attention faded, she and Steven were "the show twins." But they both craved distance from their dreadful past, and neither wanted to be pigeonholed as concentration camp survivors. "It wasn't that I thought it was a negative description, but I didn't want to be known as that. I wanted it to be a sideshow in my life, not the main event." They attended school and learned English.

Marion had a wide circle of friends throughout her school years, graduated from Barnard College, and earned a graduate degree from Columbia University. After a career in health care policy and economics with the National Academy of Sciences, she was recognized for lifetime achievement by the National Research Center for Women and Families. She married twice and was widowed; her married name is Marion Ein Lewin. She has children and grandchildren, and she lives with her partner near Washington, D.C.

Like his father, Stefan, too, changed his name, becoming Steven. He remembers his childhood as lonely. He had never experienced team sports and was never comfortable with them, typically a requisite for American boys' social lives. Encouraged by his father, he entered the Navy ROTC program while at Columbia College, which, like Barnard, is an undergraduate school of Columbia University. The twins graduated on the same day in ceremonies across the street from each other, Steven in his white Navy uniform, Marion looking strikingly like Ilse in the pre-war photo of her and Karl in Switzerland.

After graduation Steven served on active duty for four years (1960–64), leaving the Navy with the rank of lieutenant. During the time when he was a Navy press officer, he also explored a career in journalism, starting as a copy boy for the *New York Times*, carrying printed copy from one department section to another. He later purchased a small photographic equipment manufacturing business and developed it into a major company in the industry. He is married, has children and grandchildren. Every day, he raises the American flag on a twenty-foot flagpole in his yard in Rochester, New York.

Although neither twin spoke much about the Holocaust during their early years in the United States, later both committed themselves to learning about and talking about their experience. They and other family members attended the first reunion of Tröbitz survivors in 1995, fifty years after they had found refuge there.

Steven has a significant Holocaust library, made a video about Bergen-Belsen, and has taught widely about the Holocaust for over forty years. He has made it a mission to lecture about the Holocaust to various groups and in high schools and colleges throughout the United States. "For the most part," he told me, "people are curious about the

Holocaust, but have little if any knowledge. There is hardly anyone left who survived and has a broad range of knowledge beyond their remembrances. I can't play football, but I can teach the Holocaust."

Marion says that her friends were stunned, a few years ago, when she began talking and writing about her Holocaust experience. Even her son, Mark, a Washington, D.C., investor and entrepreneur, listening during a recent interview, expressed surprise at much of her story. "It's amazing! You can go through something like that and go on to live a normal, happy life."

For years, Marion had mostly held that history deep inside. Now she has given testimony at the United States Holocaust Memorial Museum and interviews to other organizations and the media. She helps to sponsor worldwide concerts of *Defiant Requiem: Verdi at Terezín*, a concert-drama of Verdi's *Requiem*, honoring its performance by Theresienstadt's imprisoned Jews before their deportation to Auschwitz.

"Even my good friends…actually until about six years ago, I never told them anything about our experience, and then, when I started writing about it, they were totally nonplussed. I do remember getting on the trains and all these horrible nightmares. You know we just sat there, wherever my parents put us, and…and…watched it all go on, not quite registering. But all the dimensions of what was going on, I remember."

Dimensions. As a very young child, Marion had understood the core of their experience. The boundaries of life under the Nazis, like barbed-wire fences, were cruel and immutable. She could not change them, but, as children do, she observed, she did what her family needed her to do, and she remembered and she held those memories deep inside until she felt ready to share them.

During their first year in the United States, the Hesses marveled at the bounty of food and goods that others seemed to take for granted. At a restaurant, Steven stuffed bread from the table into his pockets in case shortages might push them to starvation again. Ilse reminded him that they no longer needed to do that. For several years, Marion could not sleep without first putting bread or salami, any sort of food, at the foot of her bed, "just in case." She wondered about funerals and cemeteries. Why waste all that time and money when you could just dig pits for all the corpses? Even years later, when her teenaged children were late coming home, she feared that they would never return—an unwelcome echo of her terror when her mother was late returning to the barracks.

The family has pondered how they survived when others did not. At different moments, they have had different answers. Steven has said, "Why did we survive? The bottom line about survival: It was luck and more luck with the unending persistence and resourcefulness of our parents. You had NO control over living or dying." Marion agrees, but adds that their parents' determination to save all of them helped to see them through. She mentioned Ilse's dazzling diamond broach, which the family relinquished to the Nazis, hoping to delay their deportation from Westerbork and then to certain death in Auschwitz or Sobibor. Both twins also point to the fake Paraguayan passports their parents purchased that contributed to their being sent to the Sternlager in Bergen-Belsen instead of an extermination camp.

Marion says, "I never, never have a day where I don't have some thought, a special appreciation of being alive. It's not that I'm kind of noble in any way, but I do realize how lucky, how extraordinarily lucky, I was not only to survive, but to go on to have, you know, a beautiful life. We were condemned to death. Under 5 percent of

Jews deported from Holland survived. I believe we are the only surviving twins."

Once in an interview with the Holocaust Museum, Ilse explored the difference between surviving and recovering your life:

> I do not think that I was left with any hatred, bitterness, complexes, traumas. It was a happening in our lives which we did not call for. Someone…a terrible tragedy made a decision for us, and it is nothing [that] we could fight. So, we survived it, and we just look to a future. We do not look back so much. The only thing we do—we *think* back…. We have a different language. A train doesn't mean for us a transportation to a beautiful vacation spot. It means to us Bergen-Belsen, Westerbork, Auschwitz, Theresienstadt. A *selection* to us is a word which doesn't have a meaning it does for the normal people…. My husband and myself, we could discuss everything…. Even if we didn't talk at all we understood each other…. this is the language of the survivors.

After Carl passed away, Marion, Steven, and Ilse revisited the site of Bergen-Belsen for the fiftieth reunion of their liberation. The camp, of course, had changed dramatically. Instead of encountering mud and putrid, decaying corpses, in 1995 attendees walked on green grass, listened to speeches describing the camp experience, and read memorial markers. A visitor at that event told Marion he thought things in the camp hadn't really been so bad and that much of what was written about it was propaganda. She replied, "I happen to disagree. I'm a survivor." He apologized and walked away.

Ilse later said that at perhaps her lowest point, imprisoned in Bergen-Belsen and feeling that she could not go on, she told herself that she must—her implacable spirit of resistance and determination to defend her family giving her the strength she needed.

Over the years, when she heard people in America complain about small things in daily life, as she told a reporter for the *Washington Post*, she thought, but didn't say, "You should only know." Ilse Hess died in 2003, at the age of eighty-nine.

■   ■   ■

In 1940, some 143,000 Jews lived in the Netherlands, about 80,000 in Amsterdam. By early 2022, the Jewish population in Amsterdam had declined to 12,000. Significant ongoing Dutch efforts to combat embedded antisemitism have met with mixed success. In 2021 in Amsterdam, King Willem-Alexander and Jewish representatives unveiled the sculptural Holocaust Memorial of Names, first proposed in 1947. It attracts some vandalism. Jewish cemeteries have been defaced. In recent years, in the interest of traffic requirements, practically the entire Jewish Quarter of Amsterdam was demolished. There is a square in the city dedicated to Lodewijk Visser, the first Jewish judge on the Netherlands Supreme Court and an outspoken resister of Nazi persecution. He died while under a deportation order. His wife died in Westerbork, and a son died at Mauthausen. Yet, today, the square is dominated by an elaborate streetcar stop. In Amsterdam, as in cities worldwide, guards stand at synagogue doors during religious services.

Yet significant Dutch efforts to promote justice and historic memory continue. The Hollandsche Schouwburg, where Karl worked and Amsterdam's Jews were gathered for deportation to Westerbork, is under renovation to become a National Holocaust Museum. Anne Frank tours of Amsterdam and of the Anne Frank House, where the Frank family hid in a tiny apartment near the Hesses' former home, are major tourist destinations attracting more than a million international visitors every year.

■ . ■ ■

Having lived in the United States almost eighty years, the twins often feel that they've escaped the burden of the past. But at times, unpredictably, Amsterdam, Westerbork, Bergen-Belsen, and Tröbitz come to mind—flashes of their experience invade their days and nights and occupy their hearts. For years, Marion has devoted significant effort to Holocaust groups and events, battling to keep crucial elements of the Holocaust—apathy, ignorance, cruelty—on people's mind. Steven plunges continually into learning more, reading more, teaching others what happened.

Whether avoiding or confronting the Holocaust, for them there is no true liberation, no escape from remembering. The memories rise up at a charity banquet when Marion sees that there is far too much food and it will be wasted. Sometimes she still finds herself amazed that people have an array of delicious food to *choose* from. During classes that Steven teaches about the Holocaust, he feels stricken when students tell him they believe that Jews are crazy about money. Their experience pursues them like the monster it was—and does not leave them. With no distance from that which they carry inside, they face it, learn from it, endure it, and escape it in their own ways, again and again.

Marion Ein Lewin: Heroes and Miracles

My brother and I were nine years old when we came to the United States. We had never attended regular school, did not know the language, and in many ways were starting life anew. Initially, we were placed in kindergarten in a public school on the Upper West Side of Manhattan not far from where we were living, close to our relatives on 162nd Street and Riverside Drive. "Hamburg on the Hudson" they called that area of the city because it was full of German Jewish refugees. Our school had sliding doors separating the different classes, and every few weeks, as our language skills improved, those doors were opened for us so we could "slide" into the next grade as we progressed to the third grade, the proper class for our age.

During the early months of our coming here, Steven and I were regularly pulled out of school to be showcased at some event or other, the young Holocaust twins who had survived against impossible odds and were now warmly welcomed in America. We had tea with Eleanor Roosevelt, lunch with the mayor of Chinatown, were recorded at the Voice of America, and were greeted at the United Nations. It was all special, even if we hardly understood the details. One day I asked my mother why we were doing all this show-and-tell rather than being at school with our new friends. "Because of your Holocaust history and miraculous survival," she answered. I remember the look on my lovely mother's face when I responded, "I don't want to be known just as a Holocaust survivor, I also want to be seen as an American girl."

In many ways, I wanted to turn my back on the past and start life over. My parents were the same way. Of course, the horror of their experience would be with them always, but now there was a living to be made, a good education for their children to be sought, work to find, a new language and culture to be learned. It was not a turning away from what had happened to us, but the need to make room for starting over, knowing you could never fully catch up. Too much had been stolen and forever lost.

My history made me always want to be surrounded with lovely and pretty things after years of living in filth and degradation. There is never a day that fresh flowers are not prominent in my home. Even today, when I write a note to a friend or send a card for special occasions, I draw a flower next to my signature, a symbol of hope and renewal.

From the day we arrived in the United States, my parents encouraged us to do our best, to be good citizens and not to feel we were owed something for what we had gone through. We were blessed to come to America, a country of freedom and opportunity, and that was enough of a gift. I was fortunate to have a wonderful career in health policy in our nation's capital, Washington, D.C., working in the Congress, prominent think tanks, and for the last twelve years before I retired, at the National Academy of Sciences. My work focused mostly on improving health care access for the poor and underserved. The books I wrote and edited make a small contribution to the ongoing challenge of making health care more effective and affordable. In more recent years I have become involved in theater, serving on boards and committees.

In her seventies, my mother moved from our house in Queens to Chevy Chase, Maryland, to be closer to me. On a regular basis when we were out and about, she would suggest, "Let's stop for

Kaffee and *Kuchen*" (coffee and cake). There was always this special magic of sitting together, unrushed and unafraid. I don't remember chairs in Bergen-Belsen. Animals don't sit in chairs, and that is what we were. It was during those special moments that she would talk about her memories, focusing primarily on her happy youth and early years of marriage before the Holocaust. Her most painful memories were the loss of her beloved parents and the circumstances of their deaths, which she only learned about much later. My parents were true heroes; what they endured, what they did to protect my brother and me can never be fully put into words. Without question, they were the link to our survival.

My father died from pneumonia in 1981 when his tired and damaged lungs gave out. I was at his side the night he passed away. His mind was clear as a bell. He wanted to tell me three things. "Take good care of Mommy" was first. "I hope for the survival of Israel." In the camps, the dream of Israel, a land, a home where Jews would not be persecuted was a daily prayer, often the last utterance of a dying skeleton. And the last concern he wanted to share with me—"I worry about the future of democracy. It is such a special gift and if not protected can so easily disappear." I had no idea why the enduring value of democracy was on his mind, but how prophetic those words were, as we now witness democracy under threat in this country and around the globe.

In recent years, several extraordinary revelations filled in missing pieces of our family's history; they are part of the reason for this book. On September 19, 2018, Yom Kippur, I received a call from a senior attaché at the Polish embassy in Washington, D.C., who beseeched me not to hang up on this out of the blue, improbable call. So I listened as he told me about Konstanty Rokicki, a distinguished Polish diplomat who during World War II worked in the Polish Legation in exile in Bern, Switzerland. Operating under constant danger of being betrayed, Rokicki forged hundreds if not a thousand Paraguayan passports that prevented many recipients of these documents from being shipped to an extermination camp. The attaché told me that only very recently an official, if still partial, list of families who had received these passports, was made public. Our names were on that list. The lingering question of why we were sent to Bergen-Belsen, where there was at least some chance for survival, finally had an answer.

That October I was invited as a guest to attend a ceremony in Bern to mark the removal of Rokicki from his pauper's grave (he had died ill and penniless) to a place of honor. Poland's president Andrzej Duda and many other dignitaries came for the event. After the fanfare was over, I walked over to Rokicki's new flower-bedecked resting place and thanked him for his priceless gift to our family.

At the height of the COVID-19 crisis in April 2020, I wrote an op-ed piece in the *Los Angeles Times* on "My Childhood Memories of the Holocaust in a World of COVID-19," which reflected on the heroic and merciful acts of first responders and volunteers risking their lives to help others survive. These selfless acts reminded me of my parents and others at Bergen-Belsen who never lost their humanity and the grace to care for others when the struggle to stay alive was a full-time endeavor. The op-ed was accompanied by a picture of my brother and me at age six, wearing traditional Dutch costumes, the last pictures taken of us before we were sent to Westerbork.

A reader in Los Angeles with a Dutch background recognized the embroidery style on my outfit and immediately identified it as coming from Urk, a small fishing village an hour northeast of Amsterdam. With the help of the town's historian and former policeman, we discovered that our beloved nanny, Marretje, had come from Urk, and the handmade outfits had come from her family. Additional new information came to light in a later *LA Times* article by the award-winning journalist Steve Lopez. His inquiries led him to Marretje's daughter, Ellen Hoogenstrijd, who told him that her mother loved caring for us until the occupation, when she was no longer permitted to work for a Jewish family. One of her last acts was to sew heavy winter coats for us; she had a premonition we would need them. After she left our employ, she worked with a group that, under great risk, brought food to Jewish families in need as the new Nazi regime perfected its stranglehold. Our family is indebted to Marretje for many things, including keeping safely under her bed a suitcase that my parents had given her and that she returned to us after the war. Among other treasured mementos, the suitcase contained precious photo albums of my parents' families, smiling faces that my brother and I never had a chance to meet because their lives were brutally snuffed out.

History has a way of coming full circle. In November 2021, with old friends, I made a nostalgic trip to Amsterdam for a special performance of *The Defiant Requiem*, and I met with Marretje's daughter. In beautiful sunshine, I walked through this city of canals close to the places where we once lived, grateful for the heroes who helped to save our lives. That our entire family, the four of us, survived the Holocaust remains a pure miracle.

Steven: Comprehending the Incomprehensible

It took a presidential visit to Germany by Ronald Reagan in May of 1985 to awaken me to the reality of being among the remnants that survived the worst evil of modern history: the slaughter of some six million European Jews by Nazi killers and their adherents during the Holocaust.

President Reagan, under pressure from German chancellor Helmut Kohl, agreed to a ceremonial visit to the German military cemetery at Bitburg where among German military graves were those of notorious Waffen-SS murderers. Kohl's intent, forty years after the end of World War II, was to erase any distinction between fallen Allied soldiers and German military dead.

The proposed visit started a firestorm of protest from the American Jewish community, and, for the first time, I thought about the unspeakable evil that we had been subjected to and somehow survived. Of course, I knew our family's history, but our young age blocked the all-important context. I spent subsequent decades filling that gap as best I could.

My twin and I were innocents at ages five, six, and seven. We were fully aware of misery, cold, filth, and hunger—always hunger. But we did not know, as our parents did through each waking, terror-filled hour, that we were marked for death, whether that day from typhus, or after a journey in a cattle car, or in a pit in an eastern forest.

Our liberation from a cattle car train, "The Lost Transport," by advancing Soviet forces came at the end of April 1945 in the tiny farm village of Tröbitz in eastern Germany. Of the two thousand dying Jews locked in boxcars for fourteen days, more than five hundred died on the journey or shortly after we were freed.

I consider that my life started in that village. The weather was beautiful, there was food to be found or stolen. We discovered what it was like sleeping in a real bed, washing ourselves and brushing our teeth.

After returning to Amsterdam and eventually "to America!" everything was new. We spoke Dutch. Apparently, no one else did, so we focused on learning a new language, going to school, buying Juicy Fruit chewing gum from penny vending machines.

As the years passed, I realized I was and would be an outsider. My total ignorance of sports and disinterest in any sport would last forever. It was painful at times because it would separate me from "all-American boys." To this day I joke: "To me a quarterback is change at a cash register." I remember at age fourteen in summer camp, the captain of the softball team (or was it hardball?—the smaller one that could really hurt), would pick his team saying, "You get Hess, we had him last time." The things you never forget. It would have been nice to hit a home run or throw a football just once. It wasn't in the cards.

I came out of the concentration camp with "fussy" eating habits that also became permanent and a source of embarrassment. I saw myself, and still do, as a loner, but comfortable in my own skin. I never thought about Nazis consciously or saw myself as "scarred," but I was. My sister was not.

I did eventually find my own path. Although I never really had "goals" or specific career aspirations, I turned out to be a good businessman and enjoyed long years of success. I learned to fly my own plane and enjoy boating. In January 2023, I was presented with the 2022 Lifetime Distinguished Eagle Scout Award, given for service to the nation and to the community. It was one of only eighteen awards in the U.S. for that year.

To this day, I am amazed that all of us survived. The odds were totally against it.

■　　■　　■

In her testimony for the United States Holocaust Memorial Museum, Ilse responded to a question about how her family managed to live through that maelstrom of evil: "People always ask us, 'How come you survived?' And I do not know why. It was not luck. It was not special strength. It was not special treatment. It was not special food. I just think we survived to tell the tale."

Acknowledgments

Every book is a journey of discovery. When dark truths are revealed along that path, the quest can be painful. In this story, despite the pervasive darkness of the Holocaust, a belief in a brighter reality is also ever-present. I'm fortunate and grateful to those who appear in this moving story and offer an uplifting vision of the human condition. I am grateful also to others who are unseen in the story, but who traveled this path with me and helped to make this book possible.

The Hess family has been central to this book in every possible way. As explained in the author's note, both Karl and Ilse Hess left crucial records of their experience, Karl with his memoir and Ilse through interviews, including her testimony for the United States Holocaust Memorial Museum. The Hess twins, Marion and Steven, supported this book thoughtfully, generously, and spent hundreds of hours answering my questions, providing documents, checking and rechecking facts. The family has been a guiding light for me with their courage, honesty, and dedication to high purposes. Karl and Ilse urged the twins to give back to America for providing the family with freedom, safety, and opportunity. Marion and Steven have done so, unstintingly, all their lives.

Marion's partner, Ambassador Stuart Eizenstat, has stood resolutely beside Marion, supporting her efforts to tell her family's Holocaust story. In 2020, he encouraged Marion to write an article pointing out some parallels between inspiring medical workers and volunteers toiling to see the country through the scourge of COVID—acts of selfless courage—and prisoners in Bergen-Belsen who helped other prisoners, at times sharing their last crumbs of bread despite their own dire condition. Her essay moved *Los Angeles Times* reporter Steve Lopez to write the 2021 article about the Hess twins that eventually inspired me to write this book. My thanks also to Steven's children, who provided careful and valuable editing help with the book manuscript.

The Anne Frank House in Amsterdam is an invaluable resource that attracts over a million international visitors annually. Not as well known is the organization's research about Anne's life and the history of the Nazi era in the Netherlands; for instance, the Anne Frank House has put recent allegations about the source of the Franks' betrayal into a more accurate context: that the truth will probably never be known. Two Anne Frank House historians offered substantial insights helpful to this book. Gertjan Broek and Bas von Benda-Beckmann have gone above and beyond their usual roles to support the accuracy of this book. I'm indebted to them for their time, expertise, and thoughtful suggestions.

The Bergen-Belsen Memorial in Lower Saxony, Germany, preserves the memory of the Holocaust through the lens of that concentration camp, educating young and old with sensitivity and careful research. I'm indebted to Bernd Horstmann, curator for the memorial's Register of Names and Permanent Exhibition who found documents for me that I wouldn't have known existed, and explained intricacies of the running of the camp that were difficult to find from other sources. My appreciation also to Jakob Ruehe, our caring and highly knowledgeable guide at the memorial. Jakob spent an entire day with my husband, Sidney, and me, answering questions even before we knew to ask them.

The United States Holocaust Memorial Museum, with its vast resources, tireless experts, library of Holocaust testimonies, and guardianship of historical records has also been central to my work, with special thanks to Michael Berenbaum, rabbi, scholar, teacher, filmmaker, and former Project Director of USHMM. For nearly twenty years, he has been supportive, instructive, and inspiring to me in my writing about the Holocaust. Also at USHMM, my gratitude to Rebecca Erbelding, historian, curator, and author; Anatol Steck, International Archival Programs project director; Michlean Amir, survivor, author, and resource coordinator; Dr. Patricia Heberer Rice, senior historian; Megan Lewis, reference librarian; and Laura Boughton, Holocaust Education program coordinator, all of whom, over a long stretch of time, have offered their knowledge and guidance. Special thanks to Marion Stokvis, Bergen-Belsen survivor, whose letters to Marion Ein Lewin (Marion Hess) and Steven Hess provided information not available elsewhere.

Amsterdam resident during the German occupation, Lolke Wilders, now a U.S. citizen, cheerfully offered hours of conversation in his home and over the phone, describing life in Amsterdam under the Nazis. Over some years before she passed away, Alice Resseguie, a survivor, talked to me extensively about her family's life in Trier, Germany, under the Nazis. She told me that in 1935, after her mother heard Hitler's Nuremburg speech, her mother said, "Hitler is going to shit on us [Jews]," and she insisted that the family send their daughters to the United States as soon as possible. When the family was expelled from their home to make room for "Aryans," feisty Alice unsuccessfully urged her mother to argue, to fight back, and the family was forced to move. With permission of the Resseguie family, Robin Marks-Fife recently loaned me the Resseguie family's scrapbook about Alice, containing photos and descriptions of the family's experience compiled with Alice before her passing. Hilde Geisen (née Geisenheimer), a Theresienstadt survivor and my friend, now deceased, spent countless hours translating documents and discussing with me her life in Germany and during four years in the camp. I miss her.

My thanks also to Julie-Marthe Cohen, devoted curator of cultural history at the Jewish Historical Museum of Amsterdam; to Rotterdam Museum conservator and historian Rob Noordhoek; University of Oregon librarians, including Kathy Stroud and those who keep the Special Collections and Archives, including Lauren Goss, and Randy Sullivan, digital reproductions manager.

Coos Wever, descendant of a Holocaust victim and coproducer of a film about the Lost Train, wrote the best existing historical account of the Lost Train's journey and those prisoners who perished, including where and when they died, as the subject of his master's thesis. Formerly Dutch, now a resident of Israel, he cheerfully offered his knowledge and support. Rainer Bauer, German businessman, now a resident of Tröbitz, was instrumental in collecting and publishing information about the Lost Train, those who died and where they died, and provided significant information for this book. Bauer worked with Erika Arlt, who passed away in 2015, to gather the information. He continues to keep the memory of Tröbitz Jews alive through memorial sites and events in the town; in 2018, Bauer published *Erika und Richart Arlt: Zwei Leben für die DDR*, about the lives of Erika and Richard Arlt. My gratitude also to Berthold Weidner, chief executive of Weidner Händle Atelier, one of Germany's foremost corporate graphic design studios. He provided the invaluable, detailed map showing the paths of the three Bergen-Belsen trains, including the Lost Train. That map is part of a Bergen-Belsen Memorial display at the Atelier in Stuttgart, Germany.

Lub van den Berg, of Urk, Netherlands, retired police officer, and now a board member of the Friends of Urk, discovered and provided incredible photos and information about the Hess family, about their addresses in Amsterdam, and about their Dutch nanny, Marretje Pasterkamp, and her remarkable family. Marion and Steven Hess have recently connected with the Pasterkamp family, offering their gratitude. Hendrina Schindeler, native Dutch speaker now living in the United States, enthusiastically translated numerous documents for Steven Hess, a great help in research.

Weather experts: E. Andriessen at the KNMI (Dutch National Weather Service) Climate Desk; Annette Dietrich in the National Meteorological Library in Germany; and Walter Koelschtsky, manager for Climate and Environment in Deutscher Wetterdienst (German Weather Service), kindly helped me access historical weather information. Walter chillingly and unforgettably observed,

"Of course, in 1944/45 you really could call it [the weather during the Battle of the Bulge and the unbearable cold at Bergen-Belsen] 'winter,' compared to the rainy season today, but [freezing temperatures and heavy snow] weren't unusual then."

Peter Schaapman, Dutch historian and specialist in World War II history, created History Walks, guided tours through Amsterdam's historical sites focusing on the Holocaust. He spent a full day taking me through a maze of sites that brought that history close and made it feel so real that sometimes I felt like listening for German jackboots echoing on the stone streets behind me.

Judith Ventura and Micha Naim, siblings, shared my exploration of their murdered grandparents' history in Vienna, helped me in countless ways, and became my close friends. Their cousins, Anni Berger Goldschmidt and Loli Berger Fischbein, survivors now deceased, also supported my search for information and my understanding of life under the Nazis in Vienna. Another Berger cousin, Peter Wulkan, offered access to priceless Vienna Holocaust history through family records preserved for nearly a century. With endless patience, Dr. Herbert Koch, now retired, guided me through deep and revealing history at the Vienna City Archives—the Wiener Stadt- und Landesarchiv, with its records from "time out of mind." Franklin Schwartz, a Belarus state–approved guide, led my husband, Sidney, and me through the countryside near Minsk, explaining wartime and Holocaust history, and opening a window into Sidney's family history. That journey would not be possible without him, or now, under current international conditions, at all.

I am deeply indebted to Ronald Goldfarb, my brilliant agent, and his associate, Steven Seigart. We faced headwinds early on, but

Ronald persevered and never lost faith. Regnery Publishing, with Tom Spence, Mark and Kathy Bloomfield, brilliant editor Elizabeth Kantor, astute and meticulous copy editor Joshua Monnington, Kylie Carlino, Bettina Allison, and the rest of the Regnery crew have been outstanding in their skill, patience, and unflagging support. I'm grateful to them all.

Duncan McDonald, my first journalism professor at the University of Oregon, writer, photographer, and master teacher, supported and encouraged my work with imagination and laughter from the beginning of my writing journey. Lauren Kessler, author, adventurer, and University of Oregon creative writing professor, pushed and led me and so many others on our writing paths. Bob Welch, intrepid author, my editor at *The Register-Guard*, also has been a bright light whose support made a significant difference for me, as for many other people.

My writing group stood by me, laughed and cried, and offered their wisdom and superb skills, word by word, chapter by chapter, through tight deadlines, and while working on their own books. Thank you, Amalia Gladheart, Elizabeth Lyon, Barbara Pope, Geraldine Moreno-Black, and Ellen Todras. Zanne Miller, fine editor, thank you for your time and talent.

I'm chagrinned in writing these notes of gratitude, knowing that I have very likely inadvertently omitted others. My deep apologies in advance. In addition, even given the wealth of research used to write this book, I know I cannot possibly have captured the complete story.

In my gratitude, I do not forget my family, who always believed and were quick with irreplaceable encouragement and love when obstacles seemed daunting. Thanks to Sarah, Daniel, and Jonathan Cassell, Mark and Sam Van Eeckhout, and to family friend Sarah Hipolito for uncountable ways you've supported me—smiles, jokes, wisdom, quiet when needed, conversation, and wise thoughts. Sidney, of course, you are central, and continue to amaze and inspire me. Words cannot express.

Notes

Dedication

1. Robert Frost, "The Master Speed," *A Further Range* (New York: Henry Holt and Company, 1936), 54.

Epigraphs

1. Jonathan Freedland, "*The Man Who Escaped from Auschwitz to Warn the World*" (interview by David Remnick), *New Yorker*, November 11, 2022, https://www.newyorker.com/podcast/the-new-yorker-radio-hour/the-man-who-escaped-from-auschwitz-to-warn-the-world.
2. Bob Dylan, "Long Ago, Far Away," *The Bootleg Series Vol. 9: The Witmark Demos: 1962–1964*, Legacy Records, 2010.

Works Consulted

Author Interviews with Survivors

Cantor, Hirsh Mandelevich. Survivor of Maly Trostinets. In-person interview. Minsk, Belarus. 2004.

Fischbein, Trude Berger, and Ani Berger Goldschmidt fled Vienna as young women with their family, with the Nazis close behind them. They shared family documents and stories with me in Israel in 2005.

Geisenheimer, Hilde. Survivor of Theresienstadt concentration camp. In-person interview. Eugene, Oregon. 2005–2007.

Genn, Myra. Hidden child. Lived with her mother in a hayloft in German-occupied Poland for several years. In-person interview in her New Jersey home. Summer 2004.

Goldberg, Gertrude Toch, and Herbert Toch, siblings, survived life in Vienna under the Nazis with their parents, Bernard and

Pauline Toch, before escaping to America. Now deceased, they generously provided me with important letters and photos during conversations in their home in California. 2005.

Hess, Steven. Survivor of Westerbork transit camp and Bergen-Belsen concentration camp. Interviews by phone and email. 2020–2023.

Hess (Ein Lewin), Marion. Survivor of Westerbork transit camp and Bergen-Belsen concentration camp. Interviews by telephone and email. 2020–2023.

Hilberg, Raul. Conversations with Hilberg. Letters and documents sent to Faris Cassell concerning Einsatzgruppen and transports of Jews. 2006.

Reizman, Frieda. Survivor of Minsk ghetto, author, and chairperson of Association of Ghetto Survivors, a Minsk, Belarus, organization. Reizman led me on a tour of Minsk ghetto, World War II, and Holocaust sites in Minsk, Belarus. 2004.

Resseguie, Alice. Escaped as a teenager with her sisters in 1936 from Trier, Germany, to the United States. She died in 2016. Alice spoke with me over some ten years about her experiences in Germany. After her death, I perused a family scrapbook about her life.

Walter, Marion. In-person interview over several days relating her experience as a survivor of the 1938 *Kindertransport* to the United Kingdom. Eugene, Oregon. 2005.

Wilders, Lolke. Survivor of Auschwitz II (Auschwitz-Birkenau). In-person interview. Temple Beth Israel, Eugene, Oregon. November 1, 2019.

———. Interviews in person and by phone. Eugene, Oregon. 2021–2022.

Memoirs and Interviews

Boas, Jacob. *We Are Witnesses: Five Diaries of Teenagers Who Died in the Holocaust*. New York: Henry Holt, 1995.

Butter, Irene H., John D. Bidwell, and Kris Holloway. *Shores beyond Shores: From Holocaust to Hope; My True Story*. Amherst, Massachusetts: White River Press, 2018.

Christophe, Francine. *From a World Apart: A Little Girl in the Concentration Camps*. Translated by Christine Burls. Lincoln, Nebraska: University of Nebraska Press, 2000.

Churchill, Winston. *Their Finest Hour*. Vol. 2 of *The Second World War*. London: Cassell and Co., Ltd., 1949.

Eisenhower, Dwight D. *Crusade in Europe: A Personal Account of World War II*. New York: Doubleday, 1948.

Frank, Anne. *Anne Frank: The Diary of a Young Girl*. Translated by B. M. Mooyaart-Doubleday. Originally published in Holland in 1947. New York: Pocket Books, 1972.

Frank, Otto. Booklet compiling Otto Frank's Letters to America: September 1941–1946. New York: YIVO Institute for Jewish Research, 2007.

Geismar, Daphne. *Invisible Years: A Family's Collected Account of Separation and Survival during the Holocaust in the Netherlands*. Translations by Marjolijn de Jager, Judith de Zoete-Cohen, Robert Bjornson. Boston: David R. Godine, 2020.

Herzberg, Abel J. *Between Two Streams: A Diary from Bergen-Belsen*. Translated by Jack Santcross. New York: I. B. Tauris & Co., Ltd, 1997.

Hess, Charles (Karl). *Personal Memoir of Charles Hess*. Family of Charles Hess, 2007.

[Hess, Ilse, interviewed by] Phil McCombs. "Millions Died, but These Survived." *Washington Post*. April 19, 1993.

Hess, Ilse, Steven Hess, and Marion Hess (Ein Lewin). Oral history interview conducted by Shelley Gordon for the Bay Area Holocaust Oral History Project. April 13, 1983. United States Holocaust Memorial Museum Collection. Accession #: 1999.A.0122.1396. RG#: RG-50.477.1396. https://collections.ushmm.org/search/catalog/irn47690.

Hess, Steven, and Marion Hess (Ein Lewin). Interview conducted by David Hess at Abraham Joshua Heschel School for Yom HaShoah commemoration. New York, New York. April 8, 2021. https://www.youtube.com/watch?v=5Ybh3muAXZY.

Hillesum, Etty. *An Interrupted Life: The Diaries, 1941–1943 and Letters from Westerbork*. Translated by Arnold J. Pomerans. New York: Henry Holt & Co., 1996.

Jacobs, Maria. *A Safe House: Holland 1940–1945*. Hamilton, Ontario: Seraphim, 2005.

Konig, Nanette Blitz. *Holocaust Memoirs of a Bergen-Belsen Survivor: Classmate of Anne Frank*. Translated by Rafa Lombardino. Oegstgeest, Netherlands: Amsterdam Publishers, 2018.

Lamon, Lisette. *The Most Precious Gift: Memories of the Holocaust*. New York: French Hill Publishing, 2021.

Laqueur, Renata. *Diary of Bergen-Belsen: March 1944–April 1945*. Celle, Germany: Foundation of Lower Saxony Memorials (Stiftung Niedersächsische Gedenkstätten), 2007.

Lower Saxony Memorials Foundation. *Bergen-Belsen: Catalogue Accompanying the Permanent Exhibition*. Recklinghausen, Germany: Wallstein, n.d.

Masur, Janice. *Shalom Uganda: A Jewish Community on the Equator*. Vancouver: Behind the Book, 2020.

McCarthy, Josè Campion. *Happenstance and Choices: In France, 1938 to 1969*. Eugene, Oregon: Luminare Press, 2019.

Metzger, Jackie. "Interview with Dukie Gelber, Survivor from Holland." Yad Vashem: The World Holocaust Remembrance Center. 2022. https://www.yadvashem.org/articles/interviews/duky.html.

Michel, Ernest W. *Promises Kept: One Man's Journey against Incredible Odds*. With a foreword by Leon Uris. Fort Lee, New Jersey: Barricade, 2008.

Morse, Sandell. *The Spiral Shell: A French Village Reveals Its Secrets of Jewish Resistance in World War II: A Memoir*. Tucson, Arizona: Schaffner Press, 2020.

Oestreicher, Felix Hermann. *Ein jüdischer Arzt-Kalender: Durch Westerbork und Bergen-Belsen nach Tröbitz: Konzentrationslager-Tagebuch 1943–1945*. Edited by Maria Goudsblom-Oestreicher and Erhard Roy Wiehn. Konstanz, Germany: Hartung-Gorre, 2020.

Shirer, William L. *The Nightmare Years: 1930–1940*. Vol. 2 of *20th Century Journey: A Memoir of a Life and the Times*. Boston: Little, Brown and Company, 1984.

Stokvis, Marion. Personal letter to Steven Hess and Marion Hess (Ein Lewin) recalling events they experienced in Bergen-Belsen. May 5, 1996.

Thompson, Judi. *Two Men One Message: The Lavender-Lehmann Readings*. Portland, Oregon: Blackmore & Blackmore, 2000.

Tokudome, Kinue. *Courage to Remember: Interviews on the Holocaust*. Saint Paul, Minnesota: Paragon, 1999.

Van de Perre, Selma. *My Name is Selma: The Remarkable Memoir of a Jewish Resistance Fighter and Ravensbrück Survivor.* Translated by Alice Tetley-Paul and Anna Asbury. New York: Scribner, 2021.

Vassiltchikov, Marie. *Berlin Diaries: 1940–1945.* New York: Vintage, 1985.

Verolme, Hetty E. *The Children's House of Belsen.* Perth, Western Australia: Werma Pty. Ltd., 2016.

Wilsey, Clarice. *Letters from Dachau: A Father's Witness of War, a Daughter's Dream of Peace.* With Bob Welch. Eugene, Oregon: Duncan Gardens Press, 2020.

Wycoff, Johanna. *Dancing in Bomb Shelters: My Diary of Holland in World War II.* Bloomington, Indiana: iUniverse, 2010.

Primary Historical Sources

Brown, Edgar, ed. *How to See Holland*, 13th ed. The Hague: Official Information Office for Tourists, circa 1934.

Cizes, Martha, and Leo Cizes made harrowing escapes from their home in German-occupied Vienna, through France to America between 1939 and 1941. Their letters provided critical insight to the war and the Holocaust in France during those years.

Crockett, William Day, and Sarah Gates Crocket. *A Satchel Guide to Europe.* London: George Allen & Unwin, Ltd., 1939.

Friedlander, Henry, and Sybil Milton, eds. *Bundesarchiv of the Federal Republich of Germany, Koblenz and Freiburg.* Vol. 20 of *Archives of the Holocaust: An International Collection of Selected Documents.* New York: Garland Publishing, Inc., 1993.

Handbook to Holland: With General and Railway Maps of Holland: Plans of Middelburg, Dordrecht, Delft…Etc. London: Ward, Lock and Company, Ltd., 1913.

Irvine, E. Eastman, ed. *The World Almanac and Book of Facts: 1938.* New York: New York World-Telegram, 1938.

Irvine, E. Eastman, ed. *The World Almanac and Book of Facts: 1944.* New York: New York World-Telegram, 1944.

Klamper, Elizabeth, ed. *Dokumentationsarchiv des Österreichischen Widerstandes, Vienna.* Vol. 19 of *Archives of the Holocaust: An International Collection of Selected Documents*, edited by Henry Friedlander and Sybil Milton. New York: Garland Publishing, Inc., 1991.

Lyman, Robert Hunt, ed. *The World Almanac and Book of Facts: 1936.* New York: New York World-Telegram, 1936.

Murray, John. *A Handbook for Travellers in Holland and Belgium.* London: Baedeker's London, 1923.

R. I. G. Taylor, "Report on Belsen Camp by Lt. Col. Taylor." The Liberators of Belsen Concentration Camp. https://www.belsen.co.uk/report-on-belsen-camp-by-lt-col-taylor/.

Siegel, Nina. *The Diary Keepers: World War II in the Netherlands, as Written by the People Who Lived through It.* New York: Ecco, 2023.

Time, May 20, 1940.

"Transcript of the Official Shorthand Notes of 'The Trial of Josef Kramer and Forty Four Others': Nineteenth Day Monday, 8th October, 1945." BergenBelsen.co.uk. 2015. http://www.bergen-belsen.co.uk/pages/TrialTranscript/Trial_Day_019.html.

"War Crimes Trials—Vol. II The Belsen Trial. 'The Trial of Josef Kramer and Forty Four Others:' The Trial (Evidence For The

Prosecution—Captain Derek [Derrick] A. Sington). BergenBelsen. co.uk. 2015. http://www.bergenbelsen.co.uk/pages/trial/trial/trialprosecutioncase/Trial_008_Sington.html.

Wiener Adressbuch: Lehmanns Wohnungsanzeiger: 1938. Vienna: Österreichische Unzeigen-Gesellschaft, n.d.

Yank: The Army Weekly. Vol. 4, no. 18. October 19, 1945.

Secondary Historical Sources

Aalders, Gerard. *Nazi Looting: The Plunder of Dutch Jewry during the Second World War.* Translated by Arnold Pomerans and Erica Pomerans. Oxford, United Kingdom: Berg Publishers, 2004.

Arendt, Hannah. *Eichmann In Jerusalem: A Report on the Banality of Evil.* New York: Penguin, 2006.

Berkley, George E. *Vienna and its Jews: The Tragedy of Success, 1880–1980s.* Cambridge, Massachusetts: Abt Books, 1988.

Bindoff, S. T., G. R. Crone, and F. W. Morgan. *Netherlands.* United Kingdom: Naval Intelligence Division, 1944.

Braber, Ben. "Conclusion." In *This Cannot Happen Here: Integration and Jewish Resistance in the Netherlands, 1940–1945.* Amsterdam: Amsterdam University Press, 2013.

Brenner-Wonschick, Hannelore. *The Girls of Room 28: Friendship, Hope, and Survival in Theresienstadt.* Translated by John E. Woods and Shelley Frisch. New York: Schocken Books, 2009.

Bridgman, Jon. *The End of the Holocaust: The Liberation of the Camps.* Edited by Richard H. Jones. Portland, Oregon: Areopagitica, 1990.

Browning, Christopher R., and Jürgen Matthäus. *The Origins of the Final Solution: The Evolution of Nazi Jewish Policy, September 1939–March 1942.* Lincoln and Jerusalem: University of Nebraska Press and Yad Vashem, 2004.

Bruinius, Harry. *Better for All the World: The Secret History of Forced Sterilization and America's Quest for Racial Purity.* New York: Vintage Books, 2007.

Burleigh, Michael. *The Third Reich: A New History.* New York: Hill and Wang, 2001.

Cahusac-van den Berg, Aleida Pierrette. *Unconditional Love: Life with My Mother in the 1930s.* Oegstgeest, Netherlands: Amsterdam Publishers, 2018.

Cassan, Flora. *Marking the Jews in Renaissance Italy: Politics, Religion, and the Power of Symbols.* Cambridge, Massachusetts: Cambridge University Press, 2017.

Cholawsky, Shalom. *The Jews of Bielorussia during World War II.* Amsterdam. Harwood Academic Publishers, 1998.

De Marat, Pierre. "The Power of Symbols and the Symbols of Power through Time: Probing the Luba Past." In *Beyond Chiefdoms: Pathways to Complexity in Africa*, edited by Susan Keech McIntosh. Cambridge, United Kingdom: Cambridge University Press, 2009.

Diner, Hasia R. *We Remember with Reverence and Love: American Jews and the Myth of Silence after the Holocaust, 1945–1962.* New York: New York University Press, 2009.

Downey, Kirstin. *The Woman behind the New Deal: The Life and Legacy of Frances Perkins—Social Security, Unemployment Insurance, and the Minimum Wage.* New York: Anchor Books, 2010.

Dwork, Debórah, and Robert Jan van Pelt. *Holocaust: A History.* New York: W. W. Norton & Company, 2002.

Erbelding, Rebecca. *Rescue Board: The Untold Story of America's Efforts to Save the Jews of Europe.* New York: Doubleday, 2018.

Freedland, Jonathan. "The Man Who Escaped from Auschwitz to Warn the World." Interview by David Remnick. *New Yorker Radio Hour.* November 11, 2022. Podcast. https://www.newyorker.com/podcast/the-new-yorker-radio-hour/the-man-who-escaped-from-auschwitz-to-warn-the-world.

Freund, Florian, and Hans Safrian. *Expulsion and Extermination: The Fate of the Austrian Jews, 1938–1945.* Translated by Dalia Rosenfeld and Gabriel Biemann. Vienna: Austrian Resistance Archive, 1997.

Friedländer, Saul. *The Years of Extermination: Nazi Germany and the Jews, 1939–1945.* New York: HarperCollins, 2007.

Fulbrook, Mary. *The Divided Nation: A History of Germany, 1918–1990.* New York: Oxford University Press, 1992.

Gerlach, Christian. *Extremely Violent Societies: Mass Violence in the Twentieth-Century World.* New York: Cambridge University Press, 2010.

Gilbert, Martin. *The Routledge Atlas of the Second World War.* 2nd ed. New York: Routledge, 2009.

Gladwell, Malcolm. *The Bomber Mafia: A Dream, a Temptation, and the Longest Night of the Second World War.* New York: Little, Brown and Company, 2021.

———. *Talking to Strangers: What We Should Know about the People We Don't Know.* New York: Little, Brown and Company, 2019.

Goldhagen, Daniel Jonah. *Hitler's Willing Executioners: Ordinary Germans and the Holocaust.* New York: Vintage Books, 1997.

Gruner, Wolf. *Jewish Forced Labor under the Nazis: Economic Needs and Racial Aims, 1938–1944.* Translated by Kathleen M.

Dell'Orto. New York: Cambridge University Press in association with the United States Holocaust Memorial Museum, 2006.

Hamann, Brigitte. *Hitler's Vienna: A Dictator's Apprenticeship.* Translated by Thomas Thornton. New York: Oxford University Press, 1999.

Hays, Peter. *Why?: Explaining the Holocaust.* New York: W. W. Norton & Company, 2017.

Hilberg, Raul. *The Destruction of the European Jews.* Rev. ed. New York: Holmes & Meier, 1985.

———. *The Politics of Memory: The Journey of a Holocaust Historian.* Chicago: Ivan R. Dee, 1996.

Holden, Wendy. *Born Survivors: Three Young Mothers and Their Extraordinary Story of Courage, Defiance, and Hope.* New York: HarperCollins, 2016.

Hondius, Dienke. *Return: Holocaust Survivors and Dutch Anti-Semitism. Contributions to the Study of Religion.* Westport, Connecticut: Praeger, 2003.

Horn, Dara. *People Love Dead Jews: Reports from a Haunted Present.* New York: W. W. Norton & Company, 2021.

Kolb, Eberhard. *Bergen-Belsen: From "Detention Camp" to Concentration Camp, 1943 to 1945.* 2nd ed. Göttingen, Germany: Vandenhoeck & Ruprecht, 1986.

Lee, Carol Ann. *The Hidden Life of Otto Frank.* New York: Perennial, 2003.

Mendelsohn, Daniel. *Three Rings: A Tale of Exile, Narrative, and Fate.* Charlottesville, Virginia: University of Virginia Press, 2020.

Megargee, Geoffrey P. *Early Camps, Youth Camps, and Concentration Camps and Subcamps under the SS-Business Administration Main Office (WVHA).* Vol. 1 of *The United States Holocaust Memorial*

Museum Encyclopedia of Camps and Ghettos, 1933–1945. Bloomington, Indiana: Indiana University Press, 2009.

Moore, Bob. *Victims and Survivors: The Nazi Persecution of the Jews in the Netherlands, 1940–1945.* London: Hodder Education Publishers, 1997.

Morizumi, Takashi. *Children of the Gulf War: A Different Nuclear War.* Hiroshima, Japan: Global Association for Banning Depleted Uranium Weapons, 2002.

1939 Pages of Time: A Nostalgia News Report. Millersville, Tennessee: Pages of Time, 1989.

Novick, Peter. *The Holocaust in American Life.* Boston: Houghton Mifflin, 1999.

Office of Armed Forces Information and Education: Department of Defense. *A Pocket Guide to the Low Countries.* Washington, D.C.: U.S. Government Printing Office, 1953.

Orlow, Dietrich. *A History of Modern Germany: 1871 to Present.* 5th ed. New Jersey: Prentice Hall, 2001.

Presser, Jacob. *The Destruction of the Dutch Jews.* New York: E. P. Dutton & Co., 1969.

Raphael, Melissa. *The Female Face of God in Auschwitz: A Jewish Feminist Theology of the Holocaust.* London: Routledge Press, 2003.

Reilly, Jo, David Cesarani, Tony Kushner, and Colin Richmond, eds. *Belsen in History and Memory.* Portland, Oregon: Frank Cass Publishers, 1997.

Riding, Alan. *And the Show Went On: Cultural Life in Nazi-Occupied Paris.* New York: Vintage Books, 2010.

Roth, John K., and Michael Berenbaum, eds. *Holocaust: Religious and Philosophical Implications*. Saint Paul, Minnesota: Paragon House, 1989.

Roubier, Jean (photographer), and Joseph Delmelle (text). *Benelux: Holland, Belgium, Luxembourg; 100 Photographs*. Thames and Hudson: London, 1958.

Rowen, Herbert H., ed. *The Low Countries in Early Modern Times: Selected Documents*. New York: Walker and Company, 1972.

Safrian, Hans. *Eichmann's Men*. Translated by Ute Stargardt. New York: Cambridge University Press in association with the United States Holocaust Memorial Museum, 2010.

Shephard, Ben. *After Daybreak: The Liberation of Bergen-Belsen, 1945*. New York: Schocken Books, 2005.

Snyder, Timothy. *Black Earth: The Holocaust as History and Warning*. New York: Tim Duggan Books, 2015.

———. *Bloodlands: Europe between Hitler and Stalin*. New York: Basic Books, 2022.

Stigter, Bianca. *Atlas van een Bezette Stad: Amsterdam 1940–1945* [Atlas of an occupied city: Amsterdam: 1940–1945]. Amsterdam: Stichting De Gijselaar-Hintzenfonds [Foundation of Gijselaar-Hintzenfonds], 2019.

Strauss, Gwen. *The Nine: The True Story of a Band of Women Who Survived the Worst of Nazi Germany*. New York: Saint Martin's Press, 2021.

Tipton, Frank B. *A History of Modern Germany since 1815*. Berkeley: University of California Press, 2003.

Ullrich, Volker. *Eight Days in May: The Final Collapse of the Third Reich*. Translated by Jefferson Chase. New York: Liveright Publishing Corp., 2021.

Welch, Bob. *Saving My Enemy: How Two WWII Soldiers Fought against Each Other and Later Forged a Friendship That Saved Their Lives*. Washington, D.C.: Regnery History, 2021.

Weyr, Thomas. *The Setting of the Pearl: Vienna under Hitler*. New York: Oxford University Press, 2005.

Fiction

Elon, Emuna. *House on Endless Waters*. Translated from Hebrew by Anthony Berris and Linda Yechiel. New York: Washington Square Press, 2020.

Hannah, Kristin. *The Nightingale*. New York: Saint Martin's Press, 2015.

Hunter, Georgia. *We Were the Lucky Ones*. New York: Viking Penguin, 2017

Seiffert, Rachel. *The Dark Room*. New York: Vintage International, 2002.

Weil, Jiří. *Life with a Star*. Translated by Rita Klímová with Roslyn Schloss. With preface by Philip Roth. New York: Penguin, 1993.

Films

Lindwer, Willy, dir. *Goodbye Holland: The Destruction of Dutch Jewry*. Produced by AVA-Dateline Productions and Terra Film Productions. Jerusalem: Ruth Diskin Films, 2004.

Ohayon, Michèle, dir. *Steal a Pencil for Me*. Los Angeles, California: Seventh Art Releasing/Red Envelope Entertainment. 2007. Documentary about two Dutch Holocaust survivors.

Van der Burg, Michel. *Westerbork Film 2021: Complete Remastered Edition*. Filmed by Rudolf Breslauer. Settela.com. 2021.

Print Articles

Ahlrichs, Johanna, Katharina Baier, Barbara Christophe, Felicitas Macgilchrist, Patrick Mielke, and Roman Richtera. "Memory Practices in the Classroom: On Reproducing, Destabilizing and Interrupting Majority Memories." *Journal of Educational Media, Memory, & Society* 7, no. 2 (2015): 89–109.

Associated Press. "Eisenhower Regrets Policy of Total Surrender: Admits Roosevelt Erred in His World War II Goal; Says the Fear of U.S. Terms Sparred Nazis to Fight." *New York Times*, December 21, 1964.

Barenholz, Shirley. "The Lost Transport." *De TIJD*, May 5, 1995.

Bartov, Omer. "Witness to Horror: Long-Suppressed Accounts of Nazi Genocide in the Soviet Territories." *Wall Street Journal*, January 19, 2008. Book review of Rubenstein, Joshua, and Ilya Altman, eds. *The Unknown Black Book*. Bloomington, Indiana: Indiana University Press, 2008.

Bellinger, Joseph P. "The Lethal Liberation of Bergen-Belsen." *Inconvenient History* 2, no. 3 (2010).

Bennhold, Katrin. "Her Father Fled the Nazis. Now She's the U.S.'s Top Envoy in Germany." *New York Times*, June 25, 2022.

Brasz, Chaya. "Dutch Progressive Jews and Their Unexpected Key Role in Europe." *European Judaism: A Journal for the New Europe* 49, no. 1 (2016): 5–18. http://www.jstor.org/stable/43740786.

Breitman, Richard. "Hitler and Genghis Khan." *Journal of Contemporary History* 25, no. 2–3 (1990): 337–51.

"Fall of France Wakes Americans to Their Nation's Peril." *Life*, July 1, 1940.

Feifer, Gregory. "The Myths That Made, and Still Make, Russia." *New York Times*, December 25, 2022. Book review of Figes, Orlando. *The Story of Russia*. New York: Metropolitan Books, 2022.

Fritzsche, Peter. "Leaving Nazism Behind." *New York Times*, February 6, 2022. Book Review of Jähner, Harald. *Aftermath: Life in the Fallout of the Third Reich, 1945–1955*. Translated by Shaun Whiteside. New York: Alfred A. Knopf, 2021.

Gibson, Eric. "The Art of War." *Wall Street Journal*, July 9, 2022. Book Review of Rorimer, James J. *Monuments Man: The Mission to Save Vermeers, Rembrandts, and Da Vincis from the Nazi's Grasp*. New York: Rizzoli Electa, 2022.

Hasian, Marouf, Jr. "Anne Frank, Bergen-Belsen, and the Polysemic Nature of Holocaust Memories." *Rhetoric and Public Affairs* 4, no. 3 (2001): 349–74.

"Helpless Humiliation Comes to the Everyday People of France." *Life*, July 1, 1940.

Hess, Steven. "Disproportionate Destruction: The Annihilation of the Jews in the Netherlands, 1940–1945." In *The Netherlands and Nazi Genocide: Papers of the 21st Annual Scholars' Conference*, edited by G. Jan Colijn and Marcia Sachs Littell. Vol. 32 of Symposium Series. Lewiston, New York: Edwin Mellen Press, 1992.

Hett, Benjamin Carter, "The Fateful Choice: Declaring War on the United States Was a Bad Idea." Sunday Book Review. *New York Times*, January 9, 2022. Book review of Simms, Brendan, and Charlie Laderman, *Hitler's American Gamble: Pearl Harbor and Germany's March to Global War*. New York: Basic Books, 2021.

Hickley, Catherine. "Did Nazis Coerce Art Sale?" *New York Times*, July 7, 2021.

Hogervorst, Susan. "Transmitting Memory between and beyond Generations: The Rotterdam Bombardment in Local Memory Culture and Education from 1980 to 2015." *Journal of Educational Media, Memory, & Society* 7, no. 22 (2015): 66–88.

Horn, Dara. "Is Holocaust Education Making Anti-Semitism Worse?: Using Dead Jews as Symbols Isn't Helping Living Ones." *The Atlantic*, May 2023.

Horowitz, Jason. "Uncovering Secrets Buried in Vatican Archives." *New York Times*, May 28, 2022.

Kisch, Herbert. "Prussian Mercantilism and the Rise of the Krefeld Silk Industry: Variations upon an Eighteenth-Century Theme." *Transactions of the American Philosophical Society* 58, no. 7 (1968): 3–50.

Krieg, Lisa Jenny. "'Who Wants to Be Sad Over and Over Again?' Emotion Ideologies in Contemporary German Education about the Holocaust." *Journal of Educational Media, Memory, & Society* 7, no. 2 (2015): 110–28.

Lipstadt, Deborah E. "Antisemitism Here and Now." Testimony before the United States Commission on International Religious Freedom. January 8, 2020. https://www.uscirf.gov/sites/default/files/Deborah%20Lipstadt-%20Emory.pdf.

Lopez, Steve. "How a Picture in a Newspaper Unlocked Childhood Mysteries for Two Holocaust Survivors." *Los Angeles Times*, March 5, 2021.

Lucassen, Leo. "Bringing Structure Back In: Economic and Political Determinants of Immigration in Dutch Cities, 1920–1940." *Social Science History* 26, no. 3 (2002): 503–29.

Marx, Erich. "That's How It Was: A Report on Westerbork and Bergen Belsen (1945)." *Irish Pages* 9, no. 2 (2015): 72–101.

Mason, Henry L. "Testing Human Bonds within Nations: Jews in the Occupied Netherlands." *Political Science Quarterly* 99, no. 2 (1984): 315–43.

Merkin, Daphne. "Descent into Evil: A New Biography Sums Up Reinard Heydrich's Rapid-Fire Nazi Career." *New York Times*, July 31, 2022. Book review of Dougherty, Nancy. *The Hangman and His Wife: The Life and Death of Reinhard Heydrich*. New York: Alfred A. Knopf, 2022.

Moore, Bob. "The Netherlands." In *The Oxford Handbook of Fascism*, edited by R. J. B. Bosworth, 453–69. Oxford, United Kingdom: Oxford University Press, 2012.

Ravenna, Michael [pen name for Eudora Welty]. "German Home Front." *New York Times*, August 20, 1944. Book review of Hoellering, Franz. *Furlough*. New York: The Viking Press, 1944.

Roberts, Sam. "Mel Mermelstein, 95, Who Survived Holocaust and Beat Deniers in Court." *New York Times*, February 4, 2022.

———. "Vera Gissing, 93, Writer Rescued by 'Britain's Schindler,' Is Dead." *New York Times*, March 28, 2022.

Rosensaft, Menachem Z. "From 'Horror Camp' to 'Europe's Last Shtetl': What Our Fathers Saw at Bergen-Belsen." *Haaretz*, September 4, 2022.

Schmidt van der Zanden, Christine. "Holocaust Resistance." In *The Cambridge Dictionary of Judaism and Jewish Culture*, edited by Judith Reesa Baskin. Cambridge, United Kingdom: Cambridge University Press, 2014.

Siegal, Nina. "No Longer Anonymous" *New York Times*, May 19, 2021

————. "Propaganda Became Evidence." *New York Times*, July 30, 2022.

Steinhauser, Gabriele. "Germany Confronts the Forgotten Story of Its Other Genocide." *Wall Street Journal*, July 28, 2017.

Szalai, Jennifer. "The War We Revere a Little Too Much." *New York Times*, November 30, 2021.

Tammes, Peter. "Jewish Immigrants in the Netherlands during the Nazi Occupation." *Journal of Interdisciplinary History* 37, no. 4 (2007): 543–62.

Taylor, Telford. "Why the World Did Not Listen." *New York Times*, February 1, 1981. Book review of Laqueur, Walter. *The Terrible Secret: Suppression of the Truth about Hitler's "Final Solution."* Boston: Little, Brown and Company, 1981.

Van den Berg, Lub. "Jewish Twins in Urker Costumes." *Urker Volksleven*, July 2020.

Von Frijtag Drabbe Künzel, Geraldien. "Being and Belonging: Benno Premsela, Joop Voet, Sándor Baracs and the Holocaust in Nazi-Occupied Amsterdam." *Journal of Genocide Research* 21, no. 3 (2019): 418–35.

Wever, Coos. "The 'Lost Train': The Journey of the Last Evacuation Transport from Bergen-Belsen to Tröbitz, April 9–23, 1945." Master's thesis, University of Haifa Humanities Faculty, Weiss-Livnat International MA Program in Holocaust Studies, 2020.

Wijnhoven, Jochanan H. A. "Review Article." Of Presser, Jacob. *The Destruction of the Dutch Jews.* Translated by Arnold Pomerantz. New York. E. P. Dutton & Co., 1969; Wijnberg, S. *De Joden in Amsterdam, Een studie over verandering in hun attitudes* [The Jews of Amsterdam: A study of change in their attitudes]. Assen,

Netherlands: Van Gorcum, 1967. *Jewish Social Studies* 32, no. 4 (1970): 315–23.

Digital Articles

"Adolf Eichmann." In Wikipedia. December 22, 2022. https://en.wikipedia.org/w/index.php?title=Adolf_Eichmann&oldid=1128899467.

"Adolf Hitler Is Named Chancellor of Germany." History. January 27, 2022. https://www.history.com/this-day-in-history/adolf-hitler-is-named-chancellor-of-germany.

"The Amsterdam General Strike of February 1941." The National WWII Museum | New Orleans. April 10, 2018. https://www.nationalww2museum.org/war/articles/amsterdam-general-strike-february-1941.

"Anglo-Polish Alliance." In Wikipedia. December 11, 2022. https://en.wikipedia.org/w/index.php?title=Anglo-Polish_alliance&oldid=1126738882.

"An Architect of Terror: Heinrich Himmler and the Holocaust." National WWII Museum | New Orleans. May 23, 2020. https://www.nationalww2museum.org/war/articles/heinrich-himmler-holocaust.

"Arthur Seyss-Inquart." In *Encyclopedia Britannica*. October 12, 2022. https://www.britannica.com/biography/Arthur-Seyss-Inquart.

"Arthur Seyss-Inquart." In Military Wiki. June 26, 2021. https://military-history.fandom.com/wiki/Arthur_Seyss-Inquart.

"Auschwitz." In United States Holocaust Memorial Museum Holocaust Encyclopedia. March 16, 2015. https://encyclopedia.ushmm.org/content/en/article/auschwitz.

Battersby, James Larratt. *The Holy Book of Adolf Hitler.* Southport, England: J. L. Battersby, 1952. https://www.jrbooksonline.com /PDF_Books/HolyBookOfAdolfHitler.pdf.

"Battle of the Atlantic." In *Encyclopedia Britannica.* August 27, 2022. https://www.britannica.com/event/Battle-of-the-Atlantic.

"Battle of the Bulge." History. July 22, 2020. https://www.history .com/topics/world-war-ii/battle-of-the-bulge.

Beevor, Antony. "'The Fall of Berlin 1945.'" *New York Times,* September 8, 2002. https://www.nytimes.com/2002/09/08/boo ks/chapters/the-fall-of-berlin-1945.html.

"Benito Mussolini." In *Encyclopedia Britannica.* August 30, 2022. https://www.britannica.com/biography/Benito-Mussolini.

"Bergen-Belsen Concentration Camp." In Wikipedia. May 26, 2023. https://en.wikipedia.org/wiki/Bergen-Belsen _concentration_camp.

"Breif van de Minister van Financiën [Dutch Minister of Finance report 6 on reparations]." Tweede Kamer der Staten-Generaal. 1997–1998. https://zoek.officielebekendmakingen.nl/kst-25839 -2.pdf.

"British Response to V1 and V2." The National Archives (United Kingdom). 2008. https://www.nationalarchives.gov.uk/educati on/resources/british-response-v1-and-v2/.

"British U-Class Submarine." In Wikipedia. October 22, 2022. https:// en.wikipedia.org/w/index.php?title=British_U-class _submarine&oldid=1117604272.

"Buchenwald Concentration Camp." In Wikipedia. December 20, 2022. https://en.wikipedia.org/w/index.php?title=Buchenwald _concentration_camp&oldid=1128473620.

"Camp Songs." Music of Remembrance. https://www.musicofre membrance.org/show-details/camp-songs.

Chen, C. Peter. "The Danzig Crisis: 24 Oct 1938–29 Aug 1939." World War II Database. May 2007. https://ww2db.com/battle _spec.php?battle_id=162.

———. "Netherlands." World War II Database. June 2011. https:// ww2db.com/country/netherlands.

"Coining a Word and Championing a Cause: The Story of Raphael Lemkin." In United States Holocaust Memorial Museum Holocaust Encyclopedia. https://encyclopedia.ushmm.org/content/en/ article/coining-a-word-and-championing-a-cause-the-story-of-raphael-lemkin.

"Convoy." In *Encyclopedia Britannica*. October 30, 2019. https:// www.britannica.com/topic/convoy-naval-operations.

"The Days of Liberation." qooh.org.uk. 2021. https://www.qooh. org.uk/?page_id=1629.

"Death of Adolf Hitler." In Wikipedia. December 17, 2022. https:// en.wikipedia.org/w/index.php?title=Death_of_Adolf_Hitler&o ldid=1127932997.

"Der Verlorene Zug: 10. April–23. April 1945." https://upload.wi kimedia.org/wikipedia/commons/e/ee/Verlorener_Zug.png.

DeZeng, Henry L., IV. "Luftwaffe Airfields 1935–45 the Netherlands." August 2014. http://www.ww2.dk/Airfields%20-%20 Netherlands.pdf.

Dowell, Stuart. "Slovakian Invasion: The Long Forgotten Story of How Slovak Troops Helped Hitler Defeat Poland." The First News. September 1, 2018. https://www.thefirstnews.com/ article/slovakian-invasion-the-long-forgotten-story-of-how -slovak-troops-helped-hitler-defeat-poland-1997.

"Draw Me the Story of the Jews in the Netherlands." Montreal Holocaust Museum. https://museeholocauste.ca/en/activities /draw-me-story-jews-netherlands-holocaust/.

"Dutch Citizens Resist Nazi Occupation, 1940–1945." Global Nonviolent Action Database. May 27, 2011. https://nvdatabase. swarthmore.edu/content/dutch-citizens-resist-nazi-occupation-1940-1945.

"Dutch Famine of 1944–1945." In Wikipedia. December 2, 2022. https://en.wikipedia.org/w/index.php?title=Dutch_famine_of_19 44%E2%80%931945&oldid=1125206128.

"Eastern Front (World War II)." In Wikipedia. December 14, 2022. https://en.wikipedia.org/w/index.php?title=Eastern_Front_(Wo rld_War_II)&oldid=1127366060.

Egan, Charles E. "All Reich to See Camp Atrocities." *New York Times*, April 24, 1945. https://www.nytimes.com/1945/04/24/ar chives/all-reich-to-see-camp-atrocities-allies-will-billboard-scenes-in. html.

"Elbe Day." Google search. https://www.google.com/search?clien t=safari&rls=en&q=elbe+day&ie=UTF-8&oe=UTF-8.

"Elbe Day." In Military Wiki. January 19, 2021. https://military-history.fandom.com/wiki/Elbe_Day.

Frabotta, Kyle. "The Mindset of the Hitler-Jugend." Harold Marcuse. June 2004. https://marcuse.faculty.history.ucsb.edu/cl asses/133p/133p04papers/KFrabottaHitlerYouth046.htm.

Gedenkstätte Bergen-Belsen. https://bergen-belsen.stiftung-ng.de/.

"German and Allied Bombing Raids on the Netherlands (in Numbers)." Institute for War, Holocaust and Genocide Studies. https://www.niod.nl/en/frequently-asked-questions/german-and -allied-bombing-raids-netherlands-numbers.

"German Occupation of the Rhineland." The National Archives (United Kingdom). 2008. https://www.nationalarchives.gov.uk /education/resources/german-occupation/.

"German Revolution of 1918–1919." In Wikipedia. November 1, 2022. https://en.wikipedia.org/w/index.php?title=German_Rev olution_of_1918%E2%80%931919&oldid=1119407219.

"German World War I and II Poem/Song: Wir fahren gegen Engeland." Children in History. June 8, 2015. https://www.hist clo.com/essay/war/ww2/air/eur/bob/phase/bobp-gconf01.html.

"Georgy Zhukov." In Wikipedia. December 21, 2022. https://en .wikipedia.org/w/index.php?title=Georgy_Zhukov&oldid=112 8726779.

Gerstenfeld, Manfred. "Investigating Much, Paying Little: The Dutch Government and the Holocaust Asset Inquiries." *Jerusalem Viewpoints*, no. 424. February 15, 2000. https:// jcpa.org/article/investigating-much-paying-little-the-dutch -government-and-the-holocaust-asset-inquiries/.

"Gertrude van Tijn Collection." Center for Jewish History Archives. March 26, 2015. https://archives.cjh.org/repositories/5/resourc es/6781.

"Go In-Depth." Anne Frank House. https://www.annefrank.org /en/anne-frank/go-in-depth/.

Golden, Lester. "WWII Mythology Tour: The Netherlands." Lessons from History. December 1, 2020. https://medium.com/ lessons-from-history/wwii-mythology-tour-the-netherlands- 1da9113ab649.

"Hanns Albin Rauter." In Wikipedia. July 28, 2022. https://en.wi kipedia.org/w/index.php?title=Hanns_Albin_Rauter&oldid=11 01021203.

"Heinrich Himmler." In Wikipedia. December 15, 2022. https://en.wikipedia.org/w/index.php?title=Heinrich_Himmler&oldid=1127584663#Marriage_and_family.

"Heinz Guderian." In Wikipedia. December 19, 2022. https://en.wikipedia.org/w/index.php?title=Heinz_Guderian&oldid=1128387632.

"Hitler Youth." In United States Holocaust Memorial Museum Holocaust Encyclopedia. December 10, 2020. https://encyclopedia.ushmm.org/content/en/article/hitler-youth-2.

"Hitler Youth." In Wikipedia. November 18, 2022. https://en.wikipedia.org/w/index.php?title=Hitler_Youth&oldid=1122587147#World_War_II.

Hoberman, J. "A Novelist Chronicles the Panic of War while Living through It." *New York Times*, September 9, 2022. Book review of Serge, Victor. *Last Times*. Translated by Ralph Manheim. New York: New York Book Review Classics, 2022.

"Hollandsche Schouwburg—National Holocaust Memorial." European Observatory on Memories. https://europeanmemories.net/memorial-heritage/hollandsche-schouwburg-national-holocaust-memorial/.

Hornig, Frank, and Michael Sontheimer. "German History Museum Tells Story of Hitler's Life." ABC News. October 13, 2010. https://abcnews.go.com/International/germanys-hitler-exhibition/story?id=11871127.

"How Europe Went to War in 1939." Imperial War Museums. 2022. https://www.iwm.org.uk/history/how-europe-went-to-war-in-1939.

"Inflation Calculator." CPI Inflation Calculator. 2022. https://www.officialdata.org/us/inflation/.

"Joseph Goebbels." In Wikipedia. December 17, 2022. https://en.wiki pedia.org/w/index.php?title=Joseph_Goebbels&oldid=112 7894294.

"The JUST Act Report: Slovakia." U.S. Department of State. https:// www.state.gov/reports/just-act-report-to-congress/slovakia/.

Klug, Adam. "The German Buybacks, 1932–1939: A Cure for Overhang?" *Princeton Studies in International Finance*, no. 3 (1993). https://ies.princeton.edu/pdf/S75.pdf.

"Krefeld." In Wikipedia. November 22, 2022. https://en.wikiped ia.org/w/index.php?title=Krefeld&oldid=1123192950#The_Je ws_of_Krefeld.

Landé, Peter. "The Lost Train: Bergen-Belsen to Tröbitz." JewishGen. August 10, 2008. https://www.jewishgen.org/datab ases/holocaust/0170_lost_train.html.

Le Clerc Phillips, R. "Germans Take Steps to Prevent Suicides." *New York Times*, September 6, 1925. https://timesmachine.nyt imes.com/timesmachine/1925/09/06/99357199.html?pageNum ber=NaN.

Leffler, Melvyn P., Andrew Preston, Christopher Nichols, David Milne, Beverly Gage, David Farber, Geoffrey Kabaservice et al. "America First: The Past and Future of an Idea." Edited by Melvyn P. Leffler and William Hitchcock. *Passport*, September 2018: 33–51. https://shafr.org/sites/default/files/passport-09 -2018-america-first-essays.pdf.

"Liberation of Auschwitz Concentration Camp." In Wikipedia. October 20, 2022. https://en.wikipedia.org/w/index.php?title =Liberation_of_Auschwitz_concentration_camp&oldid=1117 153186.

"The Liberation of the Netherlands." Government of Canada. January 27, 2020. https://www.veterans.gc.ca/eng/remembrance /classroom/fact-sheets/netherlands.

"Liberation of the Netherlands and Capitulation of Germany." Juno Beach Centre. March 28, 2014. https://www.junobeach. org/canada-in-wwii/articles/liberation-of-the-netherlands -and-capitulation-of-germany/.

"List of Specifications of Submarines of World War II." In Wikipedia. August 23, 2022. https://en.wikipedia.org/w/index .php?title=List_of_specifications_of_submarines_of_World_War _II&oldid=1106262475.

"List of Submarines of World War II." In Wikipedia. December 13, 2022. https://en.wikipedia.org/w/index.php?title=List_of_subm arines_of_World_War_II&oldid=1127228551.

"The Lost Train." In Wikipedia. October 30, 2022. https://en.wik ipedia.org/w/index.php?title=The_Lost_Train&oldid=1119096951.

Lucassen, Leo. "Bringing Structure Back In: Economic and Political Determinants of Immigration in Dutch Cities, 1920–1940." *Social Science History* 26, no. 3 (2002): 503–29. https://www.research gate.net/publication/236758341_Bringing_Structure_Back_In_ Economic_and_Political_Determinants_of_Immigration_in_ Dutch_Cities_1920-1940.

"Maly Trostinec," Aktion Reinhard Camps, May 28, 2006, http:// www.deathcamps.org/occupation/maly%20trostinec.html.

"A Map of the Bergen-Belsen Concentration Camp in the Grounds of the Memorial Bergen Belsen, Lower Saxony, Germany." alamy. 2022. https://www.alamy.com/a-map-of-the-bergen-belsen- concentration-camp-in-the-grounds-of-the-memorial-bergen- belsen-lower-saxony-germany-image209389603.html.

Marcuse, Harold. "Historical Dollars-to-Marks Currency Conversion Page." Harold Marcuse. August 19, 2005. https://marcuse.faculty.history.ucsb.edu/projects/currency.htm.

"*Mein Kampf.*" In Wikipedia. December 14, 2022. https://en.wikipedia.org/w/index.php?title=Mein_Kampf&oldid=1127466880.

Mougel, Nadège. "World War I Casualties." Translated by Julie Gratz. Centre européen Robert Schuman. 2011. http://www.centre-robert-schuman.org/userfiles/files/REPERES – module 1-1-1 - explanatory notes – World War I casualties – EN.pdf.

"Nazi Camps." United States Holocaust Memorial Museum Holocaust Encyclopedia. https://encyclopedia.ushmm.org/content/en/article/nazi-camps.

"Night of the Long Knives." The History Place. 2001. https://www.historyplace.com/worldwar2/triumph/tr-roehm.htm.

"1935 Saar Status Referendum." In Wikipedia. November 25, 2022. https://en.wikipedia.org/w/index.php?title=1935_Saar_status_referendum&oldid=1123662620.

"Occupation of the Ruhr." In Wikipedia. December 14, 2022. https://en.wikipedia.org/w/index.php?title=Occupation_of_the_Ruhr&oldid=1127409982.

Petrova, Ada, and Peter Watson. "The Death of Hitler: The Full Story with New Evidence from Secret Russian Archives." *Washington Post*, 1995. https://www.washingtonpost.com/wp-srv/style/longterm/books/chap1/deathofhitler.htm.

Prenger, Kevin. "Seyss-Inquart, Arthur." Translated by Chrit Houben. Traces of War. May 16, 2020. https://www.tracesofwar.com/articles/2672/Seyss-Inquart-Arthur.htm.

"Raphael Lemkin Defines Genocide." Genocide Watch. 2014. http://genocidewatch.net/2013/03/14/raphael-lemkin-defines-genocide-2/.

Redeker, Nils, Lukas Haffert, and Tobias Rommel. "Misremembering Weimar: Unpacking the Historic Roots of Germany's Monetary Policy Discourse." Hertie School: Jacques Delors Centre. December 2019. https://www.hertie-school.org/fileadmin/user_upload/20191101_Inflation_Redeker_neues_Layout.pdf.

"Reichskommissariat Niederlande." In Wikipedia. December 22, 2022. https://en.wikipedia.org/wiki/Reichskommissariat_Niederlande.

"Reichstag Fire." In Wikipedia. November 21, 2022. https://en.wikipedia.org/w/index.php?title=Reichstag_fire&oldid=1122972188.

Rosensaft, Menachem Z. "Asserting Their Jewish Identity: My Mother's Testimony in the First Nazi War Crimes Trial, 75 Years Ago." Just Security. September 17, 2020. https://www.justsecurity.org/72455/asserting-their-jewish-identity-my-mothers-testimony-in-the-first-nazi-war-crimes-trial-75-years-ago/.

"Schiphol." War over Holland—May 1940: The Dutch Struggle. December 17, 2021. http://www.waroverholland.nl/index.php?page=schiphol-airbase.

"Seyss-Inquart, Arthur." Shoah Resource Center: The International School for Holocaust Studies. https://www.yadvashem.org/odot_pdf/Microsoft%20Word%20-%206018.pdf.

"Seyss-Inquart, Arthur (1892–1946)." Encyclopedia.com. June 22, 2022. https://www.encyclopedia.com/history/encyclopedias-almanacs-transcripts-and-maps/seyss-inquart-arthur-1892-1946.

Siegal, Nina. "She Discovered What Happened to 400 Dutch Jews Who Disappeared." *New York Times*, March 16, 2022. https://www.nytimes.com/2022/03/16/arts/design/nazis-dutch-jews-disappearance.html.

Simkin, John. "Unemployment in Nazi Germany." Spartacus Educational. January 2020. https://spartacus-educational.com/GERunemployment.htm.

"Slovak Republic (1939–1945)." In Wikipedia. November 26, 2022. https://en.wikipedia.org/w/index.php?title=Slovak_Republic_(1939–1945)&oldid=1123848102.

"Submarines World War 2." Harwich & Dovercourt: A Time Gone By. https://www.harwichanddovercourt.co.uk/submarines-wwii/.

TimesMachine. *New York Times*, 2022. War reports from 1940 through 1945. http://timesmachine.nytimes.com.

Tolischus, Otto D. "Reich Adopts Swastika as Nation's Official Flag; Hitler's Reply to 'Insult.'" *New York Times*, September 16, 1935. https://timesmachine.nytimes.com/timesmachine/1935/09/16/93486011.html?pageNumber=1.

Trueman, C. N. "The U-Boat War 1940." History Learning Site, May 18, 2015. https://www.historylearningsite.co.uk/world-war-two/war-in-the-atlantic/the-u-boat-war-1940/.

"U-Boat." In *Encyclopedia Britannica*. October 28, 2022. https://www.britannica.com/technology/U-boat.

"U.S. Contribution to the Liberation of the Netherlands." U.S. Embassy and Consulate in the Netherlands. https://nl.usembassy.gov/our-relationship/75-years-of-liberation-of-the-netherlands-75liberationnl/.

"Volunteer Legion Netherlands." In Military Wiki, September 5, 2022. https://military-history.fandom.com/wiki/Volunteer_Legion_Netherlands.

"Volunteer Legion Netherlands." In Wikipedia. March 15, 2023. https://en.wikipedia.org/wiki/Volunteer_Legion_Netherlands.

"V-Weapons." In Wikipedia. October 27, 2022. https://en.wikipe
dia.org/w/index.php?title=V-weapons&oldid=1118561152.

"Was Churchill Really Worried about the Battle of the Atlantic?
And If So, Why?" Churchill Archive for Schools, 2022. https://
www.churchillarchiveforschools.com/themes/the-themes
/key-events-and-developments-in-world-history/was-churchill
-really-worried-about-the-battle-of-the-atlantic-and-if-so-why.

"Wesel." In Wikipedia. December 2, 2022. https://en.wikipedia
.org/w/index.php?title=Wesel&oldid=1125134845.

"World War II: 1939-1945; The Impact of WWII on Women's
Work." Striking Women | Women and Work. https://www
.striking-women.org/module/women-and-work/world-war
-ii-1939-1945.

"World War II: The Soviet Advance to the Oder, January–February
1945." In *Encyclopedia Britannica*. August 30, 2022. https://
www.britannica.com/event/World-War-II/The-Soviet
-advance-to-the-Oder-January-February-1945.

Archives, Museums, and Tours of Historical Sites

Anne Frank House. Amsterdam, Netherlands. 2022.

Belarusian State Museum of the History of the Great Patriotic War.
Minsk, Belarus. 2004.

Bergen-Belsen Memorial. Lohheide, Germany. October 2022.

Dokumentationsarchiv des österreichischen Widerstandes
(Documentation Center of Austrian Resistance). Vienna, Austria.
2004.

Jabotinsky Institute. Tel Aviv, Israel. 2005.

The Jewish Museum of the City of Vienna. Vienna, Austria. 2004.

The Jewish Museum in Prague. Prague, Czech Republic. 2004.

Oregon Jewish Museum and Center for Holocaust Education. Portland, Oregon. 2020.

Terezín Memorial. Terezín, Czech Republic. 2004.

United States Holocaust Memorial Museum. Washington, D.C. 2019.

Wiener Stadt- und Landesarchiv (Vienna City Archives). Vienna, Austria. 2004

Yad Vashem—The World Holocaust Remembrance Center. Jerusalem, Israel. 2005.

Index

This photograph of Stefan and Marion Hess in Dutch costume, which appears on the back cover, is one of the last pictures of the twins before they and their parents were deported to Bergen-Belsen. It was taken in 1942 by German-Jewish photographer and Dutch Resistance member Leo Fischer, who would be murdered by the Nazis. *Courtesy of the Hess family*